A HERITAGE OF GOOD TASTES

Historic Alexandria, Virginia

Acknowledgements:
  The Twig wishes to express its appreciation to the following organizations for providing prints of Alexandria's historic sites:
    The Alexandria Bicentennial Corporation
    The Bank of Virginia
    Don Cannavaro
    The Lee-Jackson Memorial, Incorporated
    The Northern Virginia Regional Park Authority
    Paden Printing and Publishing Company, Incorporated
    The Virginia Trust for Historic Preservation

In addition, sincere thanks is extended to John Exley for the cover design and divider page artwork and to Melanie Modlin for editing of historic narratives.

Copyright © 1980
By The Twig, Junior Auxiliary of the Alexandria Hospital
Alexandria, Virginia

First printing	10,000 books	October, 1980
Second printing	10,000 books	July, 1982
Third printing	20,000 books	February, 1985

International Standard Book Number 0-9613588-0-7
Printed in the United States of America
Wimmer Brothers Fine Printing and Lithography
Memphis, Tennessee 38118

"Cookbooks of Distinction"℠

An Invitation to Alexandria

Alexandria is an historic seaport city offering a special charm to its visitors. Scottish merchants first settled in the area and established a tobacco warehouse on the shore of the Potomac. The city received its charter from the General Assembly in 1749 and was named for John Alexander, an early settler and owner of the land on which the town was built. During colonial days, Alexandria prospered as a thriving port. Merchants and sea captains built their typically English style row houses near the water, an area now called the Port Section.

George Washington as a 17 year old apprentice helped to survey the city, lay out the street plan and designate the building plots. Washington continued his association with the city throughout his life. It was in Alexandria that he transacted his business, attended meetings and worshipped at Christ Church. Frequently, he traveled from Mount Vernon to play cards, attend the theatre or dance at various balls and stayed overnight with friends. Washington drilled his troops in Market Square before leaving for the French and Indian War and he reviewed his troops for the last time in front of Gadsby's Tavern.

Alexandria was a center of great activity during the Revolutionary War. Washington, Madison and General "Light Horse Harry" Lee frequently consulted with colleagues in the city's homes and taverns. The seaport was a landing point for French volunteers and Hessian prisoners of war were quartered in the city. Alexandria's importance grew as more and more trade resulted from the clipper ships making port from around the world. Activity rivalled that of New York and Boston. Gracious homes, schools, churches, and a library were built as prosperity abounded. The city became a center of culture and commerce.

(continued on next page)

Five days after the burning of the White House in August, 1814, Alexandria capitulated to the British in a bloodless surrender. The naval forces demanded food, material and munitions from the city's warehouses. Loading these stores on their ships and additional ships appropriated from the harbor, they proceeded downstream after burning all barges and ships remaining in the harbor. Fortunately, the city had escaped the fate of the Nation's Capitol.

The Civil War was a difficult time for Alexandria and its citizens. Southern sympathies were sorely tried by the occupation of Federal troops. Many residences, schools and other large buildings were converted to hospitals for wounded and convalescing Union soldiers. Prison ships were anchored in the harbor. The city's economy was severely damaged. No fighting occurred however, and forts were constructed around the city as part of the Defenses of Washington. Ironically Robert E. Lee's hometown remained an occupied city during the entire war.

Today many of the historic sites in the city have been restored to share with citizens and visitors this heritage from the past.

For Further Information

Alexandria Bicentennial Center
201 South Washington Street
Alexandria, Virginia 22301
Phone: (703) 750-6677

Alexandria Tourist Council
221 King Street
Alexandria, Virginia 22301
Phone: (703) 549-0205

Profits from the sale of A HERITAGE OF GOOD TASTES go to The Twig, the Junior Auxiliary of The Alexandria Hospital, to be used to provide financial aid to indigent hospital patients, to purchase needed medical equipment and to provide nursing scholarships for students in the Alexandria Hospital School of Nursing.

Table Of Contents

The pineapple was the colonial symbol of hospitality. Schooners from the West Indies brought these rare and highly perishable fruits to colonial ports such as Alexandria. Hosts and Hostesses went to great lengths to serve this tropical fruit to guests. The special welcome of the pineapple was represented in furniture, moldings, stencils, brass work and damask of the time. Many colonial Christmas decorations centered around the pineapple.

The Twig has tested and edited the recipes in this cookbook and extends its special welcome to you as you use our favorite recipes.

Menus

Planning a Dinner Menu

Choose the main dish first, planning the other courses around the entrée.

Select a starchy food and a vegetable and/or salad. Be sure the dishes complement each other by keeping in mind the importance of contrasts in flavor, color and texture.

Think about bread or rolls.

Decide on dessert. Consider a light dessert with a heavy dinner and a more elaborate dessert when a light dinner will be served.

Give attention to the extras, such as beverages, adding an appetizer, and making a special garnish.

Presentation is important. Food tastes better and is more festive when it is beautifully decorated.

To Serve Company You Will Want to Plan On . . .

Beef—¼ to ½ pound of boneless meat per person, taking into consideration the mix of guests (young and old, male and female) and the number of other dishes.

Fish (filets)—About 4 ounces per person.

Oysters and Shrimp—From 6 to 12 per person. Less if used as an appetizer, more if served as the main course.

Poultry—About 4 ounces baked, boneless meat, or ¼ to ½ chicken.

Vegetable Salads—⅔ to 1 cup per serving.

Vegetables—½ cup per serving.

Ice cream—Approximately ½ to ¾ cup per serving.

Food for a Cocktail Party, Tea, or Reception—10 bites per person. For a cocktail buffet, plan heavier, more substantial food and up to 15 bites per person depending on the hours of the event and the type of group.

The Lyceum
Washington and Prince Streets

Constructed in the Doric Temple style in 1839, the Lyceum was one of the few Greek Revival buildings in Alexandria and one of a small number built in the state of Virginia. Benjamin Hallowell, a Quaker schoolmaster, served for a time as the City Surveyor, and also as the first president of the Alexandria Water Company. In 1834, he and a group of like-minded citizens established the Alexandria Lyceum Company, which held weekly lectures and debates in Hallowell's school or in various halls.

By 1838, Lyceum Company membership had grown considerably and the group considered constructing permanent facilities of its own. The Alexandria Library had also outgrown its quarters, so the two organizations agreed to share a new building.

The first floor of the Lyceum housed the library and had a large reading room. A large lecture room, complete with marble busts of Cicero and Seneca, occupied the second floor. The building quickly became Alexandria's cultural center, presenting musical concerts in addition to more scholarly fare.

During the Civil War, the Lyceum was converted into a hospital. The building never regained its cultural eminence. In 1868 the company sold the Lyceum to John B. Daingerfield for use as a residence.

MENUS

Morning Coffee

Quiche Lorraine   Cucumber Sandwiches   Spinach Swinger

Lemon Squares   Strawberry Bread

Pecan Tarts

Coffee Punch   Spiced Tea

Bridge Luncheon

C's Crab Delight

Hot Fruit Salad   Layered Salad

French Peach Tart

White Wine

Bridesmaid's Luncheon

Chicken Chutney Salad

Spinach Squares Hollandaise   Red Raspberry Mold

Spoon Rolls

Lemon Ice   Mexican Wedding Cakes

May Punch

Company Breakfast

Sherried Grapefruit

Monterey Oven Omelet

Sausage Stuffed Tomatoes   Hot Biscuits

Fresh Strawberries with Devonshire Cream

Coffee or Tea

Christening Brunch

Champagne Punch

Deluxe Company Crepes with Assorted Fillings

Crab Imperial

Bacon and Eggs Mornay

Fresh Asparagus or Broccoli   Cinnamon Rolls

Christening Cake

or

Petit Fours

Picnic

Cold Tomato Soup

Pasties

Potato Pickups   Dilled Blue Lake Beans

Crazy Chocolate Cake

Wolf Trap Picnic

Chilled Consommé with Lemon Slice

Salmon Mousse

Tomato Salad   Asparagus Vinaigrette

Crusty French Bread

Exquisite Pie

Super Bowl Supper

Cheese Beer Soup

Simple Stew

Spinach Salad

Dilly Bread

Seven Layer Cookies

Theatre Supper

Onion Soup

Steak Diane

Cheesy Potatoes

Hearts of Palm Salad

Rum Pie

Summer Cook-Out

Icy Lemon Soup

Marinated Grill-Broiled Chicken

Copper Carrot Pennies   Ratatouille

Monterey Dilled Pumpernickel

Pineapple Delight

Winter Cook-Out

Broccoli Soup

Grilled Leg of Lamb

Potato Princess   Asparagus Amandine

Spiced Peach Salad

Herb Bread

Lemonade Pie

Hungarian Dinner

Kaposzta (Stuffed Cabbage)

Baked Carrots and Apples   Braised Onions

Beet Mold

Cherry Flan

Italian Dinners

Tuscan Chicken

Funghi All'Olio e Limone   Risotto Alla Milanese

Confetti Salad

Cappucino Parfait with Blonde Brownies

or

Mixed Antipasto

Rice, Endive and Tomato Soup

Veal Picatta

Fettucini with Sesame Seeds   Zucchini Gaetano

Biscuit Tortoni

Kentucky Derby Party

Hot Chipped Beef Dip

Barbeque on Cocktail Rolls

Shrimp Mold

Vegetable Dip with Crudités

Pecan Tarts

Fresh Strawberries

Mint Juleps   Tea Punch

Cocktail Party

Spinach Balls   White Oaks Paté

Asparagus Canapés   Hot Crab Spread

Dried Beef Dip in Round Rye   Belle Haven Shrimp Dip

Marinated Mushrooms   Curried Hot Hors d'Oeuvres

Frozen Daiquiries   Rosé Punch   Whiskey Sours

Cocktail Buffet

Hot Crab Dip

Marinated Eye of Round

Curried Egg Mold   Fresh Vegetables and Crudités

Spinach Balls   Potatoes Muscovite

Cheese Puffs

Miniature Cheesecakes

Crème de Menthe Balls   Curried Cashews   Glazed Pecans

Thanksgiving Dinner

Easy Lobster Bisque

Roast Turkey

Cornbread Stuffing

Zesty Mashed Potatoes   Party Broccoli

Sandra's Cranberry Casserole

Sally Lunn Bread

Glorious Pumpkin Pie

15

Christmas Open House

Smithfield Ham with Biscuits

Marinated Eye of Round

Salmon Mousse

Cherry Tomatoes Stuffed with Pimento Cheese

Stuffed Brussel Sprouts

Hot Crab Dip   Curried Chicken Balls

Charleston Egg Nog   Champagne Punch

Christmas Dinner

Elba's Onion Soup

Roast Duck

Tangerine and Yam Stuffing

Onion Cauliflower Bake   Buttered Green Beans

Cucumber Mold

Traditional Christmas Pudding

Hors D'Oeuvres, Canapés and Appetizers

Artichoke Appetizer

Preheat: 350 degrees

½ cup chopped onion
½ cup water
4 eggs, well beaten
¼ cup bread crumbs
½ teaspoon salt
⅛ teaspoon pepper

⅛ teaspoon oregano
2 to 3 drops Tabasco
2 cups shredded Cheddar cheese
2 6-ounce jars marinated artichokes, chopped

Cook onion in water until tender (about 5 minutes) and drain. Combine eggs, crumbs, salt, pepper, oregano and Tabasco. Stir in onion, cheese and artichokes. Put in 11 x 7 x 1-inch greased pan. Bake at 350 degrees for 20 to 25 minutes. Cut in 1-inch squares. Serve warm.

Note: Can be made ahead and frozen. Just reheat.

Mrs. Gerald B. File

Asparagus Canapés

Preheat: 350 degrees
Yield: 36 canapés

1 tablespoon mayonnaise
1 15-ounce can asparagus
1 loaf Pepperidge Farm thin-sliced bread
Melted butter

8 ounces Roquefort cheese at room temperature
8 ounces cream cheese at room temperature
1 egg, beaten

Cut crust from bread. Roll bread flat and spread with mixture made of both cheeses, mayonnaise and egg combined. Roll one stalk of asparagus in each bread slice. Secure with pick. Dip each bread roll in melted butter. Place in freezer for a short time. Cut each roll into thirds. Bake at 350 degrees for 15 minutes.

Note: These can be made ahead and frozen until you want to serve.

Mrs. G. Ray Lewis

Carlyle House

Historic Carlyle House was built in 1752 by the Scottish merchant John Carlyle for his bride, Sara Fairfax. It is a stately stone mansion designed after "Craigiehall," an imposing manor house in West Lothian, Scotland. Carlyle House was a center of social and political activity in the early days of Alexandria. Important leaders such as George Washington were frequent visitors.

Carlyle House was the scene of an important historical event in April of 1755. The British General Edward Braddock met with five colonial governors to discuss ways of forcing the colonists to finance England's military campaign against the French and Indians. This meeting was the beginning of "taxation without representation," and eventually led to the Stamp Act, a significant cause of the American Revolution.

Carlyle House contains a number of objects which date from the 17th and 18th centuries. The Carlyle family Bible and a portrait of John Carlyle's mother are among the memorabilia on display. The 18th century kitchen in the basement is well stocked with utensils of the period.

Stuffed Brussels Sprouts

Yield: approximately 72

½ pound blue cheese, softened
¼ pound ricotta cheese
2 tablespoons softened butter

Cayenne to taste
Salt to taste
2½ pounds brussels sprouts

Sieve the two cheeses and butter into a bowl. Add cayenne and salt to taste. Mix well. Chill until firm but still of spreading consistency. Cook the brussels sprouts in boiling salted water for 10 minutes or until tender. Drain and refresh them under running cold water. Pat the brussels sprouts dry, remove centers with small melon-ball cutter. Fill a pastry bag fitted with a star tip with blue cheese mixture; pipe into each sprout.

Mrs. Donald Burchell

Cucumber Sandwiches

Serves: 20

1 package whipped cream cheese
1 package Good Seasons Italian
  salad dressing mix

Cucumber for slicing
1 package pumpernickel bread, party
  sandwich size

Combine cream cheese and salad dressing mix. Spread small amount of mixture on each slice of bread. Slice cucumber and place one slice on each cream cheese bread slice.

Mrs. Daniel Little

Crab Toast

Preheat: 450 degrees
Serves: 6

10 slices white bread, each cut
  into 4 squares
1 8-ounce can crabmeat
⅓ cup mayonnaise

1 teaspoon lemon juice
1 teaspoon sherry or white wine
Salt and pepper to taste
Cayenne pepper

Mix crabmeat, mayonnaise, lemon juice, wine, salt and pepper. Spread mixture on bread squares. Sprinkle lightly with cayenne and bake in 450 degree oven for 10 minutes, or until toast is just browned. Serve at once.

Mrs. Robert E. Applegate

Ham Roll-Ups

Yield: 80

1 3-ounce package cream cheese
   with chives
1 8-ounce package plain cream
   cheese
8 large stuffed green olives,
   chopped

6 tablespoons mayonnaise
¼ teaspoon prepared mustard
⅓ package dry onion soup mix
1 teaspoon Worcestershire sauce
8 or 9 slices cold Danish ham,
   approximately ⅛-inch thick

Mix cream cheeses, olives, mayonnaise, mustard, soup mix and Worcestershire sauce well. Spread mixture ⅛ inch thick on ham slices, roll as jelly roll. Wrap each in plastic wrap and chill. Just before serving, slice in ¼-inch slices and serve on Triscuits or other crackers.

Note: Can be frozen, defrost 2½ hours.

Mrs. Brian J. Bowden

Cheese Puffs

Preheat: 450 degrees
Yield: 25 to 30

½ cup shredded sharp white
   Cheddar cheese
1 4-ounce container whipped
   cream cheese
1 egg

1 teaspoon chives
1 teaspoon lemon juice
Dash of pepper
4 slices bacon, cooked and crumbled
4 frozen patty shells, thawed

Combine cream cheese, egg, lemon juice, chives and dash of pepper. Beat well. Stir in Cheddar cheese and bacon. Chill. Roll one of the patty shells to 8 x 4-inch rectangle. Cut into 2-inch squares. Top each square with a rounded teaspoon of filling. Fold to form triangle or square. Repeat with remaining shells. Chill until ready to bake. Place in 450 degree oven. Immediately reduce temperature to 400 degrees; bake 12 to 15 minutes.

Mrs. Renny H. Barnes

Curried Chicken Balls

Yield: 5 dozen

1 8-ounce package cream cheese
4 tablespoons mayonnaise
2 cups cooked chicken, chopped
1½ cups chopped, blanched
   almonds

3 tablespoons chopped chutney
1 teaspoon salt
2 teaspoons curry powder
1 cup grated coconut

Thoroughly cream the cheese and mayonnaise. Add chicken, almonds, chutney, salt and curry powder. Mix until well blended. Shape into walnut-sized balls. Roll each ball in coconut. Chill.

Note: May be frozen or made one day ahead.

Mrs. Donald Burchell

Zucchini Chips

Zucchini, sliced ⅛ to ¼-inch thick
1 can flat beer

Pancake mix
Cooking oil

Pour beer slowly into bowl containing the dry pancake mix to make a very thick batter. Dip zucchini slices into batter and fry in ½ inch deep cooking oil until both sides are browned.

Mrs. Robert Silver

Spinach Balls

Preheat: 350 degrees
Yield: 60 to 70 balls

2 10-ounce packages frozen
   spinach, cooked and
   well-drained
2 cups stuffing mix
1 cup grated Parmesan cheese

6 eggs, beaten
¾ cup butter, softened
Salt
Pepper

Combine all ingredients, mixing well. Roll into balls the size of walnuts. Freeze. Before serving, place on cookie sheet still frozen. Bake 10 minutes at 350 degrees.

Another variation: Add 2 chopped onions, 1 teaspoon garlic salt, ½ teaspoon thyme and ½ teaspoon MSG before rolling into balls. With additional ingredients, cooking time may be increased to 20 minutes.

Mrs. Lewis B. Puller, Jr.

Mozzarella Carozza
(Fried Cheese)

Serves: 1

1 slice of Italian bread
1 slice Mozzarella cheese
2 eggs, beaten
Flour

Bread crumbs
1 tablespoon butter, melted
½ teaspoon chopped garlic
Chopped parsley

Put slices of bread and cheese together. Dip in eggs. Flip on both sides in the flour. Dip again in the eggs, flip on both sides in bread crumbs. Deep fat fry. Combine butter, garlic and pinch of parsley. Pour butter on top of fried cheese and bread.

Geranio Restaurant

Potatoes Muscovite

Yield: 36

36 small potatoes, peeled and
    trimmed into 1¼-inch balls
1 pint sour cream

1 2-ounce jar red caviar
1 2-ounce jar black caviar

In a kettle, cook potatoes in boiling salted water until they are tender. Drain the potatoes and let them cool until they can be handled. Remove the centers with a small melon-ball cutter. Half fill each potato with sour cream, top half the potatoes with red caviar and half with black caviar.

Mrs. William T. Mahood

Marinated Mushrooms

Serves: 8 to 10

1 pound fresh mushrooms
2 tablespoons lemon juice
¼ cup olive oil
1 tablespoon minced parsley
½ teaspoon salt
½ teaspoon sugar

½ cup cider vinegar
⅛ teaspoon pepper
1 tablespoon oregano
1 tablespoon minced onion
1 clove garlic, minced

Place mushrooms in water with lemon juice. Bring to a boil; lower heat and simmer one minute. Drain. Combine mushrooms and remaining ingredients. Put in jar and refrigerate.

Mrs. Thomas F. Shea

Mushroom Rounds

Preheat: 400 degrees

1 loaf thin sliced fresh bread
  (Arnold Diet or Pepperidge
  Farm)
3 tablespoons chopped shallots
1 pound finely chopped
  mushrooms
3 tablespoons flour

4 tablespoons butter
1 cup heavy cream
½ teaspoon salt
⅛ teaspoon cayenne
1 tablespoon chopped parsley
1½ tablespoons chopped chives
½ teaspoon lemon juice

Trim bread and cut in 1-inch rounds. Butter small muffin tins. Bake the bread which has been pressed into the bottom of the tins for 8 to 10 minutes at 400 degrees. Cool. Brown shallots in 3½ tablespoons butter. Add finely chopped mushrooms (a food processor is the fastest). Sauté 10 to 15 minutes until dry. Add flour, remaining butter and heavy cream. Mix well, bring to a boil and simmer. Add salt, cayenne, parsley, chives and lemon juice. Mix well and mound in shells. Freeze. Do not defrost. Bake at 350 degrees for 20 minutes.

Note: Freeze on a cookie sheet and put the frozen rounds in a plastic bag.

Mrs. Stephen A. Sharp
Mrs. Timothy R. Geary

Kate's Shrimp Saganaki

Yield: 3 dozen

1 pound raw medium shrimp
1 10-ounce package frozen
  artichoke hearts
¼ cup olive oil
¼ pound small mushrooms
2 cloves garlic, finely minced

½ teaspoon salt
Freshly ground black pepper
½ teaspoon oregano
2 tablespoons lemon juice
2 tablespoons finely chopped parsley

Blanch artichokes in boiling salted water for 2 minutes. Drain. Heat olive oil in frying pan, add shrimp and mushrooms. Cook, stirring until shrimp turn pink. Add artichokes, garlic, salt, pepper and oregano. Heat through. Sprinkle with lemon juice and stir lightly to blend flavors. Sprinkle with parsley.

Mrs. John Smithers

HORS D'OEUVRES, CANAPÉS AND APPETIZERS

Spicy Shrimp

Serves: 6 to 8

3 tablespoons vegetable oil
1 pound shelled, deveined shrimp
 or 10 ounces frozen shrimp
3 tablespoons green onion, finely
 chopped
2 tablespoons candied ginger,
 finely chopped
1 clove garlic

3 tablespoons chili sauce
1 tablespoon catsup
2 tablespoons dry white wine
1½ teaspoons soy sauce
1 teaspoon sugar
½ teaspoon salt
¼ teaspoon dried crushed red peppers
 (optional)

Heat oil in skillet, add shrimp and onions. Stir fry for 2 minutes. Combine ginger, garlic, chili sauce, catsup, wine, soy sauce, sugar, salt and red pepper. Pour over shrimp in skillet. Stir rapidly for 1 minute. Serve with cocktail picks or on a bed of lettuce.

Mrs. Donald Burchell

Shrimp Balls

Yield: 3 dozen

1 pound raw shrimp, shelled and
 chopped
¼ pound water chestnuts, finely
 chopped
1 egg
½ teaspoon salt

Dash of pepper
1 teaspoon mashed ginger root
1 fresh scallion, white part only, finely
 chopped
1 tablespoon dry white wine

Mix all ingredients well. Form into small balls and deep fry in vegetable oil until golden brown. Serve immediately.

Ms. Cynthia Byrnes

Anchovy Tomatoes

2 pints cherry tomatoes
1 8-ounce package cream cheese

1 tube anchovy paste

Core the tomatoes and place upside down to drain. Soften cream cheese and mix with anchovy paste. Spoon or pipe with star tube and pastry bag into each tomato. Chill and serve.

Mrs. Daniel Little

Sesame Seed Wafers

Preheat: 325 degrees
Yield: 100

2 cups brown sugar
1 cup plain flour
½ teaspoon baking powder
¼ teaspoon salt

1 egg, beaten
¾ cup butter
1 teaspoon vanilla
¾ cup sesame seeds, toasted

Cream the butter and sugar; add beaten egg, then flour sifted with salt and baking powder. Add vanilla and sesame seeds. Drop by teaspoon on a greased cookie sheet. Bake in 325 degree oven. *Cook quickly*—watch carefully, until they turn brown. Allow to cool one minute before removing from pan.

Note: An old Charleston recipe

Mrs. F. Eugene Brown, Jr.

Toasted Onion Sticks

Preheat: 350 degrees
Yield: 54 sticks

1 2-ounce package dry onion soup mix
¾ cup butter or margarine, softened

1 loaf sliced white bread (about 20 slices)

Blend onion soup mix into butter. Let stand at room temperature until you are ready to toast the sticks. Trim crusts from bread. Spread with onion butter; cut each slice into 3 strips. Place on greased baking sheet and bake at 350 degrees for about 10 minutes, or until golden.

Ms. Elizabeth J. Noyes

Water Chestnut Nibbles

Preheat: 400 degrees
Serves: 16 to 20

1 can water chestnuts, drained
Brown sugar

Slices of bacon, cut in half

Roll chestnuts in brown sugar. Wrap each one in bacon slice and secure with toothpick. Place in 400 degree oven for 12 minutes or until bacon is brown.

Mrs. Herbert Stewart

White Oaks Pâté

Serves: 20

2 pounds chicken livers
3 Mackintosh apples
3 medium white onions

1 pound fresh mushrooms
1/4 pound butter
Salt and pepper to taste

Peel and slice onions, apples and mushrooms. Sauté in butter until onions are translucent. Add chicken livers and simmer until well done. Drain off excess liquid and put mixture into blender and purée. Shape pâté on one or two large serving plates and chill. Serve with crackers.

Mrs. Timothy J. O'Shaughnessy

Mock Liver Pâté

1 pound liverwurst
1/4 cup brandy
1/2 cup sour cream

1/4 cup grated onion
1 teaspoon prepared mustard

Mash liverwurst. Add remainder of ingredients and mix until smooth. Chill 2 hours.

Mrs. Lawrence O. McKnelly

Shrimp Pâté

Serves: 25

2 1/2 cups shelled, cleaned, cooked
   shrimp
1/2 cup (or more) dry vermouth
1 envelope plain gelatin
1/4 cup cold water

1/4 cup boiling water
1 teaspoon instant chopped onion
2 cups mayonnaise
1 teaspoon lemon juice
1/4 teaspoon salt

Blend shrimp and vermouth in blender until smooth. Soften gelatin in water, then add boiling water. Add instant onion to gelatin. Also add mayonnaise. Fold in shrimp and vermouth mixture, lemon juice and salt. Put in a 1-quart mold. Chill. Serve with crackers.

Mrs. Thomas Ryan

Steak Tartare

Yield: 2 to 3 cups

1 pound ground sirloin or filet
  (ground once)
¼ cup minced scallions or onion
Catsup to taste
1 teaspoon Dijon mustard
1 teaspoon Worcestershire sauce
½ cup chopped parsley

Tabasco
2 tablespoons capers
½ can anchovies—broken up
Grand Marnier
Cognac
Salt
Pepper

Add all ingredients to meat according to taste. Serve on pumpernickel or rye bread with sweet butter.

Mrs. James S. Brady

Chutney Cheeseball

2 8-ounce packages cream cheese
1 10-ounce jar chutney, drained
½ teaspoon curry powder

½ teaspoon dry mustard
Sliced almonds

Mix all ingredients and roll in sliced almonds. Refrigerate.

Note: Good served with rice crackers.

Mrs. Alfred E. T. Rusch

Jezzabelle

1 12-ounce jar pineapple preserves
1 12-ounce jar apple jelly
1½ ounces dry mustard

6 tablespoons horseradish
1 8-ounce package cream cheese

Mix ingredients together and refrigerate overnight. Pour over block of cream cheese and serve with large plain crackers. Makes sufficient sauce for several blocks of cream cheese.

Mrs. Thomas T. Bellino

Dried Beef Dip in Round Rye

Serves: 8 to 10

1 whole loaf round rye bread (1 or
   2 pound)
1 cup sour cream
1 cup mayonnaise
1½ teaspoons grated fresh onion

Dash of garlic powder
1 teaspoon chopped parsley
1 teaspoon dill seed
2 ounces dried beef, minced

Slice off 2 to 3 inches from the top of the loaf and scoop out the center, leaving crust shell intact. Blend all ingredients together and pour into bread shell. Refrigerate for at least 4 hours. When serving, pile bread chunks around loaf for dipping.

Mrs. Michael Cericola

Dr. David's Beef Jerky

Preheat: 185 degrees
Yield: 50 strips

2 flank steaks
Japanese soy sauce

Lemon pepper marinade
Garlic salt

With a very sharp knife, strip all fat from steaks. Cutting along the grain, cut 1-inch wide and ¼-inch thick strips of meat. Dip in the soy sauce. Do not marinate. Place strips on aluminum foil-covered cookie sheets. Sprinkle strips with marinade and garlic salt. Place in warm oven, 185 degrees to 200 degrees for 5 to 6 hours, or until all moisture has left meat. It may be helpful to turn meat once or twice. Cool meat strips and store in a glass jar.

Mrs. David Redding

Chicken Liver Pâté

Yield: 5 cups

2 cups butter
2 pounds chicken livers
2 medium onions, quartered
1 teaspoon curry powder
¼ teaspoon salt

¼ teaspoon pepper
¼ teaspoon paprika
2 tablespoons cognac
¼ cup sliced stuffed olives
  (optional garnish)

Melt ½ cup butter in pan. Add livers, onions, curry powder, paprika, salt and pepper. Cover and cook over low heat 8 minutes. Blend mixture in blender or food processor until smooth. Add cognac and remaining butter and blend. Chill until firm. Can be put in 5 to 6-cup mold. Garnish with olives.

Note: Can be made ahead and frozen. Good food processor recipe.

Mrs. Caswell O. Hobbs

Spinach Spread

Yield: 2 to 3 cups

10-ounce package frozen chopped
  spinach
½ cup minced parsley
2 tablespoons minced onion

⅓ cup mayonnaise
2 tablespoons sour cream
Salt
Pepper

Cook spinach, drain and press out all liquid. Stir in parsley, onion, mayonnaise, sour cream, salt and pepper. Cover and chill to allow flavors to blend. Serve with crackers.

Note: Super for summer—nice and cool!

Mrs. Renny H. Barnes

Hot Artichoke Dip

Preheat: 325 degrees

1 8-ounce jar marinated artichoke
  hearts, drained and chopped

1 cup mayonnaise
1 cup Parmesan cheese, grated

Mix all ingredients and bake at 325 degrees for 20 minutes. Serve hot with wheat crackers.

Mrs. H. Franklin Green, III

Guacamole I

6 ripe avocados, peeled and pitted
4 teaspoons wine vinegar
3 teaspoons olive oil
1 to 2 teaspoons chili powder
¼ teaspoon cumin

1½ tablespoons salt
3 tomatoes, chopped
½ cup chopped onions
2 minced jalapeno peppers

Mash avocado until creamy with vinegar, oil and spices. Mix in tomatoes, onion and peppers.

Mrs. John E. Davey

Guacamole II

Yield: 2 cups

2 large ripe avocados, peeled and diced
2 medium tomatoes, peeled and diced
¼ cup mayonnaise

¼ cup chopped, canned green chili peppers
2 tablespoons prepared yellow spicy brown mustard
1 teaspoon garlic salt

Combine all ingredients in container of blender and blend until smooth. Serve with corn chips, cherry tomatoes or cauliflower.

Mrs. Richard W. Klein, Jr.

Dilly Shrimp Dip

1 5-ounce can shrimp
¼ cup milk
¼ cup mayonnaise
1 8-ounce package cream cheese, softened

1 tablespoon finely chopped onion
1 teaspoon Accent
⅛ teaspoon salt
½ teaspoon dried dill weed
½ teaspoon Tabasco

Drain shrimp and rinse in cold water. Chop finely. Gradually blend milk and mayonnaise into cream cheese. Beat until smooth. Add onion, Accent, salt, dill and Tabasco. Mix well. Stir in shrimp. Chill until serving time. Garnish with whole shrimp and sprig of dill. Serve with crackers.

Mrs. H. Franklin Green, III

Chafing Dish Broccoli Dip

Makes 4 cups

3 ribs celery, chopped
1 4½-ounce can chopped
  mushrooms
1 chopped onion
3 tablespoons butter
1 6-ounce roll garlic cheese

1 10-ounce package frozen chopped
  broccoli
1 10-ounce can cream of mushroom
  soup
Tabasco
Worcestershire sauce

Sauté celery, mushrooms and onion in butter. Cook broccoli. Melt cheese roll. Add soup (undiluted), broccoli and sautéed vegetables. Season to taste with Tabasco and Worcestershire sauce. Serve in chafing dish.

Note: Good with fresh vegetables or chips.

Mrs. Carlyle C. Ring, Jr.

Belle Haven Shrimp Dip

Serves: 50

5 pounds cooked shrimp
4 8-ounce packages cream cheese
1½ cups mayonnasie
⅔ cup lemon juice
1 large onion, grated
6 or more drops Tabasco

4 ounces catsup
4 tablespoons Worcestershire sauce
2 tablespoons sour cream (only to
  thicken)
1½ teaspoons salt

Blend cream cheese, mayonnaise, lemon juice, onion, Tabasco, catsup, Worcestershire sauce and salt. Add shrimp and chill. Remove from refrigerator ½ hour before serving. If thin, add sour cream.

Note: Best if made 24 hours before serving.

Belle Haven Country Club

Jackie's Hot Crab Dip

Preheat: 325 degrees

1 pound backfin crab
16 ounces cream cheese, softened
½ pint sour cream
4 tablespoons mayonnaise
½ teaspoon lemon juice

1 teaspoon dry mustard
Dash of onion salt
1 cup shredded Cheddar cheese (save
⅓ cup for topping)
Dash of paprika

Blend all ingredients except crab in a blender. Fold in crab. Bake at 325 degrees for 30 to 45 minutes. Top with remainder of cheese. Serve with crackers.

Ms. Elizabeth J. Noyes

Hot Crab Dip for 25

1 8-ounce package cream cheese
1 10¾-ounce can tomato soup
1 pound Cheddar cheese, shredded

2 16-ounce cans crabmeat
Dash of Worcestershire sauce
Dash of Tabasco sauce

Melt cream cheese in double boiler. Add soup, cheese, crabmeat, Worcestershire sauce and Tabasco. Serve in a chafing dish to keep hot. Serve with small slices of pumpernickel bread.

Mrs. Edward McDonough

Crab Spread

12 ounces cream cheese, softened
1 tablespoon lemon juice
1 tablespoon Worcestershire sauce
1 tablespoon grated onion

½ bottle chili sauce
1 6½-ounce can crab meat, drained
Dried parsley

Blend cream cheese, lemon juice, Worcestershire sauce and onion. Spread in the shape of a flat loaf to form bottom layer. Spread on chili sauce for next layer. Form third layer with crab meat. Sprinkle parsley to cover crab. Cover tightly with plastic wrap and allow to stand overnight in the refrigerator to strengthen flavor. Remove from refrigerator ½ hour before serving for easier spreading.

Mrs. Stephen A. Sharp

Cheese Fondue

Serves: 6 to 8

1½ pounds Swiss cheese, shredded
4 tablespoons all-purpose flour
3 cups dry white wine
Pinch of white pepper

Dash of ground nutmeg
2 tablespoons kirsch, brandy or cognac
Bite-size pieces of French bread (cut so
  each will have a bit of crust on it)

Dredge cheese with flour. Set wine over low heat on stove and cook until air bubbles rise to surface (never let wine reach boiling point). Stir with silver fork. Add cheese little by little; keep stirring. Be sure each lot is melted before adding more. Keep stirring until mixture is bubbling lightly. Add seasonings and liquor to cheese mixture; blend well; pour into warmed fondue pot. Keep heat under pot very low—do not let boil. Spear bread on fondue fork and dunk.

Note: Add chef's salad, assorted fresh fruit and cookies to complete this fondue party.

Ms. Elizabeth J. Noyes

Hot Chipped Beef Dip

Preheat: 350 degrees
Serves: 10 to 12

1 8-ounce package cream cheese,
  softened
½ cup sour cream
¼ cup chopped green pepper

1 tablespoon chopped onion
Dash garlic salt
3 ounces chipped beef, finely chopped
1 cup pecans, chopped

Blend softened cream cheese with sour cream, green pepper, onion, garlic salt and chipped beef. Place in a 4 to 5-cup baking dish. Sauté pecans in butter and cover the cream cheese mixture. Bake for 20 minutes at 350 degrees. Put into chafing dish and keep warm. Serve with crackers.

Mrs. Timothy R. Geary

Hot Crab Spread

Preheat: 350 degrees
Serves: 6 to 8

1 8-ounce package cream cheese
1 tablespoon milk
2 teaspoons Worcestershire sauce

6 to 7 ounces crab meat, well drained
2 tablespoons chopped green onion tops
Sliced almonds

Combine cream cheese, milk and Worcestershire sauce. Add crab and onion. Turn into 8-inch pie plate or small casserole. Top with almonds. Bake for 15 minutes at 350 degrees. Serve with crackers and keep warm.

Note: Also makes an excellent filling for small pastry shells.

Mrs. E. H. Dale Gallimore

Chafing Dish Meatballs

Yield: 50 to 60 meatballs

2 pounds ground beef
1 slightly beaten egg
1 large onion, grated
Salt

1 12-ounce bottle chili sauce
1 10-ounce jar grape jelly
Juice of a lemon

Combine beef, egg, onion and salt to taste. Mix and shape into small balls. Drop into sauce made by combining chili sauce, jelly and lemon juice. Simmer until brown. Refrigerate or freeze. To serve, bring to room temperature; reheat in chafing dish. Serve with cocktail picks.

Mrs. Wiley F. Mitchell

Mustard Meatballs

Preheat: 425 degrees
Yield: about 50 meatballs

2 pounds sausage
1 cup currant jelly

¾ cup mustard
⅔ cup bread crumbs

Mix sausage and bread crumbs. Form into small balls. Bake in 425 to 450 degree oven, on a rack so that fat can drop off, about 20 minutes or until done. Mix currant jelly and mustard in double boiler and heat until melted. Add sausage balls to sauce and serve.

Mrs. Hugh C. Newton

Mixed Antipasto

Serves: 4

4 slices Prosciutto ham
4 peppers in vinegar
2 celery hearts
4 green olives

4 black olives
4 artichoke hearts in oil
1 4-ounce jar pimento
4 anchovy fillets in oil

On a large platter arrange all ingredients in any attractive manner of your own choice, and serve.

Note: Fresh Italian bread, or garlic bread complements this appetizer.

Mrs. Stephen L. Echols

Artichoke Hearts in Patty Shells

Preheat: 375 degrees
Serves: 6

1 package frozen patty shells (6)
2 3-ounce packages cream cheese
  and chives, softened
2 tablespoons butter, softened
1 egg

4 to 6 drops Tabasco sauce
⅛ teaspoon Worcestershire sauce
Pepper to taste
¼ teaspoon garlic powder
6 artichoke hearts, packed in water

Bake patty shells according to directions. Remove inner circle and hollow out shells. Set aside and cool. In medium-sized bowl, cream the cream cheese and chives with butter using an electric mixer on medium speed. Add egg, beat well. Add Tabasco, Worcestershire sauce, pepper and garlic powder, beat well again. Place spoonful of cream cheese mixture in bottom of each patty shell. Place an artichoke heart on top of cheese mixture and cover each heart with another spoonful of mixture. Place patty shells on ungreased cookie sheet and bake at 375 degrees for 10 minutes or until cheese mixture is bubbly.

Note: If used as a side dish, serve with plain meat as it is very rich.

Mrs. Thomas T. Bellino

Joanne's Caponata
(Eggplant Appetizer)

Yield: 4 cups

1 pound eggplant, peeled into
   ½-inch cubes
1 cup minced celery
5 tablespoons olive oil
1 cup minced onion
1½ cups drained, coarsely chopped
   Italian plum tomatoes

2½ tablespoons red wine vinegar
2 teaspoons sugar
2 tablespoons sliced green olives
1 tablespoon capers
2 anchovy filets, minced (optional)
¼ cup pine nuts
Salt and pepper

Sprinkle eggplant with salt and allow to drain in collander for 30 minutes. Pat dry with paper towels. In large skillet cook celery in 2 tablespoons olive oil, stirring for 10 minutes. Add onions and cook until tender. Transfer celery and onion to another bowl. Sauté eggplant in remaining oil until lightly browned. Return onion and celery to skillet. Add tomatoes. Mix vinegar and sugar and pour into skillet. Add olives, capers and anchovies. Bring entire mixture to a boil and simmer 15 minutes stirring occasionally. Add pine nuts and salt and pepper to taste. Chill. Serve with crackers.

Note: Keeps in refrigerator 3 to 4 weeks.

Mrs. Donald Burchell

 Always chill melons at least 12 hours before serving if you want them to be really cold.

Cantaloupe-Shrimp Cocktail

Serves: 6 to 8

2 large ripe cantaloupes
½ to ¾ pound cold cooked shrimp
1 cup whipping cream

2½ tablespoons catsup
Juice of 1½ lemons
Salt and pepper to taste

Halve 2 large ripe cantaloupes and discard the seeds. Remove the flesh with a melon ball cutter. Pile the melon balls in 6-8 stemmed glasses with the cold cooked shrimp. For the dressing, combine the heavy cream with the catsup and lemon juice. Season dressing well with salt and pepper and stir briskly with a whisk to thicken slightly. Chill.

Mrs. Timothy J. O'Shaughnessy

Pecan Dip

Preheat: 350 degrees
Serves: 10 to 20

1 8-ounce package cream cheese
1 tablespoon milk
1 small jar chipped beef
1 8-ounce carton sour cream

1/4 cup diced onions
1/2 cup chopped pecans
1/4 cup diced green pepper

Mix together all ingredients except pecans. Chop pecans and put on top of mixture. Bake in oven 15 minutes at 350 degrees. Put into chafing dish and keep warm. Serve with crackers.

Mrs. James A. Meriwether

Curried Hot Hors D'Oeuvres

Yield: 4 to 5 dozen

1 4-ounce can chopped black olives
1 4 or 6-ounce package sharp
   shredded Cheddar cheese
1 to 2 bunches green onions (use
   only green tops)

1/2 cup mayonnaise
1 teaspoon curry powder

Mix all ingredients together well. Spread on toast rounds and place under broiler one to 2 minutes, until bubbly.

Mrs. Thomas Ryan

Shrimpettes

Yield: 96

1/2 cup margarine, softened
1 1/2 teaspoons garlic powder
1 5-ounce jar Old English
   Cheddar cheese spread

1/2 teaspoon seasoned salt
1 can medium shrimp, drained and
   chopped
1 package of 6 English muffins, split

Blend ingredients well. Spread mixture on muffins. Freeze muffins for one hour. Thaw slightly. Cut into eighths (wedges). Broil until bubbly.

Note: These keep well in the freezer.

Mrs. Alan E. Mobray

Good Dip for Chips

1 5-ounce jar pimento cheese
1 3-ounce can deviled ham
½ cup mayonnaise
2 tablespoons chopped parsley

1 teaspoon minced onion
Dash of MSG
4 drops Tabasco sauce

Beat all ingredients with mixer to blend. Chill.

Mrs. John T. Ticer

Mock Boursin

1 8-ounce package cream cheese
4 ounces whipped margarine or
  butter

Dry Italian seasoning spice
Garlic powder
Crazy Jane salt

Mix cheese and margarine together. Add spices to taste (remember the flavors will be stronger after refrigeration). Chill 4 hours or more. Serve with crackers.

Mrs. Robert B. Anderson

Taramosalata

Serves: 10-12

5 ounces carp roe caviar
10 slices dry homemade-type white
  bread, trimmed
Juice of 2 lemons

½ to 1 cup olive oil
Greek olives
Parsley sprigs
Pita or French bread

Soak all but 2 slices of bread for 5 minutes in water to cover, then squeeze out excess moisture. Add caviar and moist bread to container of food processor. Turn machine on and off until caviar and bread are well mixed. Turn on machine and add oil and lemon juice alternately in a thin stream until enough of oil has been added to produce a mixture the consistency of mayonnaise. Chill well and serve in a bowl, garnished with Greek olives and parsley and surrounded by bread.

Mrs. Johan Morrison

Polynesian Stuffed Mushrooms

Preheat: 300 degrees
Serves: 8

1 pound large fresh mushrooms
½ pound ground beef
4 tablespoons soy sauce
3 tablespoons sugar

½ medium chopped onion
1 cup bread crumbs
Salt
Pepper

Remove stems from mushrooms and discard. Brown beef partially. Combine beef with other ingredients. Stuff mushroom caps with beef mixture. Bake at 300 degrees for 15 to 20 minutes.

Mrs. Frank McCabe

Stuffed Mushrooms Parmigiano

Preheat: 350 degrees
Yield: 15

15 large fresh mushrooms
2 tablespoons butter
1 medium onion, finely chopped
2 ounces pepperoni, diced
¼ cup green pepper, finely
  chopped
1 small clove garlic, minced

12 Ritz crackers
3 tablespoons Parmesan cheese
1 tablespoon snipped parsley
½ teaspoon salt
Dash of pepper
¼ teaspoon dried oregano
⅓ cup chicken broth

Wash mushrooms. Remove stems and chop finely. Drain caps on paper towel. Melt butter. Add onions, pepperoni, green pepper, garlic and stems. Cook until vegetables are tender but not brown. Add cracker crumbs, cheese, parsley, salt, oregano and pepper and mix well. Stir in chicken broth. Spoon stuffing into mushroom caps, rounding tops. Place caps in shallow pan with about ¼ inch water covering the bottom. Bake uncovered for about 25 minutes.

Mrs. C. Mason Ebhardt

Crab Pie

Preheat: 350 degrees
Yield: one 9-inch pie

1 pound crabmeat (backfin,
  preferably)
6 eggs, beaten
2½ pints sour cream
2 cups grated sharp cheese

2 cans crushed french fried onions
Salt and pepper to taste
Tabasco to taste
2 9-inch pie shells

Bake pie shells until slightly brown. Beat eggs, crush onion rings and combine with crabmeat, sour cream, cheese, salt, pepper and Tabasco. Divide mixture into shells. Bake at 350 degrees for 25 minutes.

Note: May be used for a lunch or as an appetizer.

Mrs. Lawton Rogers

Curried Egg Mold

Yield: about 4 cups

2 envelopes unflavored gelatin
½ cup cold water
2 chicken bouillon cubes
1 cup boiling water
2 teaspoons curry powder
1¼ cups mayonnaise

2 tablespoons lemon juice
2 tablespoons Worcestershire sauce
1 tablespoon Tabasco (or less)
2 teaspoons pepper (or less)
10 eggs, hard boiled

Dissolve gelatin in cold water. Dissolve bouillon cubes in boiling water. Bring chicken bouillon to a boil. Add gelatin and stir to dissolve. Allow mixture to cool. Blend remaining ingredients and combine with cooled gelatin mixture. Use blender for a smooth consistency. Pour in 5-cup mold and chill. Serve with melba toast or crackers.

Mrs. Albert Hudson

Caviar Mousse

Chill: 2 hours
Serves: 6 to 8

1 cup cottage cheese
1 cup mayonnaise
1 cup sour cream
3 tablespoons chopped chives
1 envelope gelatin softened in 2
    tablespoons cold water
⅔ cup boiling water

2 finely chopped hard boiled eggs
Juice of ½ lemon
3 to 4 ounces caviar
Lemon slices
Watercress
Grated pepper

Blend cottage cheese, ½ cup mayonnaise, ½ cup sour cream, chives, gelatin and boiling water. Mix eggs, lemon juice and caviar. Fold into cheese mixture. Pour into 5 or 6-cup mold and chill 2 hours. Unmold. Decorate with ½ cup mayonnaise and ½ cup sour cream as a topping. Garnish with lemon slices, watercress and grated pepper.

Mrs. Robert L. Calhoun

Shrimp Mold

1 10-ounce can tomato soup
1 envelope Knox gelatin
¼ cup water
1 8-ounce package cream cheese

1 cup finely chopped celery
½ cup finely chopped onion
1 pound finely cut cooked shrimp
1 cup mayonnaise

Heat soup to boiling. Mix gelatin and ¼ cup cold water. Add to soup. Add softened cream cheese and blend. Add remaining ingredients. Pour into greased 4 or 5-cup mold and chill overnight.

Mrs. Michael E. Delnegro

Beverages

Shrub with Fruit Ice

Serves: 40 to 45

1 pint fresh orange juice
1 pint canned pineapple juice
2 cups fresh lime juice

2 quarts gingerale
1 quart raspberry ice (or sherbet)

Mix fruit juices and pour over a small block of ice. Add raspberry ice. When ready to serve, carefully add gingerale. Garnish with fresh mint and orange slices.

Mrs. E. Darryl Barnes

Christmas Punch

Serves: 20 to 25

4 bottles dry champagne
4 cups cranberry juice
½ cup orange liqueur

Sliced orange, lemon, and red and
    green cherries.

Chill all ingredients well. Just before serving, mix together and add garnish.

Mrs. John B. Allen

Spiced Perk Punch

Serves: 25

2 32-ounce bottles cranberry juice
    cocktail
1 46-ounce can pineapple juice
2 cups water
1 cup packed brown sugar
½ teaspoon salt

4 teaspoons whole cloves
12 inches stick cinnamon, broken in
    pieces
Peel of ½ orange cut in strips
3 cups light rum

In a 24-cup automatic percolator combine cranberry juice, pineapple juice, water, brown sugar and salt. Place cloves, stick cinnamon and orange peel in the coffee basket. Assemble the coffee maker; plug in and let go full cycle. Just before serving, remove the basket and add the rum.

Note: On a cold day this not only will warm your guests but it gives the house a delicious aroma.

Mrs. Robert G. Lineberry

Christ Church

Between 1767 and 1773, Alexandria was rapidly expanding. The English settlers needed a place to practice their Anglican beliefs, so James Wren designed Christ Church.

Christ Church, on Washington Street, is well known because of its association with George Washington and Robert E. Lee. It has been in continuous use longer than any other church in Alexandria.

Construction of the church was completed in 1773 by John Carlyle, a Scottish merchant and owner of Carlyle House, another Alexandria landmark. In 1818, the brick tower and unusual "pepper pot" steeple were built. The sanctuary is noted for its six-sided pulpit covered by a canopy and centered under a Palladian window. Two wooden tablets containing the Lord's Prayer, the Apostles Creed and the Golden Rule were hand-lettered by James Wren and hang on either side of the windows.

From about 1785 George Washington attended Christ Church regularly. He was the owner of pew Number 15, which he purchased for 36 pounds, 10 shillings (believed to be the highest price paid for any pew). It has been traditional for the President of the United States and his family to worship in Christ Church on the Sunday nearest to Washington's birthday and to sit in the first President's pew.

45

Leo's Margaritas

Serves: 8

16 ounces MiLemon Cocktail mix   5 ounces triple sec
26 ounces of Tequila

Mix all ingredients together. Chill. Serve over ice in salt-rimmed glasses.

Mrs. James A. Meriwether

Mexican Daiquiris

Serves: 12 to 14

1 quart rum, vodka or gin   1 tablespoon almond extract
1 12-ounce can lemonade   1 32-ounce bottle 7-Up
1 12-ounce can water

Mix 3 days ahead. Freeze. Take out 2 hours ahead. Serve with ice cream scoop.

Note: Great summer drink.

Mrs. Michael Cericola

Frozen Daiquiris

Serves: 6 twice

12 ounces frozen pink lemonade   Fifth of rum
6 ounces frozen limeade   36 ounces water

Combine and place in freezer for 24 hours or more. Serve with cherry and lime garnish.

Mrs. Frank McCabe

Kir

Yield: 1 drink

Chilled white wine, Chablis   Creme de cassis

Place ½ to 1 teaspoon creme de cassis in wine glass, fill with white wine.

Mrs. F. Eugene Brown, Jr.

Bloody Mary

Serves 6 to 8

1 46-ounce can V-8 juice
9½ ounces vodka
2 teaspoons sugar
½ teaspoon pepper
½ teaspoon celery salt

½ teaspoon MSG
8 full shakes of Worcestershire sauce
4 shakes Tabasco
4 ounces lemon juice (about 3 lemons)

Combine all ingredients. The secret is not too much vodka.

Mrs. Donald Burchell

 For a 2½ hour party, allow about half a bottle of wine or champagne, 8 ounces of liquor, 1 quart of beer or 16 ounces of mixed punch for each guest.

Frozen Whiskey Sour

Serves: 6 to 8

1 6-ounce can frozen lemonade
1 6-ounce can bourbon

1 6-ounce can water
2 or 3 dashes of bitters

Put all ingredients in the blender. Add ice to fill. Blend. Top each glass with a cherry and orange slice.

Note: The more ice—the more frozen.

Mrs. Renny H. Barnes

West Indian Yellowbird

Serves: 8

1 cup Galliano
1½ cups light rum
¾ cup creme de banana

2 cups pineapple juice
2 cups orange juice

Shake all ingredients together. Pour over ice cubes. Decorate with slice of pineapple, orange and a cherry.

Note: Recipe from Mullet Bay Hotel, St. Maarten, Dutch West Indies.

Mrs. E. David Doane

Mai Tai

Yield: 1 drink

1 ounce light rum
1 ounce dark rum
1 ounce 151 proof rum
2 ounces pineapple juice

1 ounce lemon juice
4 dashes triple sec
4 dashes orgezt
4 dashes grenadine

Put ingredients through blender and pour in tall glass of crushed ice. Decorate with fresh pineapple and a cherry.

Mrs. Thomas T. Bellino

Rosé Punch

Serves: 20

2 bottles chilled rosé wine
½ cup grenadine syrup

½ cup lemon juice
1 quart chilled gingerale

Combine all ingredients and serve immediately.

Note: For a creamy punch, spoon one pint of raspberry sherbet into the punch.

Mrs. John Smithers

May Punch

Whole fresh strawberries
May Wine, chilled

Pink champagne, chilled

Place 3 strawberries in bottom of each wine glass. Pour equal amounts of May wine and champagne into each and serve.

Mrs. Frederick McNamara

Rum Punch

Yield: 68 8-ounce cups

12 quarts 7-UP, chilled
3 fifths white rum, chilled

12 6-ounce cans frozen limeade, undiluted

Combine all ingredients. Before serving, add lime slices and ice.

Mrs. William T. Mahood

Strawberry Punch

Serves: 25

½ gallon pineapple sherbet
2 28-ounce bottles gingerale

2 large packages frozen strawberries

Chill gingerale, soften sherbet; thaw strawberries. Mix all ingredients together.

Mrs. James W. Vaughan, Jr.

Quick and Easy Sangria

Yield: 6 to 8 servings

4 cups chilled rosé wine
12 ounces frozen pink lemonade,
*   undiluted*
Juice of 1 lime

1 orange, thinly sliced
2 cups chilled club soda
1 lemon, thinly sliced
1 lime, thinly sliced

Combine wine, lemonade and lime juice. Stir well. Next stir in the soda water. Add fruit slices and serve.

Mrs. John Smithers

 Ice cubes will dilute your punches quicker than blocks of ice. Freeze your own ice in jello molds, loaf pans or plastic containers mixing half water and half appropriate juice. Also add garnish to the ice block.

Polo Smash

1 bottle bourbon (quart)
1 cup sugar

1 dozen lemons

Cut lemons in half, squeeze into an earthen crock. As you squeeze each lemon also drop in the shell. Add bourbon and sugar and stir until sugar dissolves. Cover and refrigerate over night. Remove lemons before serving. Shake with crushed ice like a cocktail and strain into chilled glasses or serve in cups packed solid with finely crushed or shaved ice.

Mrs. Warren B. Heenan

Parting Punch

Serves: 6 to 8

1 bottle dry, white Bordeaux
2 large shots brandy

Juice of 1 lemon
3 tablespoons honey

Mix all ingredients together well and heat slowly without boiling. Serve in strong glasses.

Mrs. Robert G. Lineberry

East Indian Rum Punch

Serves: 6

1 46-ounce can pineapple juice
24 ounces orange juice, prepared
½ to ¾ cup ice tea mix with
   lemon and sugar added

2 cups dark rum
Dash vanilla
Lemon or lime juice

Mix pineapple and orange juices, ice tea mix, dark rum and vanilla. Add lemon or lime juice to reach desired tartness.

Mrs. C. S. Taylor Burke, III

 To keep cold punches cold: Freeze water in heavy duty plastic bags, place in punch bowl and pour ingredients around. Before serving lift out and replace with decorative ice ring. Saves refrigerator space since punch cools on the counter top and the mixture is not diluted.

Halloween Pumpkin Punch

1 large pumpkin to serve as punch
   bowl
Apple cider, chilled

Cranberry juice, chilled
Gingerale, chilled
Rum (optional)

Slice top of pumpkin and scoop out. Use equal parts cider, cranberry juice and gingerale to fill pumpkin. Rum may be served in a decanter on the side so guests may spike punch to taste and children can enjoy the same drink as their parents.

Mrs. E.David Doane

Champagne Punch

Serves: 12

1 pint fresh strawberries
2 bottles brut champagne

1 quart club soda
¾ cup of brandy

Chill all liquids. Wash and cap strawberries. Put strawberries in bottom of punch bowl. Pour champagne and soda down the side of the bowl to retain bubbles. Float ladle on top of champagne. Fill ladle with brandy and allow to sink. Do not stir.

Mrs. E. Darryl Barnes

Citrus Sunshine Punch

Yield: 20 servings

1 6-ounce can frozen concentrated orange juice
1 6-ounce can frozen concentrated lemonade
1 quart cold water

1 6-ounce can frozen concentrated limeade
1 28-ounce bottle gingerale
Gin or vodka (optional)

Combine all ingredients except gingerale. Add gingerale, pour over ice cubes in a punch bowl and serve immediately.

Mrs. James W. Keller

Egg Nog

Yield: 2 quarts

½ fifth Irish whiskey
8 eggs, separated
¾ cup sugar

½ pint whipping cream
1 quart milk
3 ounces rum

Beat yolks and whites separately. Add sugar gradually to yolks, beating the mixture constantly. Add whiskey and rum to yolk mixture while beating mixture constantly. Add milk and mix thoroughly. Fold in egg whites and whipping cream after both have been whipped until stiff.

Note: It's better made several days prior to serving as it mellows well.

Mrs. David Redding

Charleston Eggnog

Yield: 20 punch cups

1 pint rye whiskey (or 8 ounces
   rye and 8 ounces rum)
1 quart heavy cream

10 egg whites, stiffly beaten
10 egg yolks
¾ cup sugar

Cream sugar and egg yolks thoroughly. Add whiskey slowly, stirring constantly. Add the cream (unwhipped), and fold in the stiff egg whites.

Note: Very rich.

Mrs. Donald Burchell

Mary Todd Lincoln Punch

Serves: 25

½ gallon Sauterne wine
Juice of 3 or 4 lemons
1 cup brandy
1½ cups orange Curaçao

2 bottles champagne
2 24-ounce bottles club soda
1 6-ounce package frozen raspberries,
   slightly thawed

Put slightly thawed raspberries in a loaf pan, fill with water and freeze the day before. Mix lemon juice with the wine in a punch bowl. Add brandy and Curaçco; stir lightly. When ready to serve, add champagne and soda and slide in the raspberry ice block.

Mrs. Robert G. Lineberry

Parade Punch

Yield: 40 punch cups

2 quarts lemon-lime soft drink
1 quart vanilla ice cream, softened

1 quart orange juice
1 quart orange sherbet, softened

Beat together ice cream, sherbet and juice. Add lemon-lime just before serving.

Note: A favorite of all ages.

Mrs. Phillip A. Wells

Swedish Coffee Frappé

Yield: 4 servings

1 cup strong brewed coffee
1 pint vanilla ice cream

3½ tablespoons cold milk

Place ingredients in blender and whip. Serve in tall glasses.

Note: Good for a luncheon.

Mrs. Renny H. Barnes

Hot Cranberry Wine Cup

Yield: 3 quarts

1 32-ounce bottle cranberry juice
   cocktail
2 cups water
1 cup sugar
4 inches stick cinnamon

12 whole cloves
Peel of ½ lemon, cut in strips
2 fifths dry red wine
¼ cup lemon juice

Combine cranberry juice, water, sugar, cinnamon, cloves and lemon peel in gallon pan. Bring to a boil, stirring until the sugar is dissolved. Simmer uncovered for 15 minutes. Strain. Add wine and lemon juice. Heat thoroughly but do not boil. If desired sprinkle with nutmeg when serving.

Note: When serving hot drinks and punches, a small electric warming tray will keep a pitcher or small punch bowls contents ready for refills. Also try using your chafing dishes, and even a crock pot.

Ms. Cynthia Byrnes

Coffee Punch

Serves: 24 twice

1 gallon cold coffee
2 cups sugar

1 pint whipping cream
1 gallon vanilla ice cream

Dissolve sugar in coffee. Whip cream. Mix coffee and ice cream. Fold in whipped cream.

Mrs. James W. Vaughan, Jr.

Spiced Tea

Rind of 2 lemons
Rind of 1 orange
½ cup whole cloves
5 sticks cinnamon
3 cardamon seeds

3 tablespoons ground nutmeg
1 tablespoon anise seeds
1 tablespoon whole allspice
2 tablespoons ground ginger
½ pound loose tea

In a blender, grind lemon and orange rind. Add all ingredients except the tea and whirl again. Toss with loose tea in a large bowl. Dry the mixture for two days. Store in a tight container. Use ½ to ¼ teaspoon per cup.

Ms. Elizabeth J. Noyes

Chris' Spiced Wine

Serves: 20

1 quart water
1⅔ cups sugar
12 whole cloves
4 sticks cinnamon
6 whole allspice or ½ teaspoon
   ground allspice
½ teaspoon ground ginger

Rind of 1 orange
Rind of 1 lemon
1 cup fresh lemon juice
2 cups orange juice
1 (⅘ quart) bottle Burgundy or claret
   wine

Combine water, sugar, spices and rinds in a saucepan. Bring to a boil, stirring until sugar is dissolved. Simmer 10 minutes. Remove from heat and let stand 1 hour. Strain. Add juices and wine. Heat gently; do not boil. Serve hot in mugs.

Note: Make the night before and serve at Christmas carolling parties.

Mrs. Chris W. Ragland

Soups

Peanut Butter Soup

Serves: 8 to 10

1 quart rich chicken stock
3 ounces minced onion
3 ounces minced celery
8 ounces peanut butter
3 ounces butter
1 tablespoon flour

1 cup half and half
1 teaspoon salt
¼ teaspoon pepper
4 teaspoons crumbled bacon or minced
    country ham

Simmer chicken stock, onions and celery together for 40 to 50 minutes. Strain out onion and celery and discard. Stir in peanut butter until dissolved. Mix flour with half and half, add together with remaining ingredients, simmer all together for 15 minutes. Season with salt and pepper. Garnish each serving with ½ teaspoon bacon or minced country ham.

OLD CLUB Restaurant

My Mother's Turkey Soup

Serves: 6

Turkey carcass
2 to 3 16-ounce cans whole
    tomatoes
1 48-ounce can tomato juice
1 16-ounce can peas

2 cans Veg-all
2 to 4 pieces cut up lemons
Salt
Pepper
1 to 2 tablespoons sugar

Cover turkey carcass with water and simmer for 3 hours. Cool. Pick out bones and strain. Add tomatoes, tomato juice, peas, Veg-all, lemons, and salt and pepper to taste. Cook 3 additional hours. Add sugar to taste, half an hour before soup is done.

Note: Better when refrigerated overnight to allow flavors to blend.

Mrs. John T. Ticer

LEE'S BOYHOOD HOME

Lee Boyhood Home

This house has enjoyed a rich history since it was built by John Potts in the late 18th century. William Fitzhugh, of Chatham on the Rappahannock River, purchased the elegant home as his in-town residence. George Washington often enjoyed that gentleman's hospitality. On April 3, 1777, Washington made the following entry in his diary: "In the evening went to Alexandria and lodged myself at Mr. Fitzhugh's."

This house was the one to which Revolutionary War hero Henry "Light Horse Harry" Lee brought his wife Anne Hill Carter and his children Charles Carter, Anne, Smith and Robert Edward, in 1811.

Young Robert, destined to become the great military leader of the Confederacy, explored the lively port city and was fascinated by the traffic in the harbor. It is said that he could easily identify the flags of the ships in the port from his bedroom window. Lee lived in this house until he left Alexandria to start his military career at West Point.

Another Revolutionary War hero is associated with this historic dwelling. It was in the drawing room that the Marquis de Lafayette called on the widow of his former comrade "Light Horse Harry" Lee in 1824.

Easy Lobster Bisque

Serves: 8

1 10-ounce can tomato soup
1 10-ounce can cream of pea soup
1 10-ounce can mushroom soup

1½ pounds fresh cooked lobster
1 cup sour cream
⅓ cup sherry

Combine three soups and sour cream in top of double boiler. Add lobster. Heat, then add sherry. Serve immediately.

Mrs. C. S. Taylor Burke, Jr.

Bouillabaise

Serves: 6 to 8

3 cups fish broth
½ cup salad oil
1 cup thinly sliced onion
1 clove garlic, minced
2½ cups tomatoes
½ cup fresh lemon juice
3 strips lemon peel
2 bay leaves
¼ teaspoon coarsely ground
  pepper
8 cloves, whole

1½ teaspoons salt
2 pounds fish filet, fresh or frozen
  (sole or turbot)
12 oysters (optional)
1 7 or 10-ounce can lobster or crab
  meat
10 ounces shrimp, cooked, shelled and
  deveined
½ cup sherry
2 dozen mussels or clams
1 lemon, thinly sliced

Boil shrimp in water until pink. Drain, retaining 3 cups of liquid. Combine shrimp liquid with oyster liquor to make fish broth. Heat oil in a large saucepan, and sauté onion and garlic until tender. Add the tomatoes, lemon juice and peel, seasonings and fish broth, and simmer for 30 minutes. Cut the fish filets into 2-inch pieces, and add to the mixture. Simmer an additional 8 minutes. Drop in the oysters, and simmer until the edges curl (approximately 3 minutes). Add crab meat, shrimp and sherry, and heat gently. Add well-scrubbed steamed mussels or clams, and cook 5 minutes. Garnish with lemon slices.

Note: Serve with crusty, warm French bread and crisp spinach salad and a Rhone or Bordeaux wine.

Mrs. E. Darryl Barnes

Fish Chowder

Serves: 4

1 large onion, chopped
2 tablespoons butter
2 cups water
4 potatoes, peeled and diced

1½ to 2 cups milk
1 pound white fish, cooked
2 tablespoons flour
Salt and pepper

Sauté onions in butter until yellow. Set aside. Place water and potatoes in a large pot and cook until tender, about 10 minutes. Then add milk and fish. Mix flour with small amount of cold milk and add to fish mixture to thicken. Season with salt and pepper to taste. Serve hot.

Note: Peas and carrots may also be added. This is not overwhelmingly fishy.

Mrs. Rennie H. Barnes

Crock Pot Steak Soup

Serves: 6

3 cups water
2 onions, chopped
3 ribs celery, chopped
2 carrots, sliced
1 1-pound can tomatoes
Pepper to taste
1 tablespoon MSG

1 10-ounce package frozen mixed
    vegetables
1 pound ground chuck or round
1 tablespoon beef paste (Bovril)
½ cup butter
½ cup flour

Brown beef and pour off grease. Put all ingredients except butter and flour in crock pot. Cover and cook on low for 8 to 10 hours. One hour before serving, turn pot up to high. Make a roux of butter and the flour. Stir until smooth. Pour into crockpot and stir until thick. Continue to cook soup on high until thick.

Note: Can be made ahead and frozen.

Mrs. Caswell O. Hobbs

Artichoke Soup with Red Caviar

Serves: 4

5 Jerusalem artichokes, coarsely
  chopped
3 cups chicken or veal stock
Salt and pepper to taste
1 medium onion, coarsely chopped

1 small potato, peeled and coarsely
  chopped
½ cup butter
½ cup cream

Garnish

1 egg white, stiffly beaten
1 small jar red caviar

1 tablespoon finely chopped fresh
  chives

Put artichokes, onion and potato into saucepan with butter. Sweat with lid on until soft. Add stock, checking seasonings. Purée or sieve. Add cream. Serve hot with egg white placed on top and sprinkled with red caviar and chopped chives.

Mrs. Warren B. Heenan

Cuban Black Bean Soup

Serves: 6 to 8

1 pound black beans
2 quarts water
1½ tablespoons salt
5 garlic cloves, crushed
2 tablespoons white vinegar

1½ teaspoons cumin
1½ teaspoons oregano
5 ounces olive oil
1 large onion, chopped
1 large green bell pepper, seeded and
  chopped

In 4-quart saucepan, soak beans in water overnight. Add salt and bring to boil over medium heat. Cover and simmer, stirring occasionally, until soft, about 1½ hours. In small bowl combine garlic, vinegar, cumin and oregano. Heat oil in 10-inch skillet over medium-high heat. Add onion and pepper and sauté until onions are lightly browned. Stir in garlic mixture and sauté 1 to 2 minutes more. Add to beans, cover and simmer about 1 hour, stirring occasionally. Add a generous tablespoon rice marinade to each soup bowl before serving.

Rice Marinade

1 cup cooked rice
2 tablespoons chopped onion

2 tablespoons wine vinegar
1 tablespoon olive oil

Combine rice, onion, vinegar and oil in small bowl. Cover and marinate at least 2 to 3 hours at room temperature.

Mrs. John E. Davey

Hearty Bean Soup

Serves: 6

2 16-ounce cans pinto or kidney
  beans
1 quart water
1 16-ounce can peeled tomatoes
1 cup chopped onion
½ cup Karo dark corn syrup

1 tablespoon salt
1 clove garlic, minced
1½ teaspoons chili powder
1 teaspoon dry oregano
Dash of pepper
1 cup sliced link sausages

Mix together all ingredients except sausage in a large 4-quart saucepan or soup kettle. Bring to a boil, reduce heat, cover and simmer 1½ hours. Stir occasionally to mash beans. Add sausage after soup has cooked one hour. Uncover and boil gently, stirring now and then until the soup begins to thicken, about 30 minutes.

Note: Left-over pork or ham may be substituted for sausage.

Mrs. Christopher J. Meyer

Broccoli Chowder

Serves: 4

1 10-ounce package frozen chopped
  broccoli
2 teaspoons instant minced onion
½ cup boiling water, salted

2 cups milk
1 10-ounce can condensed cream of
  potato soup
½ cup shredded Swiss cheese

Cook broccoli and onion in the boiling salted water until tender. Do not drain. Stir in milk and soup; heat through. Add cheese, stirring until melted. Cool slightly. At this point you can serve the soup or blend in the blender until smooth.

Note: May be served cold in the summer, be sure to blend if served this way.

Mrs. Renny H. Barnes

Spicy Cabbage Soup

Serves: 4

1 10½-ounce can beef broth
1½ soup cans water
3 cups finely shredded cabbage

1 15½-ounce can spaghetti sauce with
　meat

Combine beef broth and water in 3-quart saucepan and bring to a boil. Add cabbage and return quickly to a boil. Cook uncovered until cabbage is tender, 10 to 15 minutes. Stir in spaghetti sauce, heat and serve.

Mrs. William B. Knight

Cheese Beer Soup

Serves: 10 to 12

½ cup butter
1 large onion, finely chopped
½ cup flour
1 quart beer

4 cups grated Swiss cheese (or Swiss
　mixed with Monterey Jack)
2 quarts milk

Melt butter, add onion and cook several minutes but do not brown. Add flour and cook until bubbly, stirring constantly. Gradually add beer, stir until thick. Add cheese and melt. Gradually add milk; heat but do not boil. Pour into mugs or bowls, serve with parsley sprigs.

Note: Great on a cold day or while watching the ball game.

Mrs. Renny H. Barnes

Borscht

Serves: 4

3 cups beef bouillon diluted with
　equal amounts of water
1 pound stewing beef, cut into
　small cubes
1 bay leaf
1 16-ounce can sliced beets
3 tablespoons oil
1 small head cabbage, shredded

2 carrots, sliced
2 onions, chopped
1 8-ounce can tomato sauce
Salt
Pepper
Parsley or dill
Sour cream (optional)

Boil beef and bay leaf in bouillon and water. In a different pot, boil beets in 2 cups water until beets lose their color. Drain; discard beets, reserve liquid. Sauté cabbage, carrots and onions in oil until tender. To the pan add tomato sauce, beef stock, beet juice and salt and pepper to taste. Cook for one hour or more and let sit until cool. Chill in refrigerator overnight. Skim off any fat. Bring to boil and simmer for 5 to 10 minutes before serving. Serve garnished with parsley or dill and spoonful of sour cream.

Note: This is a hearty and flavorful dish. Egg noodles go well as a side dish. May easily be increased.

Mrs. Hamilton Beggs

Eckardt Gazpacho

Serves: 8

1 46-ounce can tomato juice
5 beef bouillon cubes
3 medium tomatoes, chopped
1 cup chopped unpared cucumber
¾ cup chopped green pepper
½ cup chopped scallions with tops
8 tablespoons red wine vinegar

4 tablespoons vegetable oil
1 tablespoon Worcestershire sauce
½ teaspoon hot pepper sauce
1 large clove garlic, crushed
Seasoned croutons (for garnish)
1 lime, cut in wedges (for garnish)

Heat tomato juice and bouillon cubes until cubes are dissolved. Stir in remaining ingredients and chill for at least 12 hours. Serve ice cold, over a bed of crushed ice, with seasoned croutons and a wedge of fresh lime.

Mrs. William Heenan

Elba's Onion Soup

Serves: 4

2 tablespoons melted butter
2 Bermuda onions, sliced
1½ teaspoons flour
2 10-ounce cans condensed chicken
    broth

1⅓ cups water
1 teaspoon salt
½ teaspoon white pepper
4 slices toasted French bread
4 tablespoons Parmesan cheese

Sauté onions in butter until soft and yellow, about 15 minutes. Sprinkle flour over onions and stir in. Add broth, water, salt and pepper. Heat to boiling, stirring constantly. Lower heat, cover and simmer 30 minutes. Float slice of toast in four ovenproof bowls filled with soup. Sprinkle toast with cheese. Broil 4 inches from heat until cheese turns a golden brown.

Mrs. Kevin Gallen

Onion Soup

Serves: 6

2 large yellow onions, cut in
  eighths
2 10½-ounce cans condensed beef
  broth
1 soup can water

2 tablespoons butter
2 medium white onions, cut in eighths
1 teaspoon salt
½ teaspoon black pepper

Place yellow onions, beef broth and water in blender, cover and chop, by turning control on and off 2 or 3 times. Drain through strainer reserving broth. In a large saucepan, sauté onions in butter until tender. Put white onions and reserved broth into blender and process until onions are finely grated. Add to sautéed onions and simmer 10 minutes. Add seasonings. Cover and simmer 30 minutes.

Note: Serve with thin rye slices sprinkled with Parmesan cheese.

Mrs. Robert L. Calhoun

 When making soup, remember: soup boiled is soup spoiled. The soup should be cooked gently.

Lentil Ham Soup

Serves: 10

¼ cup oil
3 cups diced cooked ham
1 ham bone
½ pound Polish sausage, cut in
  ½-inch slices
2 large onions, chopped
1 clove garlic, crushed
2 cups chopped celery with leaves

1 16-ounce can plum tomatoes
1 pound lentils
12 cups water
½ teaspoon Tabasco
1½ teaspoons salt
1 10-ounce package frozen chopped
  spinach, thawed

Heat oil. Add ham cubes, sausage, onion and garlic and cook 5 minutes. Add ham bone, celery, tomatoes, lentils, water, Tabasco and salt. Cover and cook over low heat for 2 hours. Add spinach. Cook an additional 10 minutes.

Note: This soup freezes well.

Mrs. Henry E. Thomas, IV

Potage Cressonière

Serves: 6 to 8

¼ cup butter
1 clove garlic, minced
2 cups chopped onions
1 quart thinly sliced raw potatoes
1 tablespoon salt
½ teaspoon freshly ground black
  pepper

¾ cup water
1 bunch watercress
1½ cups milk
1½ cups water
2 egg yolks
½ cup light cream

Heat the butter in a large saucepan. Add the garlic and onions and sauté until tender, about 5 minutes. Add the potatoes, seasonings and ¾ cup water. Cover and bring to a boil. Reduce the heat and simmer 15 minutes or until the potatoes are almost tender. Cut the watercress stems into ⅛-inch lengths, reserving a few sprigs for garnish. Coarsely chop the leaves. To the potato mixture, add all the watercress stems and all but a few leaves, the milk and water. Cook 15 minutes; cool slightly. Purée in blender or put the mixture through a food mill. Return to the saucepan and reheat. Blend together the egg yolks and cream. Gradually stir into the soup and cook, stirring constantly, until slightly thickened. Garnish with the remaining watercress leaves and serve immediately, or it can be served later cold.

Mrs. Stephen A. Sharp

Potage St. Germain

Serves: 6

1 one-pound ham bone
4½ cups water
⅔ cup finely chopped green onions
⅓ cup finely chopped celery
⅓ cup finely chopped carrots
½ teaspoon sugar

1 cup chicken broth
1 pound split peas
⅛ teaspoon crushed marjoram
⅛ teaspoon pepper
2½ cups milk
1 cup half and half

Place ham bone in large pot. Add water, broth and peas. Bring to a boil and simmer 30 minutes. Add vegetables and seasonings. Simmer an additional 30 to 40 minutes, stirring occasionally until peas are very soft and mixture is thick. Remove ham bone. Reserve ham meat. Gradually stir in milk and half and half. Add ham meat and simmer 10 minutes.

Mrs. C. Mason Ebhardt

Riso e Indivia al Pomodoro
(Rice-Endive-Tomato Soup)

Serves: 6

1 slice lean salt pork	10 fresh, ripe plum tomatoes
½ onion	1 bunch curly endive
½ celery stalk	Salt to taste
1 small carrot	1 quart hot water
4 sprigs parsley	1 cup long grain rice
2 tablespoons olive oil	Grated Parmesan cheese

Make a battuto (a paste made by mincing ingredients with a sharp knife) by mincing the salt pork with the onion, celery, carrot and parsley. Sauté the mixture until golden in the oil in a soup pot over medium heat; then turn off the burner. Peel tomatoes, cut them open and remove the seeds. Save all possible juice. Add the cut tomatoes to the soup pot and cook on medium high heat for about 10 minutes stirring frequently. Wash and chop the endive, add to the soup pot, still on medium high heat, and cook for 3 to 4 minutes. Add hot water and bring to a boil; add the rice and continue cooking until the rice is done (about 12 minutes). Taste for salt and add if necessary. Serve hot, sprinkling cheese on top of each serving.

Note: A great beginning to an Italian dinner.

Mrs. Stephen L. Echols

Mother's Vegetable Soup

Serves: 8

1½ pounds stewing beef	4 potatoes, diced
1 48-ounce can tomato juice	Other vegetables, as desired
1 16-ounce can tomatoes	Salt
1 16-ounce bag frozen mixed	Pepper
vegetables	¼ cup sugar
3 celery stalks, chopped	Water (to thin)
1 onion, chopped	

Trim fat and place meat in aluminum foil. (Do not salt and pepper). Wrap up and put in a heavy pan with water, just enough to keep from burning. Cover pan and bake in oven for 1 to 1½ hours at 350 degrees. Boil tomato juice, add other vegetables, meat, and seasoning. Simmer for 2½ to 3 hours.

Mrs. John Denson

Chilled Avocado Soup

Serves: 4 to 6

2 ripe avocados
½ cup sour cream
2 large tomatoes, peeled and
  chopped
3 cups beef bouillon

¼ cup minced green onion
2 tablespoons fresh lemon juice
Salt
Pepper

Cut avocados in half lengthwise. Remove seeds and peel. Purée halves in blender. Add remaining ingredients at once and chill.

Mrs. Hamilton Beggs

Broccoli Soup

Yield: 3 cups

1 cup milk
2 tablespoons flour
1 teaspoon salt
4 sprigs parsley
2 slices onion

¾ cup light cream
2 tablespoons butter
Pinch of pepper
1 cup celery leaves
1½ cups cooked broccoli

Blend in order given above. When well-blended, heat in double boiler, stirring occasionally. May be served iced or heated.

Variation: Spinach may be substituted for broccoli.

Mrs. C. Mason Ebhardt

Cold Cucumber Soup

Serves: 4

1 cucumber, sliced
1 10-ounce can cream of celery
  soup
1 soup can milk
½ pint sour cream
3 to 4 scallions, chopped

1 teaspoon lemon juice
1 teaspoon dill weed
Salt and pepper
4 tablespoons chopped green pepper
  (optional)

Blend all ingredients in blender and refrigerate. To serve garnish with chopped chives.

Note: This soup is better served the day after it is prepared to allow flavors to blend. Garlic salt may be used if you like this seasoning.

Mrs. C. S. Taylor Burke III

Icy Lemon Soup

Serves: 4

1 10-ounce can cream of chicken
   soup
1 cup light cream
1 tablespoon water

2 teaspoons curry powder
7 tablespoons lemon juice
Lemon slices

Put soup and cream in blender. Mix curry powder in water and pour into blender. Spin at high speed for one minute. Chill for several hours. At last possible minute before serving, stir lemon juice into the soup. Serve very cold garnished with thin slices of lemon.

Mrs. James W. Vaughan, Jr.

Vichyssoise

Serves: 6 to 8

1 medium onion, minced
3 medium leeks, minced
3 tablespoons butter
5 medium potatoes, peeled and
   diced
4 cups chicken stock or bouillon

2 cups table cream
Salt
White pepper
½ teaspoon mace
Chopped chives

Sauté leeks and onions in butter. Add potatoes and chicken stock. Simmer over medium heat until potatoes are tender. Cool slightly, then blend. Add remaining ingredients. Chill. Garnish with chives when ready to serve.

Note: Mace adds the special flavor.

Mrs. David Redding

Cold Tomato Soup

Serves: 6

1 onion, chopped
1 tablespoon butter
6 tomatoes, peeled, seeded and
   chopped
½ cup chicken broth
½ teaspoon tomato paste
½ teaspoon sugar

½ teaspoon thyme
½ teaspoon salt
¾ cup heavy cream
½ cup sour cream
¼ cup lime juice
Salt
Pepper

Sauté onion in butter, covered with a buttered round of wax paper as well as saucepan lid over moderately low heat for 15 minutes or until soft. Add tomatoes, chicken broth, tomato paste, sugar, thyme and salt. Simmer the mixture, covered for 10 minutes. Let mixture cool. In a blender or food processor, purée mixture with lime juice, heavy cream, sour cream, salt and pepper. Divide the soup among six small glass bowls, chill in freeze compartment of refrigerator for one hour. Garnish with a slice of lime and a sprig of parsley.

Mrs. Edward McDonough

Rich, Rich Cherry Soup

Serves: 4

1 1-pound can water-pack red tart pitted cherries with liquid	¼ teaspoon cinnamon
	2 strips orange peel (orange part only)
¼ cup sugar	½ cup orange juice
2 teaspoons cornstarch	½ cup red Burgundy wine
¼ teaspoon salt	Whipped cream or sour cream

Place the can of cherries and liquid in a blender reserving a few whole cherries. Add sugar, cornstarch, salt, cinnamon, orange peel and juice. Cover and blend on highest speed for 20 seconds. Pour into saucepan and cook over medium heat, stirring constantly until reaching boiling point. Continue to stir at a boil for ½ minute. Remove from heat and stir in wine. Serve hot or chilled. Garnish with whipped cream or sour cream and the reserved whole cherries.

Mrs. Warren B. Heenan

Croutons

Preheat: 400 degrees
Serves: 8

8 slices bread	8 teaspoons olive oil
1 large clove garlic, split	

Rub the bread slices on both sides with the garlic, then brush generously with the olive oil. Place the bread on a baking rack or sheet and bake at 400 degrees until golden, turning once if necessary. Cut into cubes.

Pumpkin Soup

Serves: 8

7 tablespoons butter
6 green onions, chopped
1 onion, sliced
3 cups pumpkin purée, homemade
   or canned
6 cups chicken stock

½ teaspoon salt
3 tablespoons flour
1 cup light cream
Croutons
Lightly salted whipped cream

Melt 4 tablespoons butter in a large saucepan. Sauté the green onions and onion until soft and golden. Add the pumpkin, chicken stock and salt. Bring to a boil, stirring, then simmer 10 minutes. Blend mixture in blender. Return soup to pan. Knead the flour with 2 tablespoons of butter and gradually add to the soup. Bring to a boil, beating with a whisk while it thickens. Add the cream and remaining butter. Serve garnished with the croutons and whipped cream.

 Soups, when prepared ahead, take up less refrigerator space when stored in tall plastic containers or milk cartons.

Monte Cristo

Serves: 1

3 slices white bread
1 teaspoon mayonnaise
1 teaspoon Dijon mustard
2 1-ounce slices Swiss cheese
1 1-ounce slice domestic ham,
   sliced thin

1 1-ounce slice breast of turkey,
   sliced thin
4 beaten eggs

Spread mayonnaise on two slices of bread, spread Dijon mustard on the other slice. Place 1 slice of Swiss cheese on mayonnaise-coated bread, add ham and top with mustard-coated bread. Add Swiss cheese and turkey slice and top with last piece of bread. Place ½-inch oil in frying pan; heat until hot. Dip sandwich in beaten eggs and fry until golden brown. Turn to other side and brown. Cut in half. Sprinkle with powdered sugar. Garnish with strawberry preserves.

The Federalist Restaurant
Holiday Inn, Old Town Alexandria

Salads

Apricot-Orange Freeze

Serves: 6 to 8

2 8-ounce containers orange
  yogurt
1 1-pound can apricots

½ cup sugar
⅓ cup chopped pecans

Stir yogurt in containers to blend. Drain apricots and cut up. Combine yogurt, apricots, sugar and nuts. Pour mixture into square or oblong dish. Freeze until firm. Let stand at room temperature a few minutes before serving. Cut into squares and serve on lettuce.

Mrs. William F. Clayton

Orange Sherbet Salad

Serves: 6 to 8

2 3-ounce packages orange gelatin
1 10-ounce can mandarin oranges

1 16-ounce can crushed pineapple
1 pint orange sherbet

Drain oranges and pineapple, reserving liquid. Add enough water to fruit liquid to equal 2 cups. Bring to a boil. Dissolve gelatin in liquid. Cool slightly. Stir in sherbet. Chill until syrupy. Add drained fruit and chill until firm in 6-cup mold.

Mrs. William F. Clayton

Lemon-Lime Gelatin Salad

Serves: 6

1 3-ounce package lemon gelatin
1 3-ounce package lime gelatin
1 cup boiling water
6 ounces table cream
1 cup mayonnaise

½ cup chopped nuts
12 ounces cottage cheese
1 8-ounce can crushed pineapple,
  drained

Combine lemon and lime gelatins and water. Stir until dissolved. Let cool. Mix together cream, mayonnaise, nuts, cottage cheese and pineapple. Fold pineapple mixture into gelatin. Pour into 1½ quart rectangular pyrex dish or mold. Chill.

Mrs. Michael E. Delnegro

Lee-Fendall House

Built in 1795 by Phillip Richard Fendall, a founder of the Bank of Virginia, the Lee-Fendall house was the residence of various members of the Lee family from 1785 to 1903. The house was erected on a one-half acre site purchased from General Henry "Light Horse Harry" Lee in 1784. Since that time, it has become a memorial to him.

The residence has undergone considerable remodeling during its 180-year history but currently retains the atmosphere of its earlier years. It houses a growing collection of the furniture and personal belongings of members of the distinguished Lee family.

Although "Light Horse Harry" never lived in the house, he was a frequent visitor in the company of his close friend President George Washington. Lee himself enjoyed a distinguished political career, serving as governor of Virginia from 1791 to 1794.

More recently, Lee-Fendall House was the home of labor leader John L. Lewis and his family.

Spicy Peach Cranberry Ring

Serves: 8

1 30-ounce can cling peach halves
1 teaspoon whole cloves
1 3-inch cinnamon stick
¼ cup vinegar
2 3-ounce packages lemon gelatin

1 cup fresh or frozen cranberries
½ orange, unpeeled
⅓ cup sugar
1¾ cups hot water
1 3-ounce package cherry gelatin

Drain peaches, reserving the syrup. Add enough water to syrup to make 1¾ cups. Add the cloves, cinnamon and vinegar to liquid and simmer, uncovered, for 10 minutes. Add peaches and heat slowly for 5 minutes. Remove peaches and place in a 3-quart ring mold, cut side up. Strain syrup. Measure and add enough hot water to make 1⅔ cups. Add liquid to the lemon gelatin. Dissolve and pour over peaches. Refrigerate until almost firm. Meanwhile, put cranberries and orange through a food chopper. Stir in sugar. Add 1¾ cups hot water to cherry gelatin. Cool. Add cranberry mixture. Pour over almost jelled peach mixture. Chill until firm. Unmold and serve.

Mrs. James R. Skidmore

Strawberry-Apricot Salad

Serves: 14 to 16

2 3-ounce packages strawberry
 gelatin
1 12-ounce can (2 cups) apricot
 nectar

1 30-ounce can apricots
1 16-ounce box frozen strawberries

Heat nectar and pour over gelatin. Defrost strawberries. Open and drain apricots. Cut into pieces and add to gelatin. Add strawberries to gelatin. Cool and pour into mold. Chill until set.

Mrs. James L. Howe III

Creamy Sunshine Salad

Serves: 6 to 8

1 20-ounce can crushed pineapple
1 6-ounce package apricot gelatin

2 cups buttermilk
1 large container Cool Whip

Mix pineapple and gelatin. Heat until gelatin is dissolved. Allow mixture to cool. Add buttermilk and mix well. Fold in Cool Whip. Pour into 6-cup mold. Refrigerate to congeal.

Mrs. John T. Miller

Red Raspberry Mold

Serves: 12

1 10-ounce package frozen red
   raspberries, thawed
2 3-ounce packages raspberry
   gelatin

2 cups boiling water
1 pint vanilla ice cream.
1 6-ounce can frozen pink lemonade
   concentrate, thawed

Drain raspberries and reserve syrup. Dissolve gelatin in boiling water; add ice cream and stir until melted. Stir in lemonade and reserve syrup. Chill until thickened. Add raspberries; turn into a 6 to 8 cup mold and chill until firm.

Note: A lovely and colorful addition to a luncheon. Goes especially well with poultry.

Mrs. Alfred E. T. Rusch

Spiced Peach Salad

Serves: 6 to 8

1 30-ounce can sliced peaches
¼ cup vinegar
12 cloves
3 sticks cinnamon

1 6-ounce package orange gelatin
3¾ cups liquid (drained peach juice
   and water)

Boil vinegar, liquid and spices. Cook 10 minutes; remove spices. Add gelatin. Cool till slightly thickened; add peaches. Pour into 1½-quart mold. Refrigerate.

Mrs. Frank McCabe

Frozen Fruit Medley

Serves: 8 to 10

1 3-ounce package gelatin, any
    flavor
1 cup boiling water
1 8¾-ounce can pineapple tidbits
¼ cup lemon juice
1 envelope Dream Whip

⅓ cup mayonnaise
½ cup seedless grapes
¼ cup diced cherries
½ cup chopped nuts
1 medium banana, diced

Dissolve gelatin and a pinch of salt in water. Drain pineapple, measuring syrup and adding water to make ½ cup. Stir liquid and lemon juice into gelatin. Chill until slightly thickened, approximately 1 hour and 15 minutes. Prepare whipped topping mix. Mix with mayonnaise, fruits and nuts until blended. Then, blend into gelatin. Spoon into 8 x 4-inch loaf pan. Freeze until firm. Unmold 30 minutes before slicing, garnish as desired.

Mrs. Simmons B. Savage III

Gingerale Molded Salad

Serves: 6 to 8

2 tablespoons unflavored gelatin
¼ cup water
½ cup orange juice
½ cup sugar
⅛ teaspoon salt
2 cups gingerale
Juice of 1 lemon

½ pound Tokay grapes, seeded
1 orange, peeled and sliced
1 grapefruit, sectioned
6 slices unsweetened pineapple
3 teaspoons preserved ginger, chopped
1 cup whipped cream
1 cup mayonnaise

Soak gelatin in ¼ cup water. Dissolve in boiling orange juice. Add sugar, salt, gingerale and lemon juice. Chill until nearly set. Fold in fruits and ginger. Pour into wet 6-cup mold. Chill until firmly set. Unmold onto a bed of lettuce. Serve with creamy mayonnaise made by folding in whipped cream.

Note: Good with roast pork or ham.

Mrs. Bernard P. O'Hare

Fruit Salad with Sauce

Serves: 8 to 10

2 tablespoons sugar
2 eggs, well-beaten
2 tablespoons undiluted frozen
   orange juice
2 tablespoons vinegar
1 tablespoon butter
Dash of salt

1 cup (or more) sour cream
2 cups grapes
1 cup pineapple, diced
2 cups mandarin oranges
1 cup sliced bananas
2 cups miniature marshmallows

Cook sugar, eggs, juice, vinegar. Remove from heat when thick. Add butter and salt. When cool, stir in sour cream. Pour sauce over fruit and marshmallows.

Mrs. Thomas F. Johnson

Cucumber Mold

Serves: 4

1 3-ounce package lemon gelatin
½ cup hot water
1 tablespoon lemon juice

½ cup (or more) grated cucumber
½ cup diced celery
½ pint sour cream

Dissolve gelatin in water. Add juice and cool. Add vegetables to sour cream. Then fold cucumber and celery mixture into gelatin mixture. Chill.

Mrs. Thomas F. Shea

Beet Mold

Serves: 4 to 6

1 3-ounce package lemon gelatin
1 8-ounce can diced beets
1½ cups beet juice plus water
¼ to ½ cup diced celery

1 tablespoon horseradish
¼ cup vinegar
¼ cup sugar

Mix gelatin with heated beet juice and water. Chill until partially set. Add beets. Combine celery, horseradish, vinegar and sugar; add to beet and gelatin mixture. Pour into 4 or 5 cup mold. Refrigerate until set. Unmold onto salad platter.

Mrs. Marjorie S. Cook

Spinach Swinger

Serves: 8

2 envelopes unflavored gelatin
1/4 cup water
1/2 teaspoon salt
2 tablespoons lemon juice
1 cup mayonnaise
1 10-ounce can beef consommé

1/4 cup chopped green onion
1 1/2 teaspoons hot horseradish
1 10-ounce package frozen, chopped
   spinach, thawed and well drained
1/4 pound crisp fried bacon, chopped
4 hard-boiled eggs, finely chopped

Dissolve gelatin in water. Add salt, lemon juice and mayonnaise to dissolved gelatin. Then add consommé, onion and horseradish; stir well to mix. Gradually add spinach, bacon and eggs. Pour into 1 1/2-quart mold. Serve with "horseradished mayonnaise."

Note: This salad served with ham, curried fruit and rolls is an easy and simple luncheon.

Mrs. William T. Mahood

Broccoli Molded Salad

Serves: 6

1 10-ounce package frozen chopped
   broccoli
1 10 3/4-ounce can consommé
2 tablespoons lemon juice
1 tablespoon wine (with or
   without garlic) vinegar

1 1/2 tablespoons unflavored gelatin
1/4 cup cold water
2/3 cup mayonnaise
Garlic salt (optional)

Undercook broccoli, drain and cool. Soak gelatin in water; add hot consommé, lemon juice and vinegar. Chill until syrupy (heavy but not completely set), about an hour in the refrigerator. Beat with rotary beater and add mayonnaise; beat again. (It will be fluffy after first beating). Fold in broccoli and pour into lightly greased 2-quart mold. A baking dish may be used and the salad cut into squares. Top with sauce of mayonnaise mixed with curry, dried onion and lemon juice.

Mrs. Robert H. Anderson

Tomato Salad

Serves: 8

1 10¾-ounce can tomato soup
1 3-ounce package lemon gelatin
1 cup chopped celery

½ cup chopped green pepper
1 cup cottage cheese
1 cup mayonnaise

Heat soup to boiling. Add gelatin and stir until dissolved. Cool. Add remaining ingredients. Refrigerate until congealed.

Note: Tabasco may be added for a spicy salad. Shrimp may be added for a nice luncheon salad.

Mrs. Alfred E. T. Rusch

Cole Slaw Mold

Serves: 8 to 10

1 3-ounce package lemon gelatin
½ teaspoon salt
1 cup hot water
½ cup cold water
½ cup mayonnaise
½ cup sour cream

1 teaspoon grated onion
1 tablespoon prepared mustard
2 tablespoons vinegar
1 teaspoon sugar
2 cups finely shredded cabbage

Dissolve gelatin and salt in hot water. Add cold water and chill until just syrupy. Fold in remaining ingredients except cabbage. Chill until slightly thickened. Fold in cabbage. Pour into 5 cup mold and chill until firm.

Mrs. Frank McCabe

Fruited Cole Slaw

Serves: 5

1 cup canned fruit cocktail
2 cups finely shredded cabbage
¼ cup mayonnaise

1 tablespoon lemon juice
½ teaspoon salt
Salad greens

Drain fruit, add cabbage. Blend mayonnaise, lemon juice and salt together. Add fruit mixture, toss lightly. Serve well chilled on salad greens.

Mrs. John J. Ross III

Kraut Salad

Serves: 6 to 8

1 14-ounce can sauerkraut,
  drained and chopped
1 cup diced celery
1 green pepper, chopped
1 4-ounce jar pimento

1 large onion, chopped
1½ cups sugar
⅓ cup cooking oil
2 tablespoons vinegar

Mix all ingredients and refrigerate for 24 hours before serving.

Mrs. G. Ray Lewis

Artichoke Rice Salad

Serves: 8 to 10

1 4-ounce package chicken flavored
  rice
2 7-ounce jars marinated
  artichoke hearts
¼ cup mayonnaise

¼ cup chopped green pepper
4 spring onions, chopped
12 sliced olives—optional
Curry powder to taste

Prepare rice according to directions, omitting butter. Add artichokes (quartered) to rice, reserving liquid. Add onions, green peppers and olives. Toss with dressing of mayonnaise, marinade from artichokes and curry powder. Salt and pepper to taste. Chill.

Mrs. James S. Brady

Make Ahead Cole Slaw

Serves: 20

1 head cabbage, shredded
2 carrots, grated
1 large onion, finely chopped
½ cup finely chopped green pepper
1 2-ounce jar pimento, diced

2 cups sugar
1½ cups white vinegar
1 tablespoon salt
1 tablespoon celery seed
1 tablespoon mustard seed

Mix sugar, vinegar, salt, celery seed and mustard seed. Pour over vegetables. Refrigerate at least 24 hours. (Keeps two weeks in the refrigerator).

Mrs. Thomas F. Shea

Cole Slaw for a Fortnight

Serves: 12

1 medium head cabbage, finely
   chopped
1 green pepper, chopped
1 medium onion, chopped
½ cup sugar

¾ cup white vinegar
¾ cup oil
1 teaspoon salt
1 teaspoon celery salt
1 teaspoon prepared mustard

Place in large bowl: cabbage, green pepper and onion. Sprinkle with sugar. Cover and set aside. Bring to a boil: vinegar, oil, salt, celery salt and mustard. Pour over cabbage mixture and refrigerate 24 hours before serving. Drain to serve.

Mrs. Alfred E. T. Rusch

Curry Salad

Serves: 10 to 12

½ teaspoon beef-flavored gravy
   base (Maggi's)
¼ cup hot water
1 cup mayonnaise
1 clove garlic, minced
1 tablespoon curry powder

¼ teaspoon Worcestershire sauce
6 to 8 drops Tabasco sauce
1 pound can artichoke hearts
¼ cup radish slices
Spinach or salad greens

Mix gravy base and water together; add mayonnaise, garlic, curry, Worcestershire sauce and Tabasco. Let sit overnight. Spoon dressing over spinach. Add artichoke hearts and radish slices.

Mrs. Wilson Livingood

Frito Bean Salad

Serves: 8 to 10

2 15-ounce cans kidney beans,
   drained
1 large onion, chopped
1 bell pepper, chopped

4 tomatoes, chopped
1 cup grated Cheddar cheese
1 bottle Catalina salad dressing
1 large bag Fritos, crushed

Combine all ingredients except for Fritos and salad dressing several hours before serving. When ready to serve, add salad dressing and Fritos. Toss. Serve immediately.

Mrs. Lawton Rogers

Cold Curried Rice and Peas

Serves: 6 to 8

1⅓ cups Minute Rice (cooked as
   directed)
¼ cup French dressing (cream
   style)
¾ cup mayonnaise
1 tablespoon minced onion
¾ teaspoon curry powder

½ teaspoon salt
⅛ teaspoon pepper
½ teaspoon dry mustard
1 cup diced celery
1⅓ cups frozen green peas, thawed
   and drained

Cook rice as directed. Lightly toss with French dressing. Let cool to room temperature. In a large bowl, mix mayonnaise, onion, curry, salt, pepper and mustard. Add celery, peas, rice and toss lightly. Refrigerate. Shrimp or diced chicken may be added if you wish to use it as a main dish.

Mrs. Alfred E. T. Rusch

Copper Carrot Pennies

Serves: 8

2 pounds carrots, sliced
1 green pepper
1 large onion
1 can tomato soup
½ cup salad oil

¾ cup vinegar
1 cup sugar
1 teaspoon prepared mustard
1 teaspoon Worcestershire sauce

Boil carrots in salted water until just tender. When cool, alternate a layer of drained carrots, pepper rings and onion rings. Make a marinade of soup, oil, vinegar, sugar, mustard and Worcestershire sauce, beating until completely blended. Pour over carrots. Refrigerate overnight.

Note: Keeps well in refrigerator for a week. Leftover marinade is good on salads.

Mrs. Thomas F. Johnson

Marinated Broccoli

Serves: 12

3 bunches broccoli
1 cup cider vinegar
1 tablespoon sugar
1 tablespoon dill weed
1 tablespoon MSG

1 teaspoon salt
1 teaspoon pepper
1 teaspoon garlic salt
1½ cups vegetable oil

Cut florets from broccoli. Mix all remaining ingredients in large bowl. Add broccoli florets and marinate for at least 24 hours in refrigerator.

Ms. Cynthia Byrnes

Baked Bean Salad

Serves: 8

1 16-ounce can of B & M baked
   beans
5 green onions, chopped
2 large spoonfuls India Relish

Chili sauce to taste
Mayonnaise to taste
2 to 3 stalks celery, diced

Combine all ingredients. Chill very well.

Note: Great picnic dish!

Mrs. Michael R. Ward

Green Bean Salad

Serves: 16

1 tablespoon vinegar
1 tablespoon oil
1 thinly sliced red onion
6 1-pound cans whole green beans,
   reserve liquid
1 cup sour cream

½ cup mayonnaise
1 teaspoon vinegar
1 teaspoon dry mustard
1 tablespoon horseradish
1 teaspoon chopped chives or onion
   tops

Marinate green beans in their own juice, 1 tablespoon vinegar, oil and red onion overnight. The next day drain beans and toss gently in a dressing made by combining sour cream, mayonnaise, vinegar, mustard, horseradish and chives.

Mrs. Philip A. Wells

Potato Salad

Serves: 6

3 large Idaho potatoes
½ cup chopped celery
½ cup chopped onion
2 hard boiled eggs, chopped
¼ cup chopped green pepper

¼ cup oil and vinegar dressing
½ cup mayonnaise
½ cup sour cream
1 tablespoon mustard
1 tablespoon relish

Boil potatoes and cool. Dice potatoes and eggs; combine with remaining ingredients. Chill. Serve on a bed of lettuce with garnishes.

Mrs. Jack Howard

Cucumber Salad

Serves: 6

4 cucumbers, peeled and sliced
1 cup white vinegar
¾ cup sugar

½ cup water
Fresh or dried dill
1 small onion, sliced paper thin

Place cucumber and onion slices in a glass bowl. Combine sugar, water, dill and vinegar in a saucepan. Boil. Pour over cucumber slices and refrigerate.

Note: Be sure to prepare this salad the same day you plan to serve it.

Mrs. Leon B. Ruben

Cauliflower/Green Bean Salad

Serves: 6

1 head cauliflower
1 16-ounce can green beans
½ to 1 cup mayonnaise

1 cup diced celery
Favorite oil base salad dressing

Break cauliflower into florets and cook until barely tender. Toss with salad dressing. Add drained green beans, celery and enough mayonnaise to coat vegetables. Adjust seasoning if necessary. Chill and serve.

Note: This recipe may be enlarged by increasing green beans. Be sure to use a flavorful dressing.

Mrs. Stephen Roger Shaffer

Potato Pickups

Potatoes, cubed	*Salt*
1 cup salad dressing	*Pepper*
2 tablespoons mustard	*Several stalks celery, cubed*
1 tablespoon vinegar	*Several Bermuda onions, cubed*

Cut, before boiling, the desired number of potatoes. When done, cool for ½ hour. Prepare a dressing combining salad dressing, mustard, vinegar, salt and pepper. If dressing is not thick enough add 1 tablespoon sifted flour. First put one cube of celery on a toothpick, next spear the potato and then the onion cube. Dip each toothpick with vegetables into the dressing. Put on a tray in the refrigerator one day in advance of serving.

Note: This is served on the Eastern Shore with Maryland Crabs, when you can't use forks or plates.

Mrs. Stephen A. Sharp

Marinated Tomatoes and Onions

Serves: 6

½ cup red wine vinegar	*6 large tomatoes, peeled and sliced*
⅓ cup olive oil	*2 medium red onions, sliced*
4½ teaspoons dried basil	*4½ teaspoons sugar*
1½ teaspoons dried tarragon	*Salt and pepper*
¼ teaspoon oregano	

Combine vinegar, oil, basil, tarragon and oregano. Whisk until blended. Layer half of the tomatoes in large serving bowl and cover with half of the onions. Sprinkle with half of sugar, salt and pepper to taste. Drizzle with some of the marinade. Repeat using remainder of all ingredients. Cover and chill for 2 or 3 hours before serving.

Variation: Omit sugar, sprinkle tomatoes with 2 tablespoons chopped scallions and 1 tablespoon chopped fresh parsley.

Mrs. C. Mason Ebhardt

Zucchini Mushroom Salad

Serves: 6

6 small zucchini
½ pound fresh mushrooms, sliced
⅛ teaspoon nutmeg
2 teaspoons lemon juice
¼ teaspoon thyme
¾ cup dressing (1 part white
 vinegar, 3 parts olive oil, salt,
 pepper, garlic to taste)

¼ teaspoon marjoram
¼ teaspoon dill
2 tablespoons chopped parsley
2 medium tomatoes, cut in wedges
1 green pepper, chopped
6 slices purple onions, separated into
 rings

Cook zucchini in boiling, salted water until just crisp, about 5 minutes. Drain; cool and cut into ½-inch slices; refrigerate. Wash and dry mushrooms—slice and sprinkle with lemon juice and nutmeg. Toss with ½ dressing and marinate in refrigerator. Just before serving lightly toss mushrooms, zucchini, green peppers and onion rings with remaining dressing and herbs.

Note: This is especially attractive served in a transparent bowl.

Mrs. James S. Brady

Fresh Vegetable Salad in Cream Dressing

Serves: 4 to 6

Broccoli
Mushrooms
Cucumbers
Tomatoes
Carrots
Celery
Peppers
Hearts of palm

Shallots
Water chestnuts
2 hard boiled eggs
½ cup sour cream
1 tablespoon wine vinegar
1 teaspoon salt
⅛ teaspoon pepper

To make dressing, mash cooked egg yolks and gradually stir in sour cream and vinegar, keeping smooth. Add salt and pepper. Stir well. Set aside. Place torn lettuce in large bowl; add sliced or chopped egg whites and any combination of fresh vegetables listed above. Add dressing to vegetables and toss.

Mrs. Temple C. Moore

Confetti Salad

Serves: 6 to 8

1 cup diced, peeled carrots
1 cup diced zucchini
1 cup cauliflowerets
1 cup cut-up broccoli
½ cup diced green pepper

3 radishes, sliced
10 or more cherry tomatoes
Herb-wine marinade
Romaine lettuce

In large bowl combine all vegetables. Add herb-wine marinade. Mix well. Cover and let stand in refrigerator several hours. To serve, pile vegetables on center of serving bowl lined with crisp romaine.

Herb Wine Marinade   Yield: 1 cup

¼ cup white wine
1 cup sour cream
½ teaspoon each oregano,
   marjoram and basil

1 clove garlic, minced
1 teaspoon sugar
½ teaspoon salt

Combine all ingredients and store in covered jar.

Note: This is a nice, different salad for summer barbecues.

Mrs. Kevin Gallen

Garden Patch Salad

Serves: 6 to 8

1 16-ounce can tiny green peas,
   drained
1 12-ounce can tiny white shoe
   peg corn, drained
1 16-ounce can French cut green
   beans
1 medium onion, chopped

¾ cup celery, finely chopped
Pimento (optional)
½ cup salad oil
½ cup wine vinegar
¾ cup sugar
1 teaspoon salt
½ teaspoon pepper

Toss the drained vegetables with onions, celery and pimento. Heat oil, vinegar, sugar, salt and pepper to boiling. Pour over vegetables. Chill.

Mrs. David W. Dellefield

Summer Salad

Serves: 6

2 to 3 cups torn greens
2 cups cooked chicken
1 cucumber, sliced or diced
1 green pepper, seeded and diced
1 onion, chopped

2 firm ripe tomatoes, chopped
½ pound bacon, cooked and crumbled
1 large ripe avocado, sliced
Roasted diced almonds or sauteed
    walnuts (optional)

Chill all ingredients well. Start filling the salad bowl with a generous layer of greens. Add layer of diced chicken. Combine cucumber, green pepper and onion; layer over chicken. Sprinkle bacon as next layer. Top with avocado slices. Combine any leftover ingredients and layer over avocado. Sprinkle with nuts, if desired, and garnish with extra tomato wedges and cucumber slices. Serve with creamy cheese dressing.

Note: In place of chicken, use any leftover cooked meat: ham, beef, lamb or tuna.

Dressing

1 cup mayonnaise
1 cup sour cream
¼ cup wine vinegar

1 teaspoon mixed Italian herbs
⅛ teaspoon garlic powder
3 tablespoons grated Parmesan cheese

Combine and thoroughly blend all ingredients. Cover and chill until ready to use, at least 1 hour.

Mrs. Ronald Ziegler

New Orleans Shrimp Salad

Serves: 4

1 cup cooked rice
1 cup cooked, peeled shrimp
½ cup diced, raw cauliflower
½ cup diced green onion
½ cup diced green pepper
¼ cup chopped celery

4 stuffed olives, sliced
½ cup mayonnaise
¼ cup French dressing
½ teaspoon salt
1 tablespoon lemon juice

Combine all ingredients. Toss lightly and chill thoroughly. Serve in lettuce cups.

Mrs. Caswell O. Hobbs

Salmon Mousse

Serves: 5

1 16-ounce can salmon
2 envelopes unflavored gelatin
1 cup mayonnaise
2 tablespoons horseradish
½ cup diced celery

1 tablespoon chopped onion
2 tablespoons lemon juice
½ teaspoon paprika
¼ cup chopped olives
½ cup whipping cream

Drain salmon, reserving liquid. Remove skin and bones. Flake salmon. Add cold water to liquid to equal 1¾ cups. Soften gelatin in liquid over low heat until gelatin dissolves. Cool slightly. Blend together lemon juice, mayonnaise, horseradish and paprika. Gradually stir in cooled gelatin mixture. Chill until partially set. Fold in salmon, celery, olives and onion. Whip cream until soft peaks form. Fold into salmon mixture. Chill in oiled 6-cup mold until firm.

Note: A good company supper in the summer with a marinated vegetable, croissants and a fresh fruit dessert.

Mrs. Donald Burchell

Chicken Mousse

Serves: 16

2 envelopes unflavored gelatin
2 cups cold chicken stock
1 teaspoon salt
1 tablespoon lime juice
¼ cup sherry

1 cup chopped celery
4 cups chopped, cooked chicken
1 cup almonds
2 tablespoons chopped parsley
1 cup heavy cream, whipped

Sprinkle gelatin in one cup cold stock. Place over boiling water and stir until gelatin is dissolved. Add to remaining stock. Add salt, lime juice and sherry. Chill until mixture is the consistency of unbeaten egg whites. Add celery, chicken, ½ cup almonds and parsley. Fold in whipped cream. Pour into an 8-cup mold. Refrigerate until firm. Unmold and garnish with remaining almonds.

Mrs. William T. Mahood

Eggplant and Ham Salad

Serves: 6

1 2½-pound eggplant
Salt
½ cup flour
Oil
Dash garlic powder
Pepper
¼ cup oil
½ cup wine vinegar
Juice of 1 lemon

1 teaspoon thyme
3 bay leaves
2 teaspoons chervil
Dash of mace
Dash of nutmeg
Dash of ginger
½ pound boiled or baked ham, diced
Boston lettuce
Parsley, chopped

Quarter an unpeeled eggplant and slice into ¼-inch pieces. Lightly flour pieces, shaking off excess. Sauté in oil and drain on absorbent paper. Sprinkle with salt, pepper and a dash of garlic powder. Combine oil, vinegar, lemon juice, thyme, bay leaves, chervil and other spices in small saucepan and simmer for 5 minutes. Add sautéed eggplant and refrigerate for at least 1 hour. To serve, add diced ham to marinated eggplant mixture. Serve on Boston lettuce and sprinkle with parsley.

Note: A food processor to slice eggplant and ham reduces preparation time. A delicious summer supper.

Mrs. Kleber S. Masterson, Jr.

Hearty Supper Salad

Serves: 4

½ cup chopped onion
½ cup chopped celery
½ cup sour cream
¼ cup mayonnaise
2 tablespoons fresh lemon juice
1 tablespoon snipped parsley
1 teaspoon prepared horseradish
1 teaspoon mustard

1 teaspoon salt
¼ teaspoon oregano
⅛ teaspoon pepper
1 pound fresh mushrooms, sliced
1 pound cooked roast beef or ham, cut
  in julienne strips
Salad greens

Mix all ingredients except mushrooms, meat and greens. Toss mushrooms and meat with dressing in bowl. Refrigerate at least 1 hour. Serve on salad greens.

Mrs. Hamilton Beggs

Jellied Shrimp Mold

Yield: 2 to 3 cups

2 6-ounce cans shrimp
2 shelled, hard-boiled eggs,
   mashed
2 tablespoons capers (more if
   desired)
½ cup chopped stuffed olives

1 tablespoon chopped chives or minced
   green onion
1 envelope plain, unflavored gelatin
   dissolved in ¼ cup cold water
2 cups mayonnaise

Rinse canned shrimp under hot water in collander. Combine shrimp, eggs, olives, capers and chives. Soak gelatin in cold water for 5 mintues and dissolve over hot water. Add dissolved gelatin to mayonnaise, stirring constantly. Add to fish mixture and stir thoroughly. Turn into 5 or 6 cup mold and chill overnight until firm.

Note: In a hurry? Omit the gelatin and serve in bowl with plain crackers. Makes enough for a cocktail party.

Mrs. Thomas T. Bellino

Chow Mein Chicken Salad

Preheat: 300 degrees
Serves: 6

1 tablespoon butter or margarine
2 tablespoons Worcestershire sauce
1 3-ounce can chow mein noodles
½ cup mayonnaise
1 teaspoon onion salt

6 cups cubed, cooked chicken
1½ cups diagonally sliced celery
½ cup sliced water chestnuts
Lettuce leaves

Melt butter in shallow baking pan and combine with 1 tablespoon Worcestershire sauce. Add chow mein noodles and toss to coat. Bake in 300 degree oven for 20 minutes, stirring occasionally. Combine mayonnaise, onion salt and remaining tablespoon of Worcestershire sauce. Just before serving add dressing to chicken, celery, water chestnuts and part of chow mein noodles. Stir gently to coat. Serve on bed of lettuce leaves garnished with remaining noodles.

Note: Great summer meal, serve with marinated green beans, sliced tomatoes and a lemony dessert.

Mrs. Donald Burchell

Chicken Chutney Salad

Serves: 4

2 cups diced cooked chicken
1 13¼-ounce can pineapple
  tidbits, drained
½ cup sliced green onion
1 cup diagonally sliced celery
¼ cup salted peanuts (may be dry
  roasted)

⅔ cup mayonnaise
½ teaspoon grated lime rind
2 tablespoons lime juice
2 tablespoons chopped chutney
½ teaspoon curry powder
¼ teaspoon salt

Combine mayonnaise, grated lime rind, juice, chutney, curry powder and salt. Toss chicken, pineapple and green onion together. Combine with mayonnaise mixture. Chill. Add peanuts and celery just before serving and toss again.

Mrs. Donald Burchell

Layered Salad

Serves: 12

1 head lettuce, finely cut
7 stalks celery, finely chopped
1 large green pepper, chopped
1 medium purple onion, finely
  sliced
½ pound frozen petit pois

1-2 cups mayonnaise
4 ounces Parmesan cheese, freshly
  grated
8 carrots, shredded
12 slices bacon, crumbled

Make 24 hours ahead. Place in transparent bowl in layers: 1 inch of lettuce, sliced onion, celery, green pepper, carrots, more lettuce, peas, bacon, celery (if any left). Ice top of salad with mayonnaise; top with shredded cheese.

Variations: May use Swiss cheese and MSG to enhance flavor or dot with mayonnaise and sprinkle with 1 tablespoon of sugar on each layer.

Mrs. William E. Elwood

Hearts of Palm Salad

Serves: 6

1 14-ounce can hearts of palm
1 4-ounce jar pimento
Black olives, pitted
2 tablespoons wine vinegar

1 teaspoon mild curry powder
Salt and pepper to taste
8 tablespoons olive oil

Cut hearts of palm lengthwise into halves or quarters, depending upon size. Cut pimento into thin strips. Mix vinegar, curry powder, salt and pepper, then stir in olive oil. Arrange hearts of palm, pimento and olives on serving plates. Drizzle with vinaigrette.

Mrs. Caswell O. Hobbs

Deluxe Salad

Serves: 6

1 head lettuce, chopped
3 medium tomatoes, cut in small
    pieces
1 green pepper, chopped
1 large Bermuda onion, cut into
    rings
1 16-ounce can pitted black olives
    or 1 4¼-ounce can chopped
    black olives

¼ pound Longhorn cheese, diced
¼ cup sugar
Garlic salt
Pepper
6 tablespoons oil
2 tablespoons vinegar
6 strips bacon, cooked crisp and
    drained

Combine lettuce, tomatoes, green pepper, onion, olives, cheese and sugar. Add garlic salt and pepper to taste. Add oil and vinegar. Mix well. Sprinkle top of salad with crumbled bacon.

Mrs. John Denson

Blue Cheese Dressing

Yield: 1½ cups

1 cup sour cream
3 or 4-ounce package blue cheese
1 tablespoon dry onion flakes

Salt and pepper to taste
2 tablespoons chives

Mix all by hand and add crumbled cheese last.

Mrs. Gerald B. File

Spinach Salad with Dijon Mustard Dressing

Yield: 6 servings

1¼ pounds fresh spinach, torn
   bite-size
¼ pound fresh mushrooms, thinly
   sliced

6 slices bacon, fried until crisp and
   crumbled
2 hard boiled eggs, chopped

Dressing

1 egg, slightly beaten
¼ cup vegetable oil
Juice of one lemon
1 tablespoon grated Parmesan
   cheese

2 tablespoons Dijon mustard
1 teaspoon sugar
1 teaspoon Worcestershire sauce
½ teaspoon salt
Dash of pepper

Combine dressing ingredients in a jar; tighten lid and shake until well-blended. Chill thoroughly. Combine spinach and sliced mushrooms in a large salad bowl; cover and refrigerate. Toss spinach and mushrooms with chilled dressing until well coated. Garnish with bacon and hard-boiled eggs.

Mrs. James. A. Meriwether

Spinach Salad Dressing

Yield: 1¾ cups

1 cup salad oil
1 medium onion, grated
½ cup granulated sugar
¼ cup brown sugar
½ cup cider vinegar

⅓ cup catsup
1 tablespoon Worcestershire sauce
Salt
Pepper

Mix and serve on a salad of spinach, fresh bean sprouts, water chestnuts and sliced fresh mushrooms.

Note: Also good on fruit salad.

Mrs. Chris W. Ragland

Chinese Salad

Yield: 2½ cups

Spinach
Water chestnuts

Mushrooms
Bean sprouts

Dressing

¾ cup soy sauce
3 tablespoons fresh lemon juice
1 teaspoon sugar

1 teaspoon toasted sesame seeds
1 teaspoon chopped onion
1½ cups peanut oil

Combine all dressing ingredients except oil in blender on low speed, or in food processor equipped with a steel knife. Blend or process until onion is minced. With machine running, add oil in a thin stream and blend or process until oil is thoroughly incorporated. Pour dressing over salad ingredients and toss.

Mrs. John E. Davey

The Salad

Serves: 6 to 8

Fresh lettuce, any kind
Fresh spinach
1 14-ounce can artichoke hearts,
   drained and quartered
1 large red onion, thinly sliced

½ cup crumbled Bleu cheese
1 16-ounce can Leseur baby peas
1 11-ounce can mandarin orange
   sections or fresh grapefruit sections
2 ripe avocados

Dressing

¾ cup oil
¼ cup wine vinegar
½ teaspoon salt

¼ teaspoon sugar
¼ teaspoon pepper

Combine ingredients for dressing and marinate artichoke hearts, peas, and onion overnight. Before serving, put greens in salad bowl and add Bleu cheese, fruit, avocados and marinated vegetables with dressing. Toss and serve.

Mrs. Thomas T. Bellino

Celery Seed Dressing

Yield: 2 cups

⅔ cup sugar
1 teaspoon paprika
¼ teaspoon salt
1 teaspoon dry mustard
1 teaspoon celery seed

⅓ cup honey
⅓ cup vinegar
1 tablespoon lemon juice
1 teaspoon grated onion
1 cup salad oil

Mix dry ingredients; blend in honey, vinegar, lemon juice and onion. Add oil in slow stream, beating constantly with electric mixer, until thick.

Mrs. Richard W. Klein, Jr.

Tomato Salad Dressing

Yield: 2¼ cups

¼ cup sugar
Scant teaspoon salt
Scant teaspoon mustard
2 teaspoons Worcestershire sauce
¾ cup cooking oil

Few shakes cayenne pepper
Few shakes black pepper
¼ cup vinegar
1 cup tomato soup
2 garlic buds

Put all dry ingredients in bowl. Add tomato soup slowly; add vinegar and mix together. Put in large jar with 2 garlic buds. Shake before using. Good on salads or cold meats.

Mrs. Gerald B. File

French Restaurant House Dressing

Yield: ¾ cup

3 tablespoons Dijon mustard
½ cup olive oil
½ teaspoon salt
¼ teaspoon black pepper
2 tablespoons wine vinegar

2 tablespoons lemon juice
1 teaspoon sugar
1 clove garlic, finely minced
1 tablespoon drained capers

Beat mustard with whisk while adding oil drop by drop until a thick sauce is formed. Add remaining ingredients.

Note: Can be easily doubled; especially good with a variety of salad greens.

Mrs. Donald Burchell

Eggs, Cheese and Pastas

Bacon and Eggs Mornay

Preheat: 350 degrees
Serves: 4 to 6

1 pound bacon
¼ cup diced onion
¼ cup green pepper
¼ cup flour
1½ teaspoons salt
½ teaspoon paprika
2 cups milk

2 tablespoons mustard
Dash of Worcestershire sauce
1 cup shredded sharp cheese
⅔ cup chopped peeled tomato
8 hard cooked eggs, diced
6 English muffins or patty shells,
    for serving

Fry bacon until crisp, saving 3 tablespoons drippings. Break all but 4 strips of bacon into 1-inch lengths. Sauté onion and pepper in drippings until soft. Blend in flour, salt and paprika. Add milk and cook stirring constantly, until thickened. Add mustard, cheese, tomato and Worcestershire sauce. Stir and heat until cheese is melted. Add eggs and broken bacon. Pour into greased 9 x 13 casserole and bake in 350 degree oven for 20 to 30 minutes or until bubbly. Garnish with bacon strips.

Note: Can be made ahead.

Mrs. William E. Elwood

Broccoli and Cheese Frittata

Preheat: 350 degrees
Serves: 6 to 8

½ cup butter
3 eggs
1 cup flour
1 cup milk

1 teaspoon salt
1 teaspoon baking powder
½ pound Monterey Jack cheese, grated
4 cups chopped broccoli

Melt butter in a 7 x 11-inch baking dish. Beat eggs and add remaining ingredients, blending well. Pour broccoli mixture over the melted butter. Bake in 350 degree oven for 40 to 45 minutes. Cool 10 minutes and serve.

Mrs. Robert E. Applegate

The Bank of Alexandria

Throughout the late 1700s Alexandria grew as an important center of commerce. In 1790 the bank of Alexandria became the first bank chartered by the Commonwealth of Virginia and only the second bank south of Philadelphia. George Washington was an early depositor and share-holder. The bank offered ready capital and financial stability to enhance Alexandria's growing prosperity.

William Herbert, son-in-law of John Carlyle was responsible for the construction (1803 to 1807) of the Federal style landmark. Originally, the west section of the three story structure served as business space, while the cashier's residence occupied the east section.

In 1801, the bank was required to be rechartered under Federal jurisdiction. The event was Gadsby's Hotel with toasts to "the immortal memory of the illustrious Washington" and sixteen other worthy causes.

In 1834, a bank panic resulted from the economic uncertainty of Andrew Jackson's administration; the Bank of Alexandria failed. The building served as a Civil War hospital, an elegant hotel and as office space prior to its restoration. Most of the exterior and first floor features are original including the paneled interior shutters, the mythological freizes adorning twin north and south mantels, and the flooring as well as the cast iron studded vault door once again serving its original function.

Monterey Oven Omelet

Preheat: 350 degrees
Serves: 4 to 6

8 slices bacon, coarsely chopped
(can use a little more)
4 green onions, thinly sliced
8 eggs

½ teaspoon seasoned salt
1 cup milk
2 cups shredded Monterey Jack cheese

Fry bacon until brown, drain and crumble. Saute onions in 1 tablespoon bacon drippings until limp. Beat eggs with milk and salt. Stir in bacon, onions and 1½ cups cheese, pour into greased 2-quart dish. Bake uncovered in 350 degree oven for 35 to 40 minutes until mixture is set and top lightly browned. When almost done sprinkle with remaining cheese and return to oven until cheese melts. Serve right away.

Note: Serve for informal brunch with fruit and rolls or coffee cake.

Mrs. Raymond T. Bond

Râpée Morvandelle

Preheat: 375 degrees
Serves: 4

½ cup finely minced onions
2 tablespoons olive oil
4½ tablespoons butter
1½ cups finely diced cooked ham
4 eggs
½ clove garlic, crushed

2 tablespoons minced parsley
⅔ cup grated Swiss cheese
4 tablespoons whipping cream
Pinch of pepper
¼ teaspoon salt
3 medium-sized potatoes

Cook onions slowly in oil and 2 tablespoons butter until tender but not browned. Stir in ham and cook a moment more. In a mixing bowl, beat eggs and add garlic, parsley, cheese, cream, salt and pepper. Then blend in the ham and onions. Peel the potatoes and grate them, using large holes of grater. Squeeze water out of potatoes, a handful at a time. Stir potatoes into egg mixture. (May be refrigerated overnight at this point.) Heat 2 tablespoons butter in 11- to 12-inch baking dish; when foaming, pour in the potato and egg mixture. Dot with ½ tablespoon butter cut into pea-sized dots. Set in upper third of preheated oven and bake 30 to 40 minutes, or until top is nicely browned. Serve directly from dish.

Note: Great for a brunch served with petit pois and croissants.

Mrs. Donald Burchell

Eggs à La Viénne

Preheat: 450 degrees
Serves: 4 to 6

1 package Canadian bacon
3 to 4 slices Swiss cheese
½ pint cream

6 to 8 eggs
Parmesan cheese, grated

Line a shallow (8 x 13) pan or glass dish with Canadian bacon. Add a layer of Swiss cheese. Break eggs over all. Drizzle the cream over the eggs—leave the yolks showing. Put in 450 degree oven for 10 minutes. Sprinkle with Parmesan cheese and return to oven for 5 to 10 minutes. Cut in squares and serve. Extremely easy—but quite good.

Mrs. Lewis B. Puller, Jr.

Chili Egg Puff

Preheat: 350 degrees
Serves: 12

12 eggs
½ cup all-purpose flour
1 teaspoon baking powder
1 teaspoon salt
1 pint creamed small curd cottage
  cheese

1 pound Monterey Jack cheese,
  shredded
½ cup butter
1 cup diced mild green chilies

Beat eggs until lemon in color. Add rest of ingredients, mixing well. Add chilies last. (If mixing previous night, add chilies just before baking next morning.) Butter baking dish generously. Cook at 350 degrees until center is firm and top is brown, about 45 minutes.

Note: May be served with Hollandaise sauce. Especially nice for a brunch or midnight supper.

Mrs. Temple C. Moore

Burke Brunch Casserole

Preheat: 350 degrees
Serves: 6 to 8

1 dozen eggs
1 pound smoked sausage
1 cup grated sharp Cheddar cheese

Dash of Tabasco sauce
Salt to taste
Pepper to taste

Lightly grease a 2-quart casserole dish. Beat eggs with Tabasco and salt and pepper. Slice smoked sausage, place in casserole. Slice cheese, place on top of sausage. Pour egg mixture over all. Bake for 1 hour.

Note: This is better if assembled the day before and refrigerated overnight.

Mrs. C. S. Taylor Burke III

Sausage Strata

Preheat: 350 degrees
Serves: 6

1 pound mild bulk sausage
6 beaten eggs
6 slices bread, cubed, no crust

2 cups milk
1 cup shredded Cheddar cheese
1 teaspoon dry mustard

Sauté sausage lightly. Break into small pieces. Drain well. Beat eggs until fluffy. Add milk, mustard, bread, cheese and sausage. Place in buttered 8-inch square pan. Bake at 350 degrees for 45 minutes. Let stand several minutes before cutting.

Mrs. F. Eugene Brown, Jr.

Cheese Strata

Preheat: 325 degrees
Serves: 6

1 pound grated Cheddar cheese
9 slices white bread with crusts
   removed
Salt
Pepper

1½ tablespoons dried onion
4 eggs
3 cups milk
1 teaspoon Worcestershire sauce
1 teaspoon dry mustard

Cut 3 slices of bread into 3 strips each. Fit tightly into a lightly greased casserole. Sprinkle with salt, pepper and ⅓ of the onion. Add ⅓ of cheese. Repeat layers two more times. Beat eggs, add milk, Worcestershire sauce and mustard. Pour over bread mixture. Allow to set in refrigerator overnight. Take out two hours before baking. Bake at 325 degrees for 50 minutes..

Note: Good with many main dish meats, such as beef, pork, etc.

Mrs. Marjorie S. Cook

Basic Crepe

1 cup flour
2 eggs
1¾ cups milk

½ teaspoon salt
1 tablespoon melted butter

Mix flour and eggs with wire whisk. Add remaining ingredients. Pour 1½ tablespoons of batter into greased, hot crepe pan. Cook quickly on each side.

Mrs. H. Franklin Green III

Salmon Crepe Filling

Preheat: 375 degrees
Serves: 6 to 8

2 cloves
2 onions, peeled
¼ cup oil
¼ cup flour
¾ teaspoon salt
¼ teaspoon pepper

1 cup cream
1 cup milk
2 tablespoons sherry
2 beaten egg yolks
1 pound can red salmon
2 tablespoons Parmesan cheese

Press 2 cloves in one peeled onion. Mince remaining onion. Combine oil, salt, flour and pepper. Blend until smooth. Add whole and minced onion. Cook over medium heat stirring until thick and bubbly. Remove from heat, gradually blend in cream and milk, stirring constantly. Discard onion with cloves. Stir in sherry, set aside one cup of sauce. Add some of hot sauce to egg yolks. Blend egg yolks into remaining sauce. Bring just to boiling point. Remove from heat. Stir in salmon. Spread equal amounts down center of crepe. Fold up, and arrange in baking dish. Top with reserved sauce. Sprinkle with Parmesan cheese. Bake 25 minutes at 375 degrees. Garnish with parsley.

Mrs. Alan E. Mowbray

Chicken and Tomato Crepe Filling

Preheat: 325 degrees
Serves: 6 to 8

2 cups cooked chicken, cut in
 strips
1 cup peeled tomato, cut in strips
1 cup heavy cream
2 tablespoons canned jalapeno
 peppers

1 cup grated Gruyere cheese
Salt
Pepper
½ cup grated Swiss cheese
¼ cup grated Parmesan cheese

Mix together chicken, tomatoes, peppers, cream, Gruyere cheese, salt
and pepper. Roll in crepes. Place in buttered casserole. Cover with
Parmesan and Swiss cheeses. Bake at 325 degrees until hot and bubbly.
Run under broiler one minute before serving.

Mrs. H. Franklin Green III

Deluxe Company Crepes

Preheat: 425 degrees
Serves: 6 to 8

Filling

1½ cups diced or shredded
 chicken, seafood or ham
1 cup finely chopped mushrooms,
 sautéed in butter

¼ cup finely chopped shallots
1½ cups cooked chopped spinach, well
 drained

Sauce

6 tablespoons butter
½ cup flour
2½ cups hot chicken stock
2 egg yolks
1 cup heavy cream

Cayenne or dry mustard to taste
Salt
Pepper
1 cup grated Swiss cheese

Toss filling ingredients together to mix well. Prepare sauce by melting
butter and stir in flour. Cook for a minute, then add stock and stir over
low heat until thickened. Mix egg yolks and cream, add some of stock
mixture to yolks. Then blend egg yolks into hot sauce, return to low heat
and stir until sauce thickens. Season to taste.

Combine desired filling ingredient with half the sauce. Place large spoonful of filling on lower one-third of each crepe and roll up. Place seam side down close together in shallow buttered baking dish. Spoon remaining sauce on top, sprinkle with grated cheese. Place in preheated oven at 425 degrees and bake until sauce is bubbling and cheese topping is lightly browned.

Note: Use your favorite crepe recipe.

Mrs. Frederick McNamara

Cottage Cheese Pancakes

Serves: 4

2 eggs
12 ounces cottage cheese
2 tablespoons melted butter

¼ cup flour
1 teaspoon sugar
Dash of salt

Beat eggs until light; add cheese, butter, flour, sugar and salt. Beat only until well blended. Bake on preheated greased griddle. Serve with jelly, jam, strawberries or peaches.

Mrs. Henry E. Thomas IV

Mushroom and Sour Cream Pie

Preheat: 425 degrees
Serves: 6 to 8

½ pound small mushrooms
½ cup chopped onions
3 tablespoons margarine
1 tablespoon flour
½ teaspoon salt

¼ teaspoon paprika
Pepper to taste
9-inch unbaked pie crust
3 eggs, slightly beaten
1 cup sour cream

Sauté mushrooms and onions 4 to 5 minutes in margarine. Sprinkle with flour, salt, paprika and pepper. Set aside. Pierce pie shell, bake at 425 degrees for 8 minutes. Spread mushroom mixture over baked pie shell. Combine eggs and sour cream and pour over mushrooms. Reduce heat to 350 degrees and bake 30 minutes. Let stand 5 minutes. Serve hot, cut in wedges.

Mrs. Marjorie S. Cook

Quiche Unique

Preheat: 325 degrees
Serves: 6 to 8

¾ cup shredded Swiss cheese
¾ cup shredded Mozzarella cheese
½ cup chopped pepperoni
1 tablespoon chopped green onion
1 9-inch unbaked pie shell

3 beaten eggs
1 cup half and half
½ teaspoon salt
¼ teaspoon oregano
Parsley

Combine cheeses, pepperoni and onion; sprinkle into pie shell. Combine eggs, half and half, salt and oregano; mix well and pour over cheese mixture. Bake for 45 minutes. Allow to stand for 10 minutes before cutting. Garnish with parsley.

Mrs. Caswell O. Hobbs

Individual Shrimp Quiches

Preheat: 400 degrees
Serves: 12

Pastry for 2-crust pie
¾ cup chopped cooked shrimp
¼ cup sliced green onion
4 ounces Swiss cheese, shredded (1
  cup)

½ cup mayonnaise
2 eggs
⅓ cup milk
¼ teaspoon salt
¼ teaspoon dried dill or parsley

On floured surface roll half of pastry into 12-inch circle. Cut 6 four-inch circles. Repeat with remaining pastry. Fit pastry circles into twelve 2½-inch muffin pan cups. Fill each with shrimp, onion, and cheese. Beat eggs, mayonnaise, milk, salt and dill. Pour over cheese. Bake at 400 degrees for 15 to 20 minutes or until browned.

Note: Good for cocktails or a luncheon served with salad.

Mrs. Michael E. Delnegro

Fettucini

Serves: 6

1 pound fettucini or linguini
½ cup melted butter
1 pound ricotta cheese
1 tablespoon chopped parsley

1 cup Parmesan cheese
Salt
Pepper

Cook noodles *al dente*. Drain and return to pot. Add melted butter and ricotta. Mix. Put in serving dish. Sprinkle with parsley and Parmesan cheese.

Note: For a variation try adding toasted sesame seeds and freshly sautéed mushrooms.

Mrs. C. Mason Ebhardt

Mushroom Noodles

Preheat: 350 degrees
Serves: 6 as main dish
12 as side dish

½ pound broad noodles
3 tablespoons butter
1 small onion, chopped
¼ pound mushrooms, sliced
8 ounces cream cheese, softened
1 cup sour cream

1 10¾-ounce can cream of mushroom
  soup + ½ cup milk
½ teaspoon salt
½ teaspoon garlic salt
Dash of curry powder
½ cup unseasoned bread crumbs

Prepare noodles according to package directions. Grease a 2-quart casserole. In 2 tablespoons of butter, sauté onion and mushrooms until soft but not brown; set aside. In large bowl with electric mixer at low speed combine cream cheese, sour cream, mushroom soup, milk and seasonings. Drain noodles, stir into cream cheese mixture, add onions and mushrooms. Pour into casserole and sprinkle bread crumbs on top. Dot with remaining butter. Bake uncovered 30 minutes.

Mrs. Wilson Livingood

Noodles à La Swisse

Preheat: 350 degrees
Serves: 8

8 ounces fine noodles
1 cup cottage cheese
1 cup sour cream

1 clove garlic, finely chopped
Dash of Worcestershire sauce
1 cup grated Swiss cheese

Cook noodles. Mix with other ingredients, put in a 9 x 13-inch casserole (2 quart) and top with thick layer of grated Swiss cheese. Bake 30 to 40 minutes at 350 degrees.

Note: Can be made ahead and frozen. Bring to room temperature before baking.

Mrs. Stephen L. Echols

Stuffed Jumbo Shells

Preheat: 350 degrees
Serves: 8

1 box San Giorgio Jumbo Shells
3 cups Ricotta cheese
12-ounce package Mozzarella
    cheese, shredded
¾ cup grated Parmesan cheese
3 eggs, slightly beaten

1½ teaspoons salt
2 teaspoons chopped parsley
¾ teaspoon oregano, crushed
¼ teaspoon pepper
4 cups spaghetti sauce, meat or
    meatless

Cook jumbo shells as directed. Drain and dry. Combine cheeses with beaten eggs, salt, parsley, oregano and pepper. Fill shells with 2 table-spoons of cheese mixture. Spread a thin layer of sauce in a 9 x 12-inch rectangular baking dish. Place stuffed shells, one deep, in dish and cover with part of spaghetti sauce. Sprinkle with additional Parmesan cheese. Bake at 350 degrees for 35 minutes or until hot. Heat remaining sauce and serve with shells.

Mrs. Michael E. Delnegro

Seafood

Oyster Stew

Yield: 1 quart

1 quart salt water oysters
2 tablespoons butter
2 tablespoons celery
1 tablespoon finely chopped onion
1 quart milk or half and half

1 tablespoon Worcestershire sauce
1 teaspoon salt
1/8 teaspoon cayenne
Paprika

Melt butter, add celery and onion and cook until tender. Drain oysters, add to mixture and cook slowly until edges curl lightly. Add milk and Worcestershire sauce and heat until oysters are fully curled. Be careful not to overcook. Add salt and cayenne and serve at once, placing a lump of butter in each bowl. Garnish with paprika.

Mrs. Hamilton Beggs

Trout Bretonne

Serves: 4

4 10-ounce trout
1/2 cup flour
1/2 teaspoon salt
1/4 teaspoon pepper
1/2 cup peanut oil

1/4 cup margarine
2 cups sliced fresh mushrooms
1 tablespoon lemon juice
12 cooked shrimp, cut lengthwise
Parsley

Coat trout with flour, salt and pepper. Sauté in oil until well browned on both sides. Place on oven-proof platter and heat in 375 degree oven for 5 minutes or until done. Sauté mushrooms in same skillet. Stir in margarine, lemon juice and shrimp; heat through. Pour over fish and sprinkle with chopped parsley.

Sans Souci Restaurant

Captains Row

100 Block of Prince Street

A busy young city, Alexandria served as one of the principal ports of the nation during and after the American Revolution. Many captains whose ships docked in this deepwater harbor made Alexandria their home port and built their houses close to the Potomac. Prince Street, running perpendicular to the river, was an especially popular site.

The 28 homes in this short block were more than mere residences when they were first built. Shipping offices occupied the main level, as did display rooms for all sorts of exotic cargo. Family quarters filled the second floor, and apprentices or servants were housed in the attic, making for a sort of "upstairs-downstairs" arrangement. A notable feature of Prince Street is its cobblestone paving, which serves as a reminder to modern motorists of slower travel in colonial times. The stones are believed to have been brought to Alexandria as ballasts in the ships and laid by Hessian prisoners of General Washington.

Crab Imperial

Preheat: 450 degrees
Serves: 4

1 pound lump crab meat
4 tablespoons melted butter
2 tablespoons mayonnaise

1 teaspoon prepared mustard
Dash of Worcestershire sauce
¼ cup fine bread crumbs

Pick over crabmeat for cartilage. Mix gently with mayonnaise, mustard, Worcestershire sauce and half the butter. Spoon into 4 baking shells. Dust crumbs over top and sprinkle with remaining butter. Place shells on cookie sheet and bake 20 minutes at 450 degrees.

Mrs. E. Darryl Barnes

C's Crab Delight

Preheat: 325 degrees
Serves: 6

1 pound fresh lump crabmeat
2 hard boiled eggs
¾ to 1 cup mayonnaise
1½ teaspoons dry mustard
½ teaspoon cayenne

½ cup half and half
Pinch of salt
1 teaspoon Worcestershire sauce
Buttered bread crumbs

Gently combine all ingredients except eggs and bread crumbs. Place in buttered 2-quart casserole and top with buttered crumbs and place sliced eggs on top. Cover and bake at 325 degrees for 30 to 45 minutes. Serve with hot fruit and salad.

Mrs. Thomas T. Bellino

Coquilles St. Jacques Baumanière
(Scallops in Cream Sauce)

Preheat: 450 degrees
Serves: 4

1½ pounds scallops
1 tablespoon chopped shallots
¼ teaspoon salt
Dash of white pepper

½ cup dry vermouth
1 cup cream
1 tablespoon flour
4 tablespoons soft butter

Wash scallops and cut into quarters if using large sea scallops. Put in saucepan with shallots, salt, pepper and vermouth. Bring liquid to boil and cover saucepan. Simmer over low heat for 2 minutes *only*. Remove scallops with slotted spoon and divide into 4 scallop shells. Cook liquid remaining in saucepan over high heat until reduced to half. Add cream to reduced liquid and boil rapidly until cream is reduced and sauce is the consistency of syrup. Combine flour and butter. Reduce heat and gradually stir butter into scallop sauce. Pour sauce over scallops and sprinkle with minced parsley. Heat at 450 degrees for 5 minutes.

Note: May also be served in crepes. Roll scallops with a little sauce in each crepe. Place seam side down in baking dish and cover with remaining sauce. Cover with tin foil and cook for 5 mintues at 450 degrees. Shrimp may be substituted for, or combined with, the scallops.

Mrs. Thomas Bellino

 When poaching shrimps, scallops or other seafood, try adding ½ teaspoon caraway seeds with other seasonings to the cooking water—they seem to absorb the odor, but do not change the delicate flavor of the fish.

Lobster Thermidor

Preheat: 450 degrees
Serves: 4

2 cooked lobsters, split in half at
fish market
1 teaspoon grated onion
¼ cup butter
4 large mushrooms, minced
1 can condensed mushroom soup

2 tablespoons white wine
½ cup table cream
Freshly grated Parmesan cheese
Bread crumbs
Parsley (optional)

Remove all meat from lobsters, including claw meat; reserve cleaned body shells. Cut lobster meat into small pieces. Melt 2 tablespoons butter, add onion, mushrooms and lobster, and sauté 5 minutes. Combine soup, wine and cream in a double boiler and heat until well blended and smooth, adding minced parsley if desired. Add lobster mixture and heat gently for 5 minutes. Then, apportion among lobster shells, sprinkle thickly with grated cheese and dust with bread crumbs. Dot with remaining butter and bake in a 450 degree oven for 10 minutes, or until tops brown.

Mrs. C. S. Taylor Burke III

Shrimp De Jonge

Preheat: 325 degrees
Serves: 3 to 4

½ cup butter, melted
1 clove garlic, minced
⅓ cup chopped fresh parsley
¼ teaspoon paprika

Dash of cayenne
⅓ cup dry sherry
1 cup soft bread crumbs
2 cups cooked shrimp

Mix melted butter, garlic, parsley, paprika, cayenne and sherry in a pan. Add bread crumbs and toss. Spoon wine butter sauce over shrimp in a 1-quart (or smaller) shallow casserole and heat until bread crumbs have browned.

Mrs. Michael Cericola

Artichoke and Shrimp Casserole

Preheat: 375 degrees
Serves: 4

1 10-ounce package frozen
  artichoke hearts
¾ pound medium sized shrimp,
  cooked (if fresh, 1 pound)
¼ pound fresh mushrooms,
  minced
2 tablespoons butter

1 tablespoon Worcestershire sauce
¼ cup dry sherry
1½ cups white sauce
¼ cup grated Parmesan cheese
Salt and pepper to taste
Dash of paprika
Freshly chopped parsley

Cook artichokes according to package directions. Arrange artichokes in bottom of buttered 2½-quart baking dish. Spread cooked shrimp over artichokes. Sauté sliced mushrooms in butter for 6 minutes. Add Worcestershire sauce, salt, pepper and sherry to white sauce. Pour over contents of baking dish. Sprinkle top with Parmesan cheese, dust with paprika and bake at 325 degrees for 1 hour. Cover dish with fresh chopped parsley just before serving.

Note: 1 cup crabmeat can be substituted for shrimp. Goes well with spinach salad and French bread.

Mrs. C. S. Taylor Burke, Jr.

Shrimp Creole

Serves: 6

2 pounds shelled shrimp
1 20-ounce can tomatoes
1 10¾-ounce can tomato soup
1 10-ounce package okra

1 large onion, diced
1 green pepper, diced
¼ pound fresh mushrooms

Cook, cool and peel shrimp. Sauté onion, green pepper and mushrooms in butter. Add tomatoes, okra and soup. Simmer half an hour. Serve on a bed of rice.

Mrs. Jack Howard

Shrimp Curry

Serves: 4

⅓ cup butter
½ cup chopped onion
¼ to ½ cup chopped green pepper
2 cloves garlic, minced
2 cups sour cream
2 teaspoons lemon juice

2 teaspoons curry powder
¾ teaspoon salt
Dash of pepper
½ teaspoon ginger
Dash of chili powder
3 cups cooked shrimp

Melt butter. Add onion, green pepper and garlic. Cook until tender. Stir in sour cream, lemon juice and seasonings. Add shrimp. Heat over low heat constantly stirring. Serve over rice.

Mrs. Richard Rhame

Golden Shrimp Casserole

Preheat: 350 degrees
Serves: 6

8 slices buttered bread
2 cups shrimp
3 ounces mushrooms
½ pound sharp cheese, shredded
3 eggs
½ teaspoon salt

½ teaspoon dry mustard
Paprika to taste
Pepper to taste
Tabasco sauce
2 cups milk
Worcestershire sauce to taste

Break bread into crumbs. Place half of crumbs in greased 3-quart dish. Add shrimp, mushrooms and half of cheese. Top with remaining bread crumbs and cheese. Beat eggs and seasonings together. Add milk and pour over other ingredients. Bake for 50 to 60 minutes at 350 degrees.

Mrs. Frank McCabe

West Indian Shrimp

Serves: 6 to 8

1½ pounds cooked, cleaned shrimp
2 tablespoons olive oil
1 tablespoon angostura bitters
1 teaspoon chervil
½ teaspoon marjoram (or oregano)

½ teaspoon thyme
½ teaspoon cumin
¼ teaspoon saffron, soaked in 1
   tablespoon warm water
Grated Parmesan cheese

Place cooked shrimp in large frying pan, and sauté quickly in olive oil. Sprinkle with bitters during cooking.

Remove to a shallow 2-quart casserole and sprinkle the shrimp with herbs and saffron. Top with a generous sprinkling of grated Parmesan cheese, and broil until lightly browned (about 5 minutes). Serve with steamed rice.

Mrs. C. S. Taylor Burke, Jr.

Shrimp with Wild Rice

Preheat: 300 degrees
Serves: 8

½ cup flour
1 cup melted margarine or butter
4 cups chicken broth
¼ teaspoon white pepper
1 cup thinly sliced onion

2 cups sliced fresh mushrooms
2 pounds cooked, peeled, deveined
   shrimp
2 tablespoons Worcestershire sauce
4 cups cooked wild rice

Gradually add flour to ½ cup melted butter; cook over low heat, stirring constantly until bubbly. Gradually add broth, cook until smooth and thickened stirring constantly. Add pepper and simmer 2 or 3 minutes. Sauté onion and mushrooms in remaining ½ cup of butter. Combine white sauce, sautéed vegetables and remaining ingredients. Spoon into two greased shallow 2-quart casseroles. Bake at 300 degrees for 45 to 50 minutes or until bubbly. Transfer to chafing dish to serve, accompanied by wild rice.

Note: An excellent choice for a dinner party buffet, it can be prepared earlier and warmed at the last moment.

Mrs. Renny H. Barnes

Scalloped Oysters

Preheat: 400 degrees
Serves: 4 to 6

½ cup butter
¾ cup flour
3 teaspoons paprika
½ teaspoon black pepper
1 teaspoon salt
4 tablespoons finely chopped green
    pepper

4 tablespoons finely chopped onion
¼ teaspoon finely chopped garlic
2 tablespoons lemon juice
1 tablespoon Worcestershire sauce
1 quart oysters
Cracker crumbs

Melt butter. Add flour and cook over low heat, stirring constantly until color is dark brown. Add paprika, pepper and salt. Cook 3 minutes, then add green pepper, onion, garlic. Cook slowly for 5 minutes, remove from been heated in their own liquid. Pour into 2-quart shallow baking dish and sprinkle with cracker crumbs. Cook in 400 degree oven for 35 minutes.

Mrs. William Mahood

Oyster Corn Pudding

Preheat: 350 degrees
Serves: 6 to 8

½ cup chopped onion
3 tablespoons melted butter
1 16-ounce can cream-style corn
2 cups oysters
2 eggs, beaten

1 cup coarsely crushed soda crackers
⅔ cup milk
½ teaspoon salt
⅛ teaspoon pepper

Cook onions in butter until soft. Combine remaining ingredients and pour into 3-quart casserole. Place in moderate 350 degree oven for 60 minutes or until set.

Mrs. Patrick Vaughan

Florentine Flounder

Preheat: 350 degrees
Serves: 4

1 pound fresh or frozen flounder
   filets
2 10-ounce packages frozen
   chopped spinach
1 3-ounce package cream cheese,
   softened
1 tablespoon butter

4 teaspoons flour
⅛ teaspoon salt
Dash of pepper
¾ cup chicken broth
1 tablespoon dry white wine
1 tablespoon diced pimento
Dash of paprika

Thaw fish filets. Cook spinach and drain well. Spread spinach in a 1-quart greased casserole. Cut filets into four portions. Season with salt and pepper. Spread half of cheese on top of fish. Top with pimento. Roll up filet and place on top of spinach. In saucepan, melt butter. Blend in flour. Add broth. Cook and stir until thick and bubbly. Remove from heat and gradually blend into remaining cheese with a wisk. Add wine. Pour sauce over filets; sprinkle with paprika. Bake uncovered for 25 minutes.

Mrs. Kevin Gallen

Filet of Snapper Rome

Preheat: 350 degrees
Serves: 4

½ cup plus 1½ teaspoons butter
¼ cup lemon juice
Dash of Worcestershire sauce
4 red snapper filets
1 cup crabmeat
¼ cup melted butter

1½ teaspoons flour
½ cup half-and-half
½ teaspoon salt
Dash of white pepper
½ cup dry bread crumbs
8 green pepper strips

Combine ½ cup butter, lemon juice and Worcestershire sauce in small saucepan; cook stirring often until thoroughly heated. Place filets in a 13 x 9 x 2-inch baking pan; broil 10 to 15 minutes, basting with lemon butter. Saute crabmeat in melted butter for about 3 minutes; set aside. Melt 1½ teaspoons butter in heavy saucepan; add flour. Stir to maintain smoothness, cook 1 minute. Gradually stir in half and half; cook over medium heat, stirring constantly until thick and bubbly. Add salt, pepper and crabmeat. Spoon creamed crabmeat on top of each filet. Sprinkle bread crumbs on top, garnish with 2 strips of green pepper. Bake at 350 degrees for 10 minutes. Then broil filets just until bread crumbs are browned.

Mrs. Ronald E. McKeown

Salmon Croquettes

Preheat: 375 degrees
Serves: 4 to 6

1 16-ounce can pink salmon
1 large onion, finely chopped
Juice of 2 lemons
Salt and pepper to taste

2 large eggs, slightly beaten
1 cup milk
3½ cups saltine cracker crumbs

Mix all ingredients, reserving 1¾ cups cracker crumbs. Chill mixture for several hours. When ready to use, shape mixture into balls or patties. Roll in remaining crumbs and fry in hot fat until crisp.

Mrs. James L. Howe III

Sole with Mushrooms

Preheat: 350 degrees
Serves: 4

8 sole filets
1 tablespoon butter
4 ounces button mushrooms
1 cup milk
¼ cup white wine
2 tablespoons butter
3-4 tablespoons flour

½ cup table cream
4 tablespoons grated cheese (Parmesan
  is a personal favorite)
Pinch of dry mustard
Salt, pepper and chopped parsley to
  taste

Skin filets, if necessary. Season well with salt and pepper. Roll up from the tail and place in a buttered oven-proof dish with mushrooms which have been washed and thoroughly dried. Pour ½ cup milk and wine over and cover tightly. Bake for 15 minutes at 350 degrees or until fish is cooked thoroughly. Remove fish to serving dish and keep warm. Set aside mushrooms and reserve fish liquid. Melt butter in pan, stir in flour, remove from heat and beat in fish liquid and remaining ½ cup milk. Return to heat and bring to a boil, stirring constantly. Add mushrooms and simmer for 2 minutes. Add cheese, mustard, cream, salt and pepper to taste and heat gently. Pour over the filets and garnish with chopped parsley. Serve immediately.

Note: Prawns may be substituted for mushrooms and a level teaspoon of paprika added to the sauce. Garnish with lemon slices dipped in paprika. Goes well with broccoli or asparagus and wild/brown rice.

Mrs. Robert G. Lineberry

Fancy Fish

Preheat: Broiler
Serves: 6 to 8

6 to 8 white fish filets
Salt
Pepper
MSG
Melted butter
1 pound lump crabmeat

½ cup mayonnaise
1 beaten egg
2 to 4 tablespoons capers
Dash of cayenne
Dash of Tabasco
1 teaspoon dried mustard

Season filets with salt, pepper and MSG. Brush with melted butter. Bake until just cooked in a buttered baking dish. Mix remaining ingredients together. Pile crab mixture onto filets. Sprinkle with paprika. Put under broiler until golden.

Note: A lovely dish for entertaining. The crab mixture may be made earlier and refrigerated.

Mrs. Charles Everly

Baked Salmon

Preheat: 350 degrees

Salmon
Salt and pepper

Lemon slices
Onion

Sprinkle salmon with salt and pepper inside and out. Put lemon slices and onion, if desired, in cavity. Place on greased aluminum foil in pan. Bake at 350 degrees for one hour. Serve hot or cold.

Mrs. Kleber S. Masterson, Jr.

Salmon Loaf

Preheat: 350 degrees
Yield: 6

1-pound can salmon
½ cup chopped celery
¼ cup minced onion
1½ cups bread crumbs
1 tablespoon parsley
1 teaspoon salt

¼ teaspoon paprika
1 teaspoon pepper
½ cup milk
2 eggs, beaten
¼ cup lemon juice

Combine and spoon into greased 9 x 5 x 6-inch loaf pan. Bake 1 hour. Serve with Hollandaise Sauce.

Mrs. Bernard R. Corbett

Savoury Haddock

Preheat: 350 degrees
Serves: 4

½ pound thinly sliced bacon   *1 pound haddock filets*

Cut haddock into 1-inch cubes. Wrap each in ½ strip bacon and put on a skewer. Bake at 350 degrees until bacon is crisp. Serve on toast points.

Note: It is important to use good quality flavorful bacon.

Mrs. Warren Heenan

Paella

Serves: 6 to 8

1 teaspoon oregano
2 peppercorns
1 clove garlic
1½ teaspoons salt
6 tablespoons olive oil
1 teaspoon vinegar
1½ pound chicken, cut in pieces
2 ounces cooked ham, cut in strips
¾ to 1 pound chorizo (Spanish sausage), cut in 1½-inch pieces
1 ounce salt pork, finely chopped
1 onion, peeled and finely chopped
1 green pepper, finely chopped

½ teaspoon coriander
1 teaspoon capers
4 cups boiling water
3 tablespoons tomato sauce
2¼ cups raw rice
1 teaspoon saffron
1 pound shrimp, shelled and deveined
1½ pound lobster, cooked
1 8-ounce can peas, drained
1 quart mussels, scrubbed
12 small clams
1 can pimentos

Combine oregano, peppercorns, garlic, salt, 2 tablespoons olive oil and vinegar. Mash into a paste, and rub the chicken with it. Heat the remaining olive oil in a deep heavy skillet or kettle, and brown the chicken lightly over medium heat. Add ham, chorizo, salt pork, onion, pepper, coriander and capers, and cook 10 minutes over low heat. Then add tomato sauce and rice and cook 5 minutes. Add water, saffron and shrimp; mix and cook rapidly, covered until the liquid is absorbed (about 20 minutes). Turn rice to bottom, add lobster meat and peas, and cook, covered, an additional 5 minutes. Steam mussels and clams in a small amount of water just until the shells open. Strain the broth through a cheesecloth over the rice mixture. Heat pimentos while steaming mussels and clams. Use the mussels, clams and pimentos as garnish.

Note: Serve with Sangria or Rioja Alta and a crisp green salad.
Mrs. E. Darryl Barnes

Jambalaya

Serves: 15 to 20

5 pounds sausage, sliced
6 green peppers, coarsely chopped
12 onions, coarsely chopped
3 bunches celery, coarsely chopped
2 cups butter, melted
3 pounds uncooked long-grain rice
5 cloves garlic, chopped
Salt
Pepper

3 teaspoons thyme
5 bay leaves
2 teaspoons cayenne
2 teaspoons Tabasco
12 cups canned tomatoes
7 pounds uncooked shrimp, cleaned,
    shelled and deveined (cut in several
    pieces, if large)
16 cups tomato sauce

Sauté sausage, pepper, onion and celery until vegetables are just tender. Add tomatoes, tomato sauce and seasonings. Bring to a boil. Add shrimp and rice, cook 10 minutes. Remove from heat. Remove bay leaves. Rice should not be completely dry. Allow to rest 20 to 30 minutes before serving.

Pete Fisher, Chef
219 Restaurant

Crunchy Tuna Casserole

Preheat: 325 degrees
Serves: 6 to 8

1 6-ounce can tuna
1 3-ounce can Chinese noodles
1 10¾-ounce can mushroom soup
1 soup can of evaporated milk
1 4-ounce can mushrooms,
    undrained

1 cup chopped celery
½ cup chopped onion
Soy sauce
Potato chips
Slivered almonds

Mix all ingredients. Place in 3-quart casserole. Shake soy sauce over entire mixture. Top with crushed potato chips and slivered almonds. Bake at 325 degrees for 30 minutes.

Mrs. John T. Ticer

Meats

Pasties

Preheat: 450 degrees
Yield: 7

5 cups flour
1½ cups shortening
1¾ teaspoons salt

1½ teaspoons baking powder
1 cup water

Filling

1½ pounds sirloin, diced
¾ pound pork steak, diced
3 potatoes, diced
3 onions, sliced

Salt to taste
Pepper to taste
Butter
3 tablespoons favorite soup

Combine dry ingredients, cut in shortening, add water and stir until dough forms. Divide into 7 portions. Roll each into a circle. On bottom, in center, put a layer of diced potatoes, then meat, then onions. Salt, pepper and dot with butter and a small amount of the soup mixture. Fold crust like a turnover. Seal edges, make 2 small slits and bake. Bake at 450 degrees for 10 minutes; 375 degrees for 50 minutes.

Note: These can be frozen before baking. They are quite large and can even be eaten cold on a picnic.

Mrs. Alan E. Mowbray

Ramsay House

Ramsay House is situated three blocks from the Potomac River in the heart of Old Town Alexandria. The yellow clapboard cottage was owned by William Ramsay, a distinguished Scottish founder of the city.

William Ramsay and his wife Anne had eight children. They occupied this house only a short time before moving to a larger, finer home in the city. Ramsay, like so many of Alexandria's founders, was a hard-working, resourceful Scotsman who became very successfully involved in trade and civic affairs.

According to restoration architects, the house was constructed about 1724, nearly 24 years before the town of Alexandria was founded. Some researchers say that it may have stood in the early Scottish settlement of Dumfries, Virginia, some 30 miles down the Potomac River from Alexandria. It was moved to its present location, perhaps by barge up the river, between 1749 and 1751.

The original house contained only one room on each floor, but it was expanded to include two rooms per floor before it was moved to Alexandria. Major alterations were made on the house during the late 18th century.

After a fire in 1942, the City of Alexandria purchased the house and restored it. It was dedicated in 1956 as an historic site, marking it as the city's oldest house. Today, Ramsay House is Alexandria's official visitors center.

125

Individual Beef Wellington

Serves: 10

Meat and Marinade

1 whole filet of beef
Bacon or suet to cover filet
1 teaspoon salt
½ cup olive oil
½ cup sliced onions
½ cup sliced carrots
½ cup sliced celery

¼ teaspoon thyme
¼ teaspoon sage
1 bay leaf
10 peppercorns
2 cups dry vermouth
½ cup cognac

Sprinkle beef with salt, place in tightly fitting casserole. Cook vegetables and herbs in oil until tender. Cover with oil-vegetable mixture, vermouth, and cognac. Cover and refrigerate 24 to 72 hours, turning occasionally.

Pastry

6 cups flour
1 tablespoon salt
1 cup butter
1½ cups shortening

2 eggs, well beaten
2 tablespoons vinegar
⅔ cup cold water

Mix flour and salt. Cut in butter and shortening. Combine eggs, vinegar and water. Mix with flour until all can be formed into a ball. Divide pastry into 10 equal balls. Refrigerate until one hour before using. (If you want fancy decorations on top—make an extra half recipe of pastry).

Mushroom Filling

3 pounds mushrooms, finely
 chopped
3 tablespoons butter
⅔ cup minced shallots

¾ cup Madeira
Salt and pepper
8 ounces foie gras (optional)

Twist mushrooms in the corner of a linen towel to extract as much juice as possible. Save juice. Sauté mushrooms with shallots in butter 10 minutes. Add Madeira; boil until liquid has evaporated. Salt and pepper to taste. Beat in foie gras; refrigerate.

Preliminary Baking: Remove meat from marinade; scrape off vegetables. Reserve marinade together with mushroom juice for sauce. Place suet on top of filet roast 15 minutes in preheated 425 degree oven. Let cool or refrigerate until ready to use.

Assembling and Baking: Slice meat into 10 equal pieces. Roll out a ball of pastry into approximately a 10-inch circle. Spread some mushroom mixture in center of dough. Place filet on top and pat more mushroom mixture on top and sides. Wrap dough around filet. Seal bottom. Place seam-side down and make a small hole in top center for steam to escape. You can decorate around hole with pastry cutouts.

Refrigerate overnight or freeze. If frozen, wrap in freezer wrap. Defrost in refrigerator for 6 hours before baking. When ready to bake, brush each pastry with egg glaze (2 eggs beaten with 2 teaspoons water). Bake for 25 to 30 minutes at 425 degrees or to 140 degrees on meat thermometer inserted in center hole in pastry. Let rest 20 minutes in warm place.

Madeira Sauce

Marinade
Mushroom juices
2 cups beef bouillon

1 tablespoon tomato paste
2 tablespoons cornstarch
½ cup Madeira

Simmer marinade, mushroom juice, bouillon and tomato paste for one hour or until reduced to 2 cups. Strain, season and thicken with cornstarch blended with Madeira. Pass sauce separately.

Note: This sounds difficult but can be done in stages over a 4 or 5 day period.

Mrs. Lewis B. Puller, Jr.

Sirloin Tips Ragout Au Vin

Serves: 6

3 pounds sirloin tip cut in 1-inch cubes
3 tablespoons butter
2 ounces tomato paste
2 tablespoons wine vinegar
1 cup Burgundy wine

1 stick cinnamon
2 pounds tiny whole onions, peeled
2 bay leaves
1 teaspoon salt
¼ teaspoon pepper
1 teaspoon cornstarch

Place cubes of meat in deep saucepan with butter. Simmer meat over medium heat, stirring constantly, until meat is brown and tender. Mix tomato paste, vinegar and wine with browned meat. Add remaining ingredients except cornstarch. Simmer covered one hour. Mix cornstarch with ¼ cup water and blend into sauce.

Mrs. Jerome J. Palermino

Steak Diane

Serves: 4

6 *tablespoons butter*
2 *tablespoons shallots*
4 *portions of beef filet or sirloin*
2 *tablespoons heated brandy*
4 *tablespoons dry sherry*

2 *tablespoons chopped chives*
2 *tablespoons minced parsley*
2 *tablespoons Worcestershire sauce*
2 *tablespoons A-1 Steak Sauce*

In a large heavy skillet, melt 4 tablespoons of butter. Sauté shallots until golden. Place filets in skillet and sear quickly on both sides. Add brandy and flame. When flame dies down, add sherry, chives, parsley, Worcestershire sauce, A-1 Sauce and remaining butter. Mix well. Continue to sauté until done.

Mrs. Wallace W. Edens

Akwaknee Tenderloin Tips

Serves: 6

4 *tablespoons butter*
1 *tablespoon flour*
1 *cup beef bouillon*
1 *bay leaf*
3 *whole cloves*
2 *pounds tenderloin tips cut in*
 bias strips (sirloin can be used,
 and amount can be increased)

2 *tablespoons salad oil*
1 *medium green pepper, cut in thin*
 strips
½ *to 1 pound fresh mushrooms, sliced*
¼ *cup lemon juice*
1 *4-ounce jar pimentos, cut in strips*

Melt 2 tablespoons butter, blend flour, gradually stir in bouillon. Add bay leaf and cloves, heat, stirring constantly, bring to boil; simmer 2 minutes. Remove spices. Brown meat in hot oil, season with salt and pepper. Cook until tender. Don't put too many strips in the pan at one time. Put on paper towels. Cook mushrooms until just tender in 2 tablespoons butter. Cook green pepper until tender. Add bouillon mixture and lemon juice. Add meat. Heat until just boiling. Check seasoning. Decorate with pimento. Serve with peas and rice delux.

Note: This recipe comes from a hotel at Yosemite National Park. A good company dish with a tangy sophisticated taste. May be made ahead and reheated.

Mrs. Raymond T. Bond

Filet of Sour Cream

Preheat: 450 degrees
Serves: 6

3 pounds filet of beef or eye of
   round, rolled and tied securely
   at 1-inch intervals
½ pound onions, sliced
1 cup diced celery
⅔ cup diced carrots
1 cup diced parsnips
¼ cup diced bacon
8 peppercorns

4 whole allspice
2 bay leaves
1 teaspoon salt
Freshly ground black pepper
¼ teaspoon thyme
2 cups beef stock, and additional ¼
   cup if needed
1 tablespoon melted butter

Place the beef in a 4 to 5-quart casserole or saucepan. Add the onions, celery, carrots, parsnips, bacon, peppercorns, allspice, bay leaves, salt, a few grindings of pepper and thyme. Dribble the melted butter evenly over the meat and vegetables. The meat may be marinated in this mixture for at least 24 hours if desired. Bake the filet, uncovered, in the middle of a 450 degree oven for 25 to 30 minutes, or until the vegetables and meat are lightly browned, turning the meat once during this time. Reduce temperature to 350 degrees. Pour 2 cups of stock, first brought to a boil in a saucepan, into the casserole, and bake for 1 hour longer, turning the meat occasionally. Add more stock only if the liquid seems to be cooking away too rapidly. Arrange the beef on a platter and keep it warm in a 200 degree oven while preparing the sauce.

Sauce

1 tablespoon lemon juice
2 cups sour cream

2 tablespoons flour

Pour the contents of the casserole through a sieve, pressing hard on the vegetables with a wooden spoon before discarding them. Then return the stock to the casserole. Bring the liquid to a simmer over medium heat. In a mixing bowl, add 2 tablespoons of the casserole liquid to the sour cream, then beat in the flour with a wire whisk. Stir the mixture into the casserole. Cook for 3 to 4 minutes without boiling. Add lemon juice. Taste for seasoning. Serve the beef sliced and the sauce separately.

Mrs. William E. Elwood

Bolichi
(Stuffed Eye of the Round)

Preheat: 475 degrees
Serves: 6

3 to 4 pounds eye of the round
½ to ¾ cup chopped pepperoni
  sausage
1 medium slice cured ham,
  chopped
1 clove garlic, minced
½ green pepper, chopped

1 medium onion, chopped
1 teaspoon Worcestershire sauce
1 bay leaf
4 cloves
Salt and pepper to taste
1 10¾-ounce can consommé

Have the butcher make a pocket in the center of roast, lengthwise, leaving opposite end closed. You can do it yourself with a very sharp knife. Insert knife in one end in center of roast; repeat diagonally, making an X. Try not to go through opposite end. Mix all ingredients except consommé, bay leaf and cloves. Stuff roast with mixture, forcing to end. Flour stuffed roast, season with salt and pepper. Roast for 20 minutes. Add consommé, cloves, and bay leaf to pan. Reduce oven temperature to 325 degrees and roast for 2½ hours, basting frequently. Serve Bolichi cut in ½-inch slices. Good with brown or wild rice made with essence from pan.

Mrs. Richard L. Wallace

Beef and Onions Braised in Beer

Preheat: 325 degrees
Serves: 6

3 pounds boneless chuck cut in 2
  x 4-inch strips
¼ cup salad oil
3 to 4 large onions, thinly sliced
1 tablespoon brown sugar
1 clove garlic, minced
1 cup beef stock (may be canned)
½ teaspoon thyme
Pinch of nutmeg

1 bay leaf
1 teaspoon salt
2 tablespoons Dijon mustard
2 tablespoons wine vinegar
2 to 3 cups beer
5 slices French bread
2 tablespoons chopped parsley
1 pound fresh mushrooms

In a large heavy casserole, heat half of the oil, and brown meat a few pieces at a time. Set meat aside. In same casserole, sauté onions and mushrooms until tender, adding oil as needed. Sprinkle brown sugar over the onions and cook, stirring for a minute. Return meat to casserole and add garlic, stock, thyme, nutmeg, bay leaf, salt, vinegar and parsley, with enough beer to cover meat. Coat bread slices on one side with mustard; then place bread mustard-side down on top of meat mixture.

The bread will slowly dissolve and serve as a thickener. Bring to simmer, cover casserole and place on lower rack of oven. Cook for 2 hours or until tender. Liquid will be reduced to about half.

Note: An excellent stew that freezes beautifully.

Mrs. Renny H. Barnes

Marinated Eye of Round

Preheat: 300 degrees
Serves: 12 to 16

3 to 4 pound eye of round, cooked
   medium rare, cooled, sliced very
   thin
2 cups catsup
Juice of 1 lemon
1 teaspoon salt
½ teaspoon pepper

4 tablespoons mustard
4 tablespoons Worcestershire sauce
4 tablespoons vinegar
1 teaspoon onion juice
½ teaspoon cayenne
½ cup margarine

Heat all ingredients except beef in saucepan. Spread sliced meat in a serving dish, spooning sauce over each layer. Refrigerate (or freeze) until ready to serve. Cover with foil and heat in 300 degree oven. Serve with rolls.

Mrs. Patrick J. Vaughan

Round Steak Sauerbraten

Preheat: 350 degrees
Serves: 4 to 5

2 cups water
1½ pounds round steak, ½ to 1
   inch thick
1 tablespoon oil
1 envelope brown gravy mix
1 tablespoon instant minced onion
1 tablespoon brown sugar

2 tablespoons wine vinegar
1 teaspoon Worcestershire sauce
¼ teaspoon ground ginger
1 bay leaf
½ teaspoon salt
¼ teaspoon pepper

Cut meat in 1-inch squares. Brown meat in oil. Remove meat from skillet. Add gravy mix and 2 cups water. Bring to boil, stirring constantly. Stir in onion, brown sugar, vinegar, Worcestershire sauce, ginger, bay leaf, salt and pepper. Add meat and mix. Turn into 1½-quart casserole. Cover, bake at 350 degrees for 1½ hours. Remove bay leaf. Serve over rice or noodles.

Mrs. Carlton L. Schelhorn

Poppy Seed Pot Roast

Serves: 6 to 8

1 5-pound chuck roast
1 tablespoon paprika
2 teaspoons salt
¼ teaspoon pepper
2 tablespoons oil
2 cups water
1 bay leaf

2 teaspoons poppy seed
1 pound carrots, cut into pieces
½ 10-ounce package frozen peas
Flour
½ cup sour cream
1 4-ounce can sliced mushrooms
   (optional)

Sprinkle roast with paprika, salt and pepper. Brown in hot oil in Dutch oven. Add the water, bay leaf and poppy seed. Cover. Simmer for 2 hours and 30 minutes. Add carrots. Cook additional 40 minutes. Add peas. Cook until peas are done. Thicken broth with flour. Check seasoning, adding additional salt and paprika to taste. Add mushrooms and heat through. Remove from heat, add sour cream and mix well. Serve with noodles.

Mrs. Frederick R. McNamara

Beef and Green Peppers

Serves: 2 to 3

1 pound beef steak, sirloin
4 tablespoons soy sauce
1 tablespoon cornstarch
1 tablespoon dry sherry
1 teaspoon sugar

¼ teaspoon MSG
1 slice ginger root
4 tablespoons cooking oil
½ teaspoon salt
2 green peppers, cut in chunks

Cut beef across the grain into thin slices about 2 inches long. Mix sliced beef with soy sauce, cornstarch, sherry, sugar and MSG. Set aside. Put 2 tablespoons of oil into hot skillet over high heat. Add salt. Then add green peppers. Stir constantly, about one minute. Remove from pan. Add 2 tablespoons more of oil and the ginger. Stir in beef mixture. Cook until beef is almost done—about 2 minutes. Add green pepper and mix thoroughly. Do not overcook.

Mrs. Donald M. McNamara

Sukiyaki

Serves: 6

4 tablespoons salad oil
2 pounds sirloin (sliced thin while
   partially frozen)
½ cup beef bouillon
½ head Chinese cabbage, shredded
¾ cup soy sauce
¼ cup sugar
1 tablespoon sherry

3 onions, thinly sliced
½ cup thinly sliced celery
1 cup sliced bamboo shoots
½ pound mushrooms, sliced
2 cups shredded spinach
2 to 3 carrots, thinly sliced
4 scallions, sliced

Heat oil in large frying pan. Add meat and brown. Meanwhile combine bouillon, soy sauce, sugar and sherry. Add half of sauce mixture to pan and push meat to one side. Add cabbage, onions, celery and carrots. Cook 3 minutes over low heat, push to side. Add remaining sauce, bamboo shoots, mushrooms and spinach. Cook 3 minutes over low heat. Add scallions. Cook one minute. Serve with rice or vermicelli.

Mrs. Frank McCabe

Ropa Vieja
(Shredded Beef)

Serves: 8

2 pounds rump roast or flank
   steak
⅓ cup oil
1 onion, sliced thin
2 cloves garlic, crushed
1 10¾-ounce can tomato soup

1 large green pepper, cut into thin
   strips
1 teaspoon salt
1 bay leaf
½ cup dry wine, red or white

Stew meat until tender and can be shredded by fork into small strips. Brown garlic and onion in oil, add remaining ingredients. Cook over low heat 15 to 20 minutes, stirring occasionally.

Note: Serve with rice, black beans and a salad.

Mrs. John Smithers

Corned Beef in Foil

Preheat: 300 degrees
Serves: 6 to 8

3 to 4 pounds corned beef brisket
¼ cup water
2 tablespoons pickling spice
1 small orange, sliced

1 onion, sliced
1 stalk celery with leaves
1 carrot, sliced

Soak beef in cold water to cover for 30 minutes or longer. Pat dry and place on heavy foil. Place seasonings on top of beef with water. Seal foil and bake for 4 hours. Remove seasonings and fat from beef when done. Let set for at least 15 minutes before carving.

Note: Good served with cabbage, carrots and new potatoes.

Mrs. Alfred E. T. Rusch

Simple Stew

Preheat: 250 degrees
Serves: 6

2 pounds stewing meat, cubed
1 medium onion, sliced
1 stalk celery, cut on diagonal
6 carrots, cut in chunks
4 medium potatoes, quartered

2 teaspoons salt
1 tablespoon sugar
2 tablespoons Minute Tapioca
1 6-ounce can tomato juice

Stir together salt, sugar, tapioca and tomato juice. Place other ingredients in heavy casserole. Pour juice mixture into casserole, stir and cover. Cook four hours at 250 degrees.

Mrs. Kevin Gallen

Hong Kong Beef

Serves: 4 to 5

2 tablespoons cornstarch
Dash of pepper
2 tablespoons soy sauce
2 cups thinly sliced strips of
  cooked beef
1½ cups thinly sliced strips of
  green pepper

3 to 4 tablespoons oil
1 clove garlic, minced
3 tomatoes, peeled and cut in wedges
½ cup beef bouillon or consommé
Lemon peel strips

Combine cornstarch, pepper and soy sauce. Dredge beef in mixture and set aside. Sauté green peppers lightly in oil. Remove peppers. Add garlic and beef, sauté 2 to 3 minutes. Add peppers, tomatoes and bouillon. Cook until sauce is thickened, about 5 minutes. Serve over rice. Garnish with lemon peel, if desired.

Note: May use canned tomatoes. Great for leftovers!

Mrs. Gerald B. File

Roast Brisket of Beef

Preheat: 500 degrees
Serves: 6 to 8

4 pound beef brisket
1 package dehydrated onion soup
  mix
1 cup water

Pepper
Paprika
Garlic salt

Place brisket fat side up in roaster. Sprinkle dry onion mix over meat; dust with pepper, paprika and garlic salt. Add water. Place in 500 degree oven for 15 minutes until meat begins to brown. Turn oven down to 350 degrees, cover and cook for 2 hours, basting 2 or 3 times.

Note: Delicious sliced hot or cold.

Mrs. Leon B. Ruben

Gourmet Goulash

Serves: 6 to 8

2 tablespoons butter
2½ pounds round steak, cubed
3 cups chopped onion
1 8-ounce can tomato sauce
1 teaspoon Worcestershire sauce
1 clove garlic, minced
2 tablespoons brown sugar

1 tablespoon paprika
1½ teaspoons salt
1 teaspoon caraway seed
1 teaspoon dill seed
¼ teaspoon pepper
1 cup sour cream (optional)

Melt butter in large skillet; add meat and brown well. Add onion. Combine tomato sauce, Worcestershire sauce, garlic, brown sugar, paprika, salt, caraway seed, dill seed and pepper. Add to meat and onion and cook covered until meat is tender—about 1½ hours. If desired, add sour cream. Serve on parsley-buttered noodles.

Mrs. Herbert Stewart

Stuffed Eggplant

Preheat: 350 degrees
Serves: 10

2 medium eggplants, halved,
  unpeeled
1½ cups bread crumbs
¼ pound (plus a little extra)
  Mozzarella cheese, grated
Chopped parsley to taste
1 clove garlic, minced (optional)

2 eggs, beaten
1 16-ounce can tomatoes or pizza
  sauce
Salt to taste
Pepper to taste
Sugar to taste
1 pound ground beef, browned

Scoop out eggplant and cut into pieces. Blanch in boiling water, drain well. Add bread crumbs, grated cheese, parsley, garlic, ground beef, salt, pepper and beaten eggs. Mix well. Fill half shells with mixture. Sprinkle with additional grated cheese. Add salt, pepper and sugar to can of tomatoes. Pour tomatoes over eggplant halves and bake at 350 degrees for at least one hour. Serve as hot slices.

Mrs. John J. Ross III

Jim Brady's Prize Winning Texas Chili

Serves: 10

2 pounds round steak
1 pound fresh pork
3 tablespoons fat
3 medium onions, chopped
4 cloves garlic, minced
1 tablespoon oregano
1 tablespoon red wine vinegar
1 2.4-ounce box hot chili powder
1 tablespoon masa flour*

28-ounce can Progresso tomatoes
3 bay leaves
1 tablespoon salt
1 tablespoon cumin
1 tablespoon brown sugar
1 4-ounce can jalapeno peppers, seeded
  (add more if extra hot flavor desired)
1 pint ripe olives, sliced

* A Quaker product—like flour used to bind chili.

Cut meat into cubes. Brown in hot fat, then add chili powder and stir. In another skillet, sauté onions and garlic with jalapeno peppers until golden. Add to meat, drained tomatoes, onions, garlic, chili powder and masa flour. Cook for 20 minutes. Add remainder of spices, vinegar and brown sugar. Add olives last. Cook slowly for several hours. Serve with shredded Cheddar cheese on top. This is very hot!

Note: Recipe has won Washington Area Chili Cook-off for several years.

Mrs. James S. Brady

Chili Con Carne

Serves: 8 to 12

2 pounds ground beef
1 tablespoon shortening
1 cup diced green peppers
3½ cups canned tomatoes or
    tomato sauce
½ cup onion flakes

2 teaspoons salt
4 cups kidney beans (2 pounds canned)
4 tablespoons chili powder
2 tablespoons oregano
½ teaspoon garlic powder
½ teaspoon ground black pepper

Brown meat in shortening in a 3-quart saucepan or Dutch oven. Add green peppers and cook until limp. Stir in tomatoes, onion and salt. Cook slowly 15 minutes. Add undrained beans and remaining ingredients. Cook 10 minutes. Serve in bowls or over hot rice.

Note: Freezes well.

Mrs. Alfred E. T. Rusch

Western Hospitality Casserole

Preheat: 350 degrees
Serves: 24

4 pounds lean stew beef, cut in
    1-inch cubes
¾ cup flour
2 teaspoons salt
½ cup oil
2 cloves garlic, minced
1 onion, sliced (optional)
1 6-ounce can tomato paste
1¼ cups dry red wine

3 cups water
1 teaspoon thyme
Pinch of allspice (optional)
2 bay leaves
2 4-ounce cans mushrooms
1 8-ounce package egg noodles (bows
    or twists), cooked and drained
3 cups shredded Cheddar cheese
Parsley

Coat the meat with flour and salt. In large Dutch oven, brown meat in oil at medium temperature; drain off excess grease. Add garlic, onion, tomato paste, wine, water, thyme, allspice and bay leaves. Cover, simmer 1½ hours or until meat is tender; remove bay leaves. Stir in mushrooms and noodles; divide mixture in half and pour into two 12 x 8 x 2-inch baking dishes. May be frozen at this point, or placed in refrigerator overnight. About 1¼ hours before serving, cover with foil. Bake at 350 degrees for 1 hour. Uncover. Border each dish with half of the Cheddar cheese. Bake 15 minutes longer. Garnish with parsley.

Mrs. Timothy J. O'Shaughnessy

Hawaiian Meat Balls

Serves: 6

1½ pounds ground beef
⅔ cup cracker crumbs
½ cup chopped onions
⅔ cup evaporated milk

1 teaspoon seasoned salt
3 tablespoons shortening
Flour

Combine beef, cracker crumbs, onions, milk and salt. Mix lightly but thoroughly. Shape mixture into 30 balls. Roll in flour. Brown meatballs in shortening and drain excess fat. Prepare sweet-sour sauce. Pour over meatballs. Simmer covered for 15 minutes.

Sauce

1 13½-ounce can pineapple
  chunks
2 tablespoons cornstarch
½ cup vinegar
½ cup brown sugar

2 tablespoons soy sauce
2 tablespoons lemon juice
1 cup coarsely chopped green pepper
1 tablespoon chopped pimento

Drain pineapple chunks, reserve syrup. Measure pineapple syrup and add water to equal one cup. Blend together pineapple liquid and cornstarch until smooth. Stir in vinegar, brown sugar, soy sauce and lemon juice. Cook until thickened and clear. Add pineapple chunks, green pepper and pimento. Mix well. Cover and simmer over low heat for 15 minutes before adding to meatballs.

Mrs. John Denson

Kaposzta
(Stuffed Cabbage Rolls)

Preheat: 350 degrees
Serves: 6

1 large head cabbage
1 pound ground beef
1 cup cooked rice
1 onion, chopped
¼ cup brown sugar
1 egg, slightly beaten

½ teaspoon allspice
⅛ teaspoon garlic powder
1 27-ounce can sauerkraut
1 16-ounce can tomato sauce
Sour cream (optional)

Core cabbage. Place in saucepan with 2 inches boiling water, core down. Simmer until soft—about 10 to 15 minutes. Drain and cool. Remove leaves. Brown beef and drain. Add rice, onion, egg and seasonings. Place small amount in middle of each leaf. Roll up, tucking in edges. In a 9 x 13-inch pan combine sauerkraut, one cup tomato sauce, brown sugar. Spread over bottom of pan. Place cabbage rolls, seamside down on kraut mixture. Pour another cup of tomato sauce over top. Cover and bake one hour at 350 degrees. Serve with a dollop of sour cream.

Mrs. E. Darryl Barnes

Crafty Crescent Lasagne

Preheat: 375 degrees
Serves: 2 to 3

Meat Filling

¼ *pound sausage*	¼ *teaspoon oregano*
¼ *pound ground beef*	¼ *teaspoon salt*
⅜ *cup chopped onion*	*Dash pepper*
¼ *clove garlic*	½ *6-ounce can tomato paste*
½ *tablespoon parsley*	*12 slices Mozzarella cheese*
¼ *teaspoon basil*	*1 can refrigerator crescent rolls*

Cheese Filling

½ *cup creamed cottage cheese*	⅛ *cup Parmesan cheese*
1 small egg	

In skillet, brown sausage and ground beef; drain. Add onion, garlic, parsley, basil, oregano, salt, pepper and tomato paste. Simmer, uncovered, for 5 minutes. Combine cheese filling ingredients in separate bowl. Unroll the can of crescent rolls into 4 rectangles. On *ungreased* cookie sheet, lay dough out, overlapping edges and pressing edges to seal. Spread ½ of meat filling lengthwise on center half of dough to within 1 inch of the end. Top with cheese filling; top cheese with remaining meat filling. Place Mozzarella over last meat layer. Fold short ends of dough 1 inch over filling. Fold long ends of dough, pinch together, and brush with 1 tablespoon milk and sprinkle with 1 tablespoon sesame seeds. Bake at 375 degrees for 20 to 25 minutes or until golden brown.

Note: May be prepared ahead. Cover with plastic wrap and refrigerate 2 to 3 hours. Increase baking time 25 to 30 minutes.

Mrs. Hugh C. Newton

Creamy Lasagna Bolognese

Preheat: 375 degrees
Serves: 10 to 12

2 10-ounce packages frozen
  chopped spinach
8 ounces lasagna noodles (½
  16-ounce box)
1 pound lean ground beef
1 medium onion, minced
½ pound fresh mushrooms, sliced
1 teaspoon oregano leaves
½ teaspoon basil
¼ teaspoon pepper
Salt to taste

1 12-ounce can V-8 juice
½ cup all-purpose flour
1 cup milk
2 eggs
1 cup Ricotta or creamed cottage
  cheese
1 tablespoon parsley
1 8-ounce package sliced
  Mozzarella cheese
2 tablespoons Parmesan cheese, grated

About 1¾ hours before serving:

Thaw and completely drain frozen spinach. Cook lasagna noodles and drain completely. Over medium heat, sauté ground beef until it loses its pink color. Add onion, mushrooms, oregano, basil, pepper and 1 teaspoon salt. Continue cooking until onion is tender, stirring constantly. Add vegetable juice. In a small bowl, blend flour and milk until smooth. Gradually stir into meat mixture and cook, stirring constantly, until mixture is thickened. Set aside. Preheat oven and grease a 13 x 9-inch baking dish. In a medium bowl, combine spinach with 1 egg and ½ teaspoon salt. Spread in bottom of baking dish and cover with ½ of the lasagna noodles. In the same bowl you mixed the spinach, combine Ricotta cheese with 1 egg and blend. Spoon ½ of mixture over noodles. Top with ½ of the Mozzarella cheese slices, then ½ of the meat mixture. Repeat layers of noodles, cheeses, and sauce. Sprinkle Parmesan cheese evenly over sauce. Bake for 30 minutes until hot and bubbly. Let stand for 10 minutes for easier cutting. Garnish with parsley.

Note: May be made ahead. If frozen allow 1½ hours baking time; if refrigerated, allow 45 minutes to 1 hour. Excellent for an informal dinner party or buffet. Serve with fresh green salad and crispy Italian bread. Very worth the effort—not the usual lasagna taste.

Mrs. Bernard P. O'Hare

Texas Yum Yum

Preheat: 350 degrees
Serves 6 to 8

1 pound ground beef
1 16-ounce can tomatoes, drained
2 teaspoons salt
1 8-ounce can tomato paste
2 tablespoons sugar
2 cloves garlic, crushed
1 cup sliced mushrooms

1 8½-ounce can water chestnuts,
   drained and thinly sliced
1 cup sour cream
1 4-ounce package of cream cheese
Scallions, chopped
10 ounces egg noodles

Brown meat in garlic and add tomatoes, salt, tomato paste, sugar, mushrooms and water chestnuts. Mix sour cream, softened cream cheese and add chopped scallions. Cook egg noodles according to directions on package. Butter 4-quart casserole dish and layer ingredients beginning with noodles and ending with noodles. Cover and bake at 350 degrees for 35 to 45 minutes.

Note: Good family fare.

Mrs. Thomas T. Bellino

Spinach Fandango

Preheat: 350 degrees
Serves: 6 to 8

2 10-ounce packages frozen
   chopped spinach
1 pound ground beef
1 medium onion, chopped
1 to 2 cloves garlic, minced
2 dashes Tabasco
1 teaspoon oregano

1 10-ounce can mushrooms, drained
1 cup sour cream
1 10-ounce can cream of celery soup
Salt and pepper to taste
1 8-ounce package Mozzarella or
   Monterey Jack cheese, shredded

Cook spinach; drain well, and squeeze dry. Set aside. In a skillet, sauté ground beef, onions and garlic until browned. Add Tabasco, mushrooms, oregano, salt and pepper. Simmer 5 minutes. Add spinach, sour cream and soup. Heat thoroughly. Turn into a greased casserole and top with cheese. Bake 15 to 20 minutes until brown and bubbly.

Mrs. John B. Allen

Middle East Skillet

Serves: 6

½ cup uncooked rice
1¼ pounds ground beef
1 medium onion, chopped
¼ cup canned pineapple tidbits,
  drained
2 tablespoons raisins

2 teaspoons Worcestershire sauce
1 teaspoon curry powder
1½ teaspoons salt
1 1-pound can tomatoes
Salted cashews or peanuts, chopped

Cook and drain rice. Cook meat in skillet until it loses its red color, breaking meat up with a fork. Add rice and remaining ingredients, except nuts. Mix well, bring to a boil, cover and simmer. Stir occasionally. Cook 15 to 20 minutes. Sprinkle with nuts.

The Honorable Margaret B. Inman

Tijuana Tortilla

Preheat: 350 degrees
Serves: 12

Must be done ahead

2 pounds lean chuck ground
1 large onion, chopped
1 16-ounce can tomatoes
1 10-ounce package frozen spinach
1 10¾-ounce can cream of
  mushroom soup
1 10¾-ounce can "golden"
  mushroom soup

8 ounces sour cream
½ cup milk
½ cup butter
1 7-ounce can green chilies (or more)
12-16 flour tortillas
½ pound Cheddar cheese, grated

Sauté beef and onion; drain off fat. Drain and chop spinach. Add spinach and tomatoes to beef mixture. Line bottom and sides of shallow casserole with ½ of the tortillas. Mix chilies and ½ cheese and add to meat mixture. Spoon mixture into casserole. Place rest of tortillas on top. Mix soups, sour cream, milk and butter. Pour over meat and tortillas. Cover and refrigerate overnight. Sprinkle on other ½ of cheese and bake 45 minutes.

Mrs. E. H. Dale Gallimore

Tamale Casserole

Preheat: 350 degrees
Serves: 6

1 pound ground round steak
1 onion, chopped
1 green pepper, chopped
1 stalk celery, chopped (optional)
1 4-ounce can chopped olives
1 16-ounce can hominy, drained

2 12-ounce cans tamales, cut in half
1 10¾-ounce can cream of chicken
  soup .
Grated Monterey Jack or Cheddar
  cheese

Brown meat with onion, green pepper and celery. Drain well. Place in 3-quart casserole, add olives, hominy, tamales and soup. Top with grated cheese. Bake at 350 degrees for 30 to 40 minutes.

Mrs. Kleber S. Masterson, Jr.

Blanquette of Veal

Preheat: 375 degrees
Serves: 8

½ cup butter
4½ pounds veal, cut into 1½-inch
  cubes
Salt and freshly ground pepper
1 clove garlic, minced
1 cup finely chopped onion
4 carrots, cut in 2-inch julienne
  strips
2 packages frozen small onions,
  thawed

4 tablespoons freshly chopped dill (may
  use less)
½ cup flour
½ teaspoon nutmeg
1½ cups canned chicken broth
1 cup white wine
1 cup water
1 cup heavy cream

Heat ¼ cup butter in a large deep casserole and add the veal. Sprinkle with salt and pepper, add garlic, chopped onion and half the dill (remember less dill is needed if it is dried). Cook, stirring, without browning for 5 minutes. Sprinkle with flour and nutmeg; add chicken stock, wine and water. Bring to a boil. Cover and bake one hour at 375 degrees. Heat ¼ cup butter in a skillet, cook frozen onions and julienne carrots until wilted. Stir half this mixture into the veal. Stir in cream and bring to a boil. Spoon the veal mixture onto a serving platter or shallow tureen, garnish top with remaining onions, carrots and chopped dill to taste. Serve with rice.

Mrs. Donald Burchell

Veal and Mushrooms in Sour Cream Sauce

Serves: 6 to 8

12 veal scallops
Salt and pepper to taste
½ cup flour
6 to 8 tablespoons butter
1 cup finely chopped onion

1 pound mushrooms, sliced
¼ cup brandy
1 cup sour cream
½ teaspoon salt

Dredge veal in flour. Add salt and pepper to taste. In skillet, melt 2 tablespoons butter until bubbly. Add scallops a few at a time, add more butter as needed. Cook veal 3 minutes on each side. Remove as it browns and place on warm platter. Melt 2 more tablespoons of butter and sauté onion 3 minutes. Stir. Add 2 more tablespoons butter and stir in mushrooms. Cover skillet and cook over low heat 5 to 8 minutes or until mushrooms and onions are tender. Add brandy. Shake skillet carefully to ignite brandy. If it does not ignite then start with a match. Let flame subside and stir in sour cream and salt. Bring to a boil and correct seasonings. Return veal to skillet, spoon sauce over it, and bring sauce to boiling point, but don't boil. Serve immediately with buttered noodles.

Mrs. Thomas T. Bellino

Veal Chops Stuffed with Ham and Cheese

Serves: 6

6 veal chops, slit in the thick part
   of each chop
1 cup grated Gruyere cheese
½ cup finely chopped ham

1 finely chopped onion
4 slices bacon, diced
1 cup (or more) whipping cream

Stuff each chop cavity with grated Gruyere cheese and finely chopped ham. Cook chops slowly in clarified butter, turning frequently. Remove from pan to oven-proof dish. Cover each chop with slice of Gruyere cheese and place under broiler to brown the cheese. While chops are browning, add onion and bacon to the fat in the skillet. Cook briskly until onion is browned. Remove bacon. Add whipping cream and reduce until sauce thickens.

Note: Serve on bed of 1 pound small, red, new potatoes, sliced thin and sautéed in butter with onion and bacon. Arrange chops on the potatoes, spread sauce over the chops. Garnish with parsley.

Mrs. Tod R. Hullin

Veal Piccatta

Serves: 4

1½ pounds veal cutlets
⅓ cup flour
4 tablespoons butter
¼ cup olive oil
Juice of 2 lemons

¼ cup dry white wine or vermouth
Salt and pepper to taste
1 lemon, thinly sliced
Chopped parsley

Dredge the cutlets very lightly in the flour. Heat the butter and oil in a frying pan until quite hot, but not smoking. Quickly sauté cutlets on both sides until golden brown. Add the lemon juice and white wine, reduce the heat, and simmer for 5 minutes. Season to taste. Serve immediately, garnished with the thinly sliced lemon and parsley.

Note: Buttered noodles tossed with some toasted sesame seeds make a nice side dish to soak up some of the delicious sauce.

Variation: If more sauce is preferred, after veal is sautéed, remove from pan. Add ½ cup chicken bouillon, 1 cup white wine and ½ teaspoon salt. Cook one minute. Return veal to sauce. Cook 2 to 3 minutes until bubbly. Sprinkle with freshly ground pepper.

Mrs. Stephen L. Echols

Roast Lamb with Herbal Mustard Coating

Preheat: 350 degrees
Serves: 6

6 pound leg of lamb
½ cup Dijon mustard
2 tablespoons soy sauce
1 clove mashed garlic

1 teaspoon ground or leaf rosemary
¼ teaspoon ground ginger
2 tablespoons olive oil

Blend the mustard, soy sauce, garlic, rosemary and ginger together in a bowl. Beat in olive oil by droplets to make a mayonnaise-like cream. Paint the lamb with the mixture and set it on the rack of a roasting pan. The meat will pick up more flavor if it is coated several hours before roasting. Roast in a 350 degree oven 1¼ to 1½ hours.

Note: Burgundy wine goes well with this.

Mrs. Donald Burchell

Lamb Navarin

Serves: 12

2 tablespoons oil
2 tablespoons butter or margarine
6 to 8 pounds shoulder of lamb,
   cut in 1½ inch pieces
2 cups chopped onions
2 cloves garlic, minced
¼ cup all-purpose flour
1 teaspoon salt
¼ teaspoon pepper
2 cups dry white wine

2 8-ounce cans tomato sauce
2 13¾-ounce cans chicken broth
¼ cup chopped parsley, reserve stems
1 bay leaf
½ teaspoon thyme leaves, crumbled
2 cups cooked peas, drained (fresh or
   frozen)
2 1-pound cans small carrots, drained
2 1-pound cans white onions, drained

Heat oil and butter in large skillet over medium heat. Brown meat in batches, adding more oil to pan if necessary. Transfer meat to large Dutch oven when browned. Add onion to fat left in skillet. Cook 2 to 3 minutes, stirring occasionally. Add garlic; cook one minute. Sprinkle with flour, salt and pepper. Mix well. Add wine. Bring to a boil. Stir until all of flour mixture is dissolved. Add tomato sauce, chicken broth, parsley stems, bay leaf and thyme. Return to a boil. Pour sauce over meat. (If planning to freeze, stop cooking process at this point. Resume with instructions when mixture has been thawed.) Cover and simmer one hour and 15 minutes or until meat is tender. Discard parsley stems and bay leaf. Add vegetables. Simmer until vegetables are heated through. Sprinkle with parsley when ready to serve.

Mrs. William E. Elwood

Loin of Lamb in Puff Pastry

Preheat: 400 degrees
Serves: 2 to 4

½ cup butter
2 teaspoons rosemary
2 cloves garlic
Crushed, freshly ground
black pepper

1 tablespoon parsley, finely chopped
4 loin chops, boned
½ pound puff pastry
2 egg yolks, well-beaten

Mix butter, rosemary, garlic, pepper and parsley to form paste. Roll pastry out into 4 rectangles. Place lamb chop on pastry and spread herb butter on top of meat. Cover and seal pastry with a fork. Brush with beaten egg yolks and bake in hot oven (400 degrees) for 15 minutes, until pastry is well puffed up and golden brown. Lamb should be pink and juicy.

Mrs. Warren B. Heenan

Bengal Curry of Lamb

Serves: 4 to 5

2½ pounds lean lamb shoulder
¼ cup butter
⅔ cup chopped onion
3 tablespoons chopped or
crystallized ginger
½ teaspoon granulated sugar
⅛ teaspoon ground pepper
2 teaspoons salt
2-3 tablespoons curry powder
¼ teaspoon crushed dried mint

2 cups milk
½ cup fresh coconut milk:
1 cup shredded coconut and 1 cup
fresh scalded milk—let stand 20
minutes and strain
½ cup freshly grated or packaged
coconut
½ cup fresh lime juice
½ cup heavy cream

Cut lamb into 1-inch cubes. Melt ½ butter and sauté onion. Remove from pan. Add remaining butter and brown lamb. Return onions to pan. Add ginger, sugar, pepper, salt, curry powder, mint and milk. Mix well. Cover and simmer one hour. Add coconut milk and coconut. Cook 5 minutes. Stir in lime juice and then cream. Cook over low heat for 10 to 15 minutes or until lamb is tender. Serve on fluffy rice and with condiments, such as: peanuts, chopped tomatoes, chopped hard-boiled egg, chutney, raisins and coconut.

Note: Serve with a spinach salad and fresh strawberry pie for dessert. This dish also freezes well.

Mrs. Alan E. Mowbray

Pork Barbecue

Serves: 4

¼ cup vinegar
½ cup water
2 tablespoons sugar
1 tablespoon prepared mustard
¼ teaspoon pepper
2 slices lemon

1 medium onion
¼ cup butter
Dash of cayenne
½ cup catsup
1¼ tablespoons Worcestershire sauce
1 cup cooked pork

Combine vinegar, water, sugar, mustard, pepper, lemon, onion, butter and cayenne. Simmer mixture uncovered in a quart pan for 20 minutes. Add catsup and Worcestershire sauce and bring to a boil. Add pork and simmer until thickened. Serve with rolls.

Note: An excellent use for leftover pork roast.

Mrs. Stephen W. Rideout

Stuffed Pork to Stuff People

Preheat: 325 degrees
Serves: 4

4 2 to 2½-inch thick pork chops
with pockets
¼ cup chopped celery
½ cup chopped mushrooms
½ cup chopped onions
½ teaspoon pepper
½ teaspoon salt
1 tablespoon parsley

1 tablespoon parsley
1 tablespoon thyme
2 tablespoons grated horseradish
1 cup herb croutons
2 tablespoons water
1 egg
Several splashes of Tabasco
1 teaspoon cumin

In olive oil, sauté mushrooms, onions and celery, adding spices until oil is absorbed. Remove when slightly browned and place in bowl containing stuffing, 2 tablespoons water and Tabasco. Stir. Bind with egg. If too moist add more croutons. Stuff pork chops with this mixture. Lightly salt and pepper chops, then dust with cumin. Bake at 325 degrees until brown. Serve with wild rice and green salad.

Note: This recipe won *Chicago Today*'s Bachelor Cooking Contest in 1971.

Mrs. James S. Brady

Sweet and Sour Pork

Serves: 4

2 tablespoons bacon fat
1½ pounds boned, lean pork
shoulder, cut in thin strips
1 20-ounce can pineapple chunks
½ cup water
½ cup red wine vinegar

½ cup thinly sliced onion
¼ cup packed brown sugar
2 tablespoons cornstarch
½ teaspoon salt
1 tablespoon soy sauce
¾ cup thinly sliced green pepper

The night before: In large skillet, cook meat in hot bacon fat until golden brown on all sides. Drain pineapple, reserving syrup. Combine water, vinegar, brown sugar, cornstarch, salt, soy sauce and 1 cup pineapple syrup. Cook until clear and slightly thickened, about 2 minutes. Add meat, cook covered over low heat for 1 hour or until meat is fork tender. Refrigerate. About 30 minutes before serving, heat mixture over low heat until steaming hot. Add green peppers, onions, pineapple. Cook 2 minutes. Serve with rice.

Mrs. Frank McCabe

Spareribs with Apples and Squash

Preheat: 300 degrees
Serves: 6 to 8

4 pounds spareribs cut into
   pieces
2 tablespoons butter
½ cup minced onions
3 cups apple juice
4 apples, cored and quartered
½ cup cider vinegar

3 teaspoons brown sugar
1½ teaspoons cinnamon
2 teaspoons cornstarch
2 acorn squash, quartered
Salt
Pepper

Place ribs, meat-side up, in a large shallow roasting pan. Bake 1 hour at 300 degrees. Drain fat. Meanwhile, combine butter, onions, apple juice, vinegar, brown sugar, cinnamon, and salt and pepper to taste. Bring mixture to a boil, simmer 15 minutes. Add cornstarch to thicken. Add sauce to ribs and bake an additional hour. Add quartered apples and squash, bake a third hour.

Mrs. Bernard R. Corbett

Pork Tenderloin Filets

Serves: 6

2 pork tenderloins or cutlets,
   approximately 1½ pounds of
   meat
2 tablespoons shortening
1 chicken bouillon cube
1¼ cups water
2 tablespoons chopped onion
1 clove garlic, crushed

½ cup canned, sliced mushrooms, or
   fresh mushrooms sautéed in 2
   tablespoons butter
1 teaspoon salt
⅛ teaspoon pepper
2 tablespoons flour
¼ cup dry white wine
¼ teaspoon leaf oregano

Brown meat in melted shortening on both sides in large skillet. Drain fat. Dissolve bouillon cube in 1 cup boiling water. Add onions, garlic, mushrooms, bouillon, salt, pepper and oregano to browned meat. Cover and simmer until tender (this will take between ½ and 1 hour depending on the thickness of the pork). Combine flour and ¼ cup water until smooth. Stir into cooking liquid. Continue stirring constantly until mixture is smooth and thick. Add wine. Simmer 5 minutes.

Mrs. Hamilton Beggs

Marinated Pork Roast

Preheat: 325 degrees
Serves: 6 to 10

2 tablespoons dry mustard
2 teaspoons whole thyme leaves
½ cup dry sherry
½ cup soy sauce

2 cloves garlic, minced
1 teaspoon ground ginger
4 to 5 pound pork loin roast, boned,
   rolled and tied

Combine marinade ingredients in a shallow dish, stirring well. Place roast in dish; cover and marinate 3 to 4 hours in refrigerator, turning occasionally. Remove roast from marinade, and place on a rack in a shallow roasting pan. Bake, uncovered, at 325 degrees until meat thermometer registers 170 degrees or 2½ to 3 hours.

Sauce

1 10-ounce jar apricot preserves
1 tablespoon soy sauce

2 tablespoons dry sherry

Combine preserves, soy sauce and sherry in a small saucepan; cook over low heat, stirring occasionally, until preserves melt. Serve sauce with sliced roast.

Mrs. Donald Burchell

Polynesian Pork

Serves: 4

2 pounds pork tenderloin, cut in
   strips
2 tablespoons butter
1 13½-ounce can pineapple tidbits
½ cup Russian dressing
1½ tablespoons soy sauce

1 tablespoon vinegar
¼ teaspoon salt
¾ cup water
2 tablespoons cornstarch
2 medium green peppers, thinly sliced
Hot cooked rice

Cook pork in butter until brown, drain. Drain juice from pineapple and reserve. Combine juice with dressing, soy sauce, vinegar and salt. Stir in water which has been mixed with cornstarch. Pour sauce over meat, green pepper and pineapple. Stir until thick. Cover and simmer 45 minutes, stirring often. Serve over hot cooked rice.

Mrs. William E. Elwood

Baked Pork Chops á La Bordeaux

Preheat: 350 degrees
Serves: 4

4 heavy cut loin pork chops
Salt
Pepper
⅛ teaspoon nutmeg

⅛ teaspoon ground cloves
1 tablespoon brown sugar
1 cup Bordeaux wine
Spiced apples

Wipe chops dry and season with salt and pepper. Broil chops until golden brown on both sides. Remove and drain excess fat. Sprinkle chops with nutmeg and cloves. Add brown sugar and wine to oven-proof pan and bake covered in a 350 degree oven for 15 minutes. Remove cover and bake an additional 10 minutes. Serve on a hot platter garnished with spiced apples.

Mrs. Jerome J. Palermino

Christmas Morning Sausage Pie

Preheat: 350 degrees
Serves: 6

1 baked 9-inch pie shell
1½ pounds mushrooms
6 tablespoons butter
1 pound poached kielbasa or
   cooked sausage
1 cup heavy cream

1 tablespoon flour
1 tablespoon lemon juice
½ teaspoon salt
Pepper to taste
Chives, chopped

Sauté mushrooms in 5 tablespoons butter, add sausage and heat. Stir in cream and simmer 5 minutes. Knead flour and 1 tablespoon butter together to form "beurre manie". Add to cream in bits, stirring. Add lemon juice, salt and pepper to taste. Simmer 5 more minutes. Spoon into pie shell. Heat in 350 degree oven until warmed through. Sprinkle with chives.

Mrs. Hugh C. Newton

Smithfield Ham

Traditional Boiled Method: Cut off hock, wash and scrub with brush and soak overnight. Place ham skin-side down in ham boiler and cover with cold water. Bring to a boil on top of stove and simmer 20 minutes per pound or until paddle bone loosens. Remove ham from water.

Glaze per following recipe. Skin ham. Moisten ¾ cup brown sugar with pickle or orange juice. Add powdered cloves to mixture and sprinkle over ham. Place in 350 degree oven until glaze has set.

Night Oven Method (for hams 12-13 pounds): Prepare ham for cooking as above. Preheat oven to 375 degrees. Place ham in boiler skin-side up with 5 cups of water. Cover and place in oven. Turn temperature to 500 degrees for 10 minutes. Turn off oven for 3 hours and then again to 500 degrees for 15 minutes. Turn off and leave in oven overnight.

To store keep in cool place or refrigerated and *well* wrapped.

Mrs. Alfred E. T. Rusch

Ham with Madeira Sauce

Serves: 4

3 tablespoons butter	1 tablespoon tarragon
1 large slice precooked ham, up to 1½ inches thick	6 tablespoons dry Madeira
	½ cup heavy cream
3 tablespoons shallots, finely chopped	Salt and pepper

Melt 2 tablespoons butter in a large skillet and when foam subsides, place ham in skillet. Cook slowly 3 to 4 minutes, turn, cook other side same amount of time. Remove ham from the pan and keep warm. Sauté shallots in skillet for 2 minutes—do not brown. Add the tarragon and Madeira to the pan and cook over moderate heat, stirring until reduced by half. Add cream and continue to reduce by half. The sauce should coat a spoon. Season with pepper, may need salt (check first). Swirl in 1 tablespoon soft butter. Carve the ham slice into thin finger slices and pour the sauce over the ham.

Mrs. Frederick R. McNamara

Poultry

Brunswick Stew

Serves: 12 to 14

1 2½ to 3-pound chicken
2 quarts water
1 large can tomatoes
1 large onion, chopped
4 medium potatoes, peeled and
   diced
1 can butter beans, partially
   drained

1 large can shoe peg corn, partially
   drained
1 pound fresh okra (or 1 package
   frozen)
2 slices bacon, diced
1 heaping teaspoon sugar
1 tablespoon salt
Catsup (optional)

Simmer chicken in water for 1½ hours until tender. Pour through collander, putting stock back in pot. Add tomatoes including liquid. Add onion and potatoes. Add butter beans and accompanying liquid. Also add corn and its liquid. Add okra. Remove chicken from carcass and put back in pot. Add bacon. Season with salt and sugar. Cook slowly for 3 or 4 hours, stirring occasionally. Some catsup may be added when cooking time is completed.

Note: Freezes well.

Mrs. J. F. Moring

Blushing Chicken

Serves: 4

4 chicken breasts, may be boned
½ cup butter
½ cup dry white wine

1 10-ounce jar red currant jelly
1 cup sour cream
Salt

Wash chicken, dry, and salt. Melt butter in electric skillet and brown chicken, slowly, at 360 degrees. Add wine, pouring slowly over chicken. Cover and cook slowly for 15 minutes at 300 degrees. Melt jelly in separate pan and baste chicken thoroughly. Cook 15 minutes longer, uncovered, at 300 degrees. Turn frequently until tender. Remove chicken from pan. Add sour cream to pan juices and pour over chicken when ready to serve.

Mrs. James R. Skidmore

Gadsby's Tavern

Gadsby's Tavern combines two buildings of great importance to Alexandria in the 1700's—the City Tavern, which was built before the Revolution, and the City Hotel, which was added in 1792. They were recently restored to celebrate America's Bicentennial. Authentic colonial food and drink are served indoors and in the courtyard.

Gadsby's is especially noted for its Georgian architecture and the hanging musicians' gallery in the ballroom. George and Martha Washington attended birthday balls (in his honor) and the Alexandria Dancing Assemblies in this same ballroom. The original ballroom woodwork is now in the American Wing of New York City's Metropolitan Museum of Art, but it has been copied in detail and replaced in the tavern.

Guests of the 18th century hostel described Gadsby's as the finest public house in America during its heyday. The Marquis de Lafayette, John Paul Jones, Aaron Burr, George Mason, Francis Scott Key, and Henry Clay were among those who visited the tavern. On November 5, 1778, after dining on canvasback duck, hominy and Madeira, General Washington made his final military appearance, bidding farewell to the Alexandria Independent Infantry Blues, from the doorway of Gadsby's.

Tuscan Chicken

Preheat: 350 degrees
Serves: 2 to 4

2½ to 3 pounds fryer chicken
1 clove garlic
2 tablespoons olive oil
1 teaspoon crumbled rosemary

¼ teaspoon crumbled sage (not powdered)
Salt and freshly ground pepper
½ cup dry vermouth

Rinse chicken under cold water and pat dry. Rub bird inside and out with split garlic, then with olive oil. Place garlic inside bird. Sprinkle with herbs, salt and pepper, and roast 20 minutes. Pour vermouth over bird and continue roasting, basting every 20 minutes with pan juices. Roast 25 minutes to the pound or until leg moves easily.

Note: Delicious with Risotta ala Milanese and green beans, lightly sprinkled with basil.

Mrs. John E. Davey

Chicken Piquant

Preheat: 375 degrees

¾ cup rosé wine
¼ cup soy sauce
¼ cup oil
2 tablespoons water
2 sliced cloves garlic

1 tablespoon brown sugar
1 teaspoon ginger
¼ teaspoon oregano
1 chicken, quartered

Make a sauce from above ingredients. Pour over chicken. Bake at 375 degrees for 1½ hours. Sauce is enough for one chicken. Bake, uncovered, turning once.

Mrs. Alan E. Mowbray

Asopao De Pollo

Serves: 6 to 8

2½ to 3 pounds of chicken, cut in
    pieces
1 teaspoon oregano
2 cloves garlic, pressed or mashed
Dash of pepper
2 teaspoons salt
Juice of 1 lemon
2 cups uncooked long grain rice
2 cups water

¼ cup shortening
2 ounces salt pork, diced (or ham)
1 green pepper, chopped
1 large onion, sliced
1 tomato, cut in bits
2 tablespoons capers
2 tablespoons chopped olives
1 1-pound can peas, reserve liquid
7 cups water

The day before: Marinate chicken pieces in mixture of pulverized garlic cloves, oregano, pepper, salt and lemon juice. Rub mixture into chicken, cover, and refrigerate.

The next day: Let chicken come to room temperature. Meanwhile, soak 2 cups uncooked rice in 2 cups of water for 30 minutes. While it is soaking, melt shortening in a large skillet or Dutch oven. Add diced ham or salt pork to melted shortening and cook until browned. Add green pepper, onion slices, tomato bits, capers and olives. Cook slowly for 5 to 10 minutes. Add marinated chicken pieces and brown. Drain water off rice and discard. Add rice to skillet. Also add 7 cups fresh water and liquid from peas. Stir through mixture only until blended. Do not overmix. Cook until chicken is tender, 30 to 45 minutes. When almost done, add peas and heat through.

Note: A traditional Puerto Rican dish often used when entertaining. Usually served in individual dishes with a garnish of asparagus spears and pimentos or sprinkled with Parmesan cheese.

Mrs. James R. Skidmore

Buttermilk Chicken

Preheat: 350 degrees

Chicken pieces
Salt
Pepper

Paprika
Buttermilk
Corn flakes

Select various pieces of chicken. Salt, pepper, and paprika each piece and soak in buttermilk all day. Roll chicken in crushed corn flakes and bake at 350 degrees for 45 minutes to 1 hour. Serve hot or cold.

Mrs. Thomas T. Bellino

Chicken Sauté with Fines Herbs

Preheat: 450 degrees
Serves: 6

3 pounds chicken, cut up
5 tablespoons butter
½ teaspoon salt
¼ teaspoon pepper
½ teaspoon chervil
½ teaspoon tarragon
⅓ teaspoon thyme
½ to 1 cup dry white wine or
  Marsala

½ cup shallots or onions, chopped
1 tablespoon chives
Salt
Pepper
Lemon juice
1 can mushrooms, drained (optional)

Place chicken pieces skin side up in oven baking dish. Sprinkle with salt and pepper. Dot with 2 tablespoons of butter. Place in 450 degree oven for 20 minutes or until chicken starts to brown. Meanwhile, in a small saucepan, add chervil, tarragon, thyme and wine. Simmer. Remove from heat and let steep while chicken is browning. Sauté shallots in 3 table-spoons of butter. Mix wine, lemon juice, spices and shallots and pour over chicken. Finish cooking, approximately 30 to 40 minutes at 350 degrees or until chicken is tender.

Note: Easily doubled.

Mrs. Charles Leppert, Jr.

Korean Chicken

Preheat: 350 degrees
Serves: 4

1 chicken, cut up and skinned
Salt and pepper
1 egg yolk
2 tablespoons honey

1 clove garlic, crushed
2 tablespoons soy sauce
4 tablespoons butter

Sprinkle chicken with salt and pepper. Mix egg yolk, honey, garlic and soy sauce. Soak chicken in mixture. Place in covered baking dish and dot generously with butter. Bake 45 minutes to 1 hour.

Note: Serve with rice, steamed Chinese cabbage and warmed sake or chilled Sauterne.

Mrs. E. H. Dale Gallimore

Parmesan Cheese Chicken

Preheat: 400 degrees
Serves: 4 to 6

8 to 10 chicken pieces
1 cup Bisquick
⅓ cup grated Parmesan cheese
1 teaspoon paprika

½ teaspoon celery salt
Dash of pepper
½ cup evaporated milk
½ cup melted butter

Combine dry ingredients. Dip chicken in milk, then roll in dry mixture. Place skin side up in a greased shallow pan. Melt butter and pour over chicken. Bake at 400 degrees for one hour.

Mrs. John T. Miller

Poulet Vallée D'Auge

Serves: 4

1 3-pound chicken cut in quarters
2 tablespoons butter
¼ cup finely chopped onions
¼ cup finely chopped carrots
½ cup finely chopped mushrooms
½ cup finely chopped apples

1 tablespoon flour
1 bouquet garni (1 bay leaf, parsley, thyme, tarragon)
4 ounces Calvados wine
1½ cups cider
1 pint whipping cream

Melt butter in a Dutch oven. Brown chicken well. Add onions, carrots, mushrooms and apples to the chicken with the flour. Add bouquet garnis. Blaze with Calvados. Moisten with cider. Cover and cook 20 minutes. Remove chicken from pot. Add whipping cream. Reduce sauce until it thickens nicely. To serve, arrange chicken pieces on a platter, and pour the sauce over all. Garnish with steamed mushrooms and apples.

Mrs. Tod R. Hullin

Pollo a La Chulinclron

Serves: 4 to 6

8 to 10 chicken thighs or small
  breasts
¼ cup olive oil
1 clove minced garlic
3 small green peppers, cut in
  strips

2 small onions, sliced
½ cup finely chopped ham
1 large can pear shaped tomatoes
6 pitted black olives cut in half
6 green olives cut in half

Brown chicken in olive oil, add onions, garlic, peppers and ham. Cook 8 to 10 minutes until vegetables are soft but not brown. Add tomatoes and olives, cover and simmer 30 to 40 minutes.

Note: Serve with noodles.

Mrs. Michael Cericola

Chicken Breasts Amandine

Serves: 4

1 tablespoon butter
2 tablespoons (or more) almonds
2 whole large chicken breasts,
  skinned, boned and halved
1 garlic clove, minced

¼ pound fresh sliced mushrooms
½ teaspoon salt
¼ teaspoon pepper
1 chicken bouillon cube
1 tablespoon cornstarch

In electric skillet on medium high heat melt butter, and brown almonds, stirring constantly. Remove and set aside. Add chicken and brown all sides. Stir in garlic, mushrooms, salt, pepper and chicken bouillon cube. Add 1 cup water. Reduce heat, cover skillet and simmer 25 minutes until chicken is fork tender. In cup blend cornstarch and 1 tablespoon water until smooth. Gradually stir into hot liquid in skillet and cook, stirring constantly until thickened. On platter arrange breasts over rice, spoon on sauce. Sprinkle with almonds.

Mrs. Bernard P. O'Hare

Lemon Chicken with Artichokes

Preheat: 350 degrees
Serves: 6

6 chicken breasts
1 6-ounce jar marinated artichoke
  hearts

2 large lemons
½ cup heavy cream

Marinate chicken in mixture of liquid from artichokes and juice of one lemon. Bake uncovered at 350 degrees for one hour, turning breasts once. Add cream, artichokes and garnish with lemon slices. Return to oven for 15 minutes.

Mrs. Robert L. Calhoun

Avocado Chicken

Preheat: 350 degrees
Serves: 6

¼ cup Parmesan cheese, grated
1 teaspoon salt
2 teaspoons chopped parsley
3 chicken breasts, halved and
  boned
6 large mushrooms
2 to 3 tablespoons melted butter

1 8-ounce can tomato sauce
½ cup dry white wine
2 ripe avocados
¼ teaspoon coarsely ground pepper
1 to 2 tablespoons cornstarch
1 to 2 tablespoons water

Mix ¼ cup cheese, ½ teaspoon salt and one teaspoon parsley. Sprinkle inside of chicken breasts with mixture. Remove stems from mushrooms and save for sauce. Place mushroom cap on each piece. Roll up chicken, fastening with skewers. Brown chicken in butter and place in baking pan. In skillet combine tomato sauce, wine, pepper and ½ teaspoon salt, and parsley just to blend. Slice mushroom stems into sauce. Pour over chicken, cover and bake at 350 degrees for 45 minutes or until tender. Just before chicken is done, cut avocados lengthwise into halves; remove seeds and skin. Slice crosswise in crescents. Place chicken on warm serving platter. Blend cornstarch with water, stir into sauce in pan. Heat until thickened. Add avocados then pour over chicken. Sprinkle with additional cheese.

Mrs. Edward F. Kapusta

Chicken Olé

Serves: 4

4 chicken breasts   8 1-inch cubes jack cheese
8 flour tortillas   1 can green chilies

Steam cook chicken and tear into small pieces. Place ⅛ chicken and 1 cube cheese on each tortilla. Top with ½ teaspoon chilies (or more). Roll and fold and secure with toothpick. Fry in oil on all sides. Serve with guacamole sauce.

Note: This recipe has won many prizes in the Southwest.

Mrs. E. H. Dale Gallimore

Crab Stuffed Chicken

Preheat: 350 degrees
Serves: 8

4 large chicken breasts, halved,   5 crackers, crumbled
   skinned and boned   1 3-ounce can mushrooms, drained
4 tablespoons butter   2 tablespoons parsley
¼ cup flour   ½ teaspoon salt
¾ cup milk   Dash of pepper
⅓ cup dry white wine   1 cup shredded Swiss cheese
¼ cup chopped onion   ½ teaspoon paprika
4½ ounces crabmeat   ¾ cup chicken broth

Pound chicken pieces to make ⅛ inch thick cutlets (8 inches x 5 inches) and set aside. Melt 3 tablespoons butter, blend in flour; add milk, broth and wine. Cook and stir until mixture thickens and bubbles, then set aside. In skillet, cook onion in remaining butter until tender but not brown. Stir in crab, mushrooms, cracker crumbs, parsley, salt and pepper. Stir in 2 tablespoons of sauce. Top each chicken piece with ¼ cup of crab mixture, fold sides over and roll up each piece. Place seamside down in 12 x 7½ x 2-inch baking pan. Pour sauce over all. Bake at 350 degrees for 1 hour. Sprinkle with cheese and paprika. Bake 2 minutes more.

Mrs. John Smithers

Chicken Elizabeth

Serves: 4 to 6

4 whole chicken breasts, boned and
   split
4 tablespoons lemon juice
1 teaspoon salt
½ teaspoon pepper
¼ teaspoon nutmeg

¼ cup butter
1 small onion, finely chopped
¼ cup honey
1½ cups chicken broth
1½ cups plain yogurt

Rub all sides of chicken with lemon juice. Season with salt and pepper and let stand while you chop onion. Melt butter in large skillet. Sauté chicken breasts until golden brown on both sides. Remove to warm plate. Add chopped onion to pan and cook until transparent. Stir in honey, pepper, nutmeg, broth and yogurt and simmer 5 minutes without allowing it to reach a boiling point. Taste for seasoning, add salt and pepper if necessary. Return chicken to pan and spoon sauce over filets. Cover pan and continue cooking over low flame until chicken is tender, about 35 minutes. Serve with sauce and garnish with fresh parsley.

Ms. Elizabeth McGlohn

 Parsley keeps fresher if stored in a covered jar in the refrigerator. Always wash it in hot water for flavor retention.

Chicken Imperial

Preheat: 350 degrees
Serves: 6

6 chicken breast halves, boned
1 cup sherry
1 cup bread crumbs
1 teaspoon salt
¼ teaspoon ground pepper

1 cup grated Parmesan cheese
1 tablespoon chopped parsley
1 clove garlic, crushed
1 cup chopped almonds
¾ cup melted butter

Marinate chicken in sherry for 2 to 3 hours. Pat dry with paper towel. Combine remaining ingredients except butter and almonds. Dip chicken in butter and roll in mixture. Arrange in 13 x 9 x 2-inch baking pan. Sprinkle with almonds. Bake for 1 hour. Delicious with Gourmet Stuffed Potatoes.

Mrs. Richard L. Wallace

Chicken Rosé

Preheat: 350 degrees
Serves: 10 to 12

6 chicken breasts, split
1½ cups rosé wine
⅓ cup water
5 tablespoons brown sugar
⅓ cup soy sauce
1 clove garlic, minced

Dried tarragon
White pepper
¼ teaspoon ginger
¼ pound fresh mushrooms
Butter
Lemon juice

Arrange chicken breasts in shallow baking dish. Pour a mixture of wine, water, brown sugar, soy sauce, garlic, ginger, tarragon and pepper to taste over chicken. Cover and bake one hour at 350 degrees. Then add mushrooms sautéed in butter and lemon juice. Uncover and bake 15 or 20 more minutes.

Note: Better when made ahead of time and reheated.

Mrs. Tod R. Hullin

Sesame Chicken

Preheat: 350 degrees
Serves: 6 to 8

4 whole chicken breasts, halved,
   skinned, and boned
8 thin strips ham, 1-inch wide
16 strips Swiss cheese
1 egg
1 tablespoon water

¾ cup bread crumbs
¼ cup plus 2 tablespoons butter
1 tablespoon soy sauce
½ cup chicken broth
Sesame seeds

Fill chicken breasts with ham and cheese strips; press edges together firmly and secure with skewers. Beat egg with water. Dip chicken in egg then in bread crumbs. Sauté chicken in ¼ cup butter until golden. Place in baking dish. Combine 2 tablespoons melted butter, soy sauce, and broth. Brush chicken with sauce. Sprinkle with sesame seeds. Bake for 35 to 45 minutes at 350 degrees until tender, basting with remainder of sauce.

Mrs. John E. Davey

Szechuan Chicken

Serves: 4 to 6

1 egg white, beaten
2 tablespoons cornstarch
3 tablespoons soy sauce
1 tablespoon sherry
2 whole chicken breasts, skinned,
   boned, and cut in 1-inch cubes
½ teaspoon salt
½ teaspoon MSG

1 tablespoon vinegar
3 tablespoons sugar
1 tablespoon molasses
⅓ cup water
1 clove garlic, crushed
1 bunch chopped green onions
1 10-ounce package frozen pea pods
½ teaspoon dried red pepper

Combine egg white, 1 tablespoon soy sauce, sherry, 1 tablespoon corn-starch, and beat until frothy. Marinate chicken in mixture for ½ hour. Combine salt, MSG, remaining soy sauce, garlic, vinegar, sugar, molas-ses, water and remaining cornstarch. Sauté chicken pieces in hot peanut oil *quickly*. Remove chicken and put chopped onion and pea pods in skillet. Stir fry. Add red pepper, add chicken pieces and sauce. Bring to boil. Serve over rice.

Mrs. Henry E. Thomas, IV

Stuffed Turkey Breast

Serves: 4

4 slices raw turkey breast, 2 to 3
   ounces each
Salt
Pepper
Lemon slice
Flour
½ medium onion, chopped

4 slices bacon, chopped
1 tablespoon parsley, chopped
8 pitted prunes, cut in half
Pinch of sage
Bechamel sauce
8 slices of bread, crumbled
4½ cups grated Cheddar cheese

Beat meat lightly to tenderize. Season with salt, pepper, lemon juice and dust with flour. Sauté in butter for a very short time so that meat is still rare on inside. Meanwhile prepare stuffing. Sauté onion and bacon until lightly brown. Add parsley, prunes, sage and bread crumbs. Sauté until hot and lightly crusty. Keep hot. Place stuffing on oven-proof platter. Place four slices of turkey on top. Cover with Bechamel sauce, grated Cheddar cheese and bread crumbs. Dot with butter cubes and broil until ready, approximately 4 to 5 minutes.

Wayfarer's Chef: Jurgen Meier

Chicken Breasts Wellington

Preheat: 375 degrees
Serves: 12

6 whole chicken breasts, boned,
  split
Salt and pepper
1 6-ounce package long grain and
  wild rice
¼ cup grated orange peel
2 eggs, separated

3 8-ounce packages refrigerated
  crescent rolls
1 tablespoon water
2 10-ounce jars red currant jelly
1 tablespoon prepared mustard
3 tablespoons port wine
¼ cup lemon juice

Pound breasts with meat mallet and sprinkle with salt and pepper. Cook rice according to package directions for drier rice. Add orange peel. Cool. Beat egg whites until soft peaks form, then fold into rice mixture. On floured surface, roll two triangular pieces of roll dough into a circle. Repeat until you have 12 circles. Place chicken breast in center of each circle. Spoon ¼ cup rice mixture over chicken. Roll chicken jelly roll fashion. Bring dough up over stuffed breasts and moisten edge of dough. Press together to seal. Place seamside down on baking tray. Brush dough with slightly beaten egg yolks and a little water. Bake uncovered at 375 degrees for 45 to 50 minutes. If dough browns too quickly, cover loosely with foil. Heat currant jelly in saucepan. Stir in mustard, wine and lemon juice. Serve warm over chicken.

Mrs. Colin M. Campbell, Jr.

Tarragon Chicken Trieste

Serves: 6

½ pound fresh mushrooms
6 chicken breasts, boned
1 cup dry white cooking wine
1 cup sour cream
½ cup chopped green onions

1 box Uncle Ben's wild brown, long
  grain rice
¼ cup butter
2 teaspoons beau monde
½ teaspoon tarragon

Slice mushrooms and sauté in 2 tablespoons butter. Remove mushrooms from pan and set aside. Add remaining butter and brown chicken well. Sprinkle with beau monde while browning. Sprinkle with tarragon. Pour wine over chicken. Cover and simmer 45 minutes. Remove chicken from pan. Add sour cream to pan drippings and blend well on low heat; add mushrooms and green onions. To serve, place serving of rice on plate, place chicken on rice and spoon gravy over.

Note: Goes well with sliced, fresh fruit with celery seed dressing.

Mrs. Richard W. Klein, Jr.

Chicken Squares with Pimento Sauce

Preheat: 325 degrees
Serves: 12

1 8-ounce package herb seasoned
   stuffing
3 cups diced chicken
½ cup margarine or butter

½ cup self-rising flour
¼ teaspoon salt
4 cups chicken broth
6 slightly beaten eggs

Prepare stuffing according to package for dry stuffing. Spread in shallow 3 quart ovenproof dish. Top with layer of chicken. In saucepan melt butter, blend in flour and salt. Add cool broth. Cook and stir until thick. Stir small amount of hot mixture into eggs; return eggs to hot mixture. Pour over chicken. Bake in slow oven, 325 degrees, for 40 to 45 minutes or until set. Let stand 5 minutes. Cut in squares and serve with heated pimento sauce.

Pimento Sauce

1 10¾-ounce can of mushroom
   soup
¼ cup milk

1 cup sour cream
¼ cup chopped pimento

Mrs. Carlyle C. Ring, Jr.

Hot Chicken Salad

Preheat: 400 degrees
Serves: 6

4 cups cooked chicken
2 tablespoons lemon juice
¾ cup mayonnaise
1 teaspoon salt
2 cups chopped celery
4 hard boiled eggs, sliced
1 teaspoon minced onion

¾ cup condensed cream of chicken
   soup
2 2-ounce can pimento
1½ cups crushed potato chips
1 cup grated Cheddar cheese
⅔ cup finely chopped toasted
   almonds

Combine all ingredients except cheese, chips and almonds. Place in large shallow casserole. Top with cheese, chips and almonds. Refrigerate overnight. Bake at 400 degrees for 20 to 25 minutes.

Note: For variation omit eggs, pimentos, and soup, double lemon juice, and add 2 cups mayonnaise and 4 teaspoons grated onion. Bake 10 minutes at 450 degrees.

Ms. Elizabeth J. Noyes

Roz's Chicken Curry

Serves: 5

⅓ cup onions, chopped
1 cup diced, pared eating apples
3 tablespoons butter
3 tablespoons flour
⅜ teaspoon salt
Dash of pepper
1½ tablespoons curry powder

¾ cup light cream
¾ cup chicken broth
1 large and 1 small can sliced
 mushrooms
3 tablespoons lemon juice
3 cups diced cooked chicken

In top of double boiler, over direct heat, cook onion and apple in butter until tender. Remove from heat, blend in flour, salt, pepper and curry powder. Add cream and broth. Place over boiling water and stir until thickened. Cover and cook 10 minutes. Add mushrooms, lemon juice and chicken. This can be made ahead and reheated. Serve over rice.

Toppings, served separately

Chopped hard-boiled eggs
Crumbled bacon
Chopped green pepper
Toasted, shredded coconut

Chutney
Chopped peanuts
Chopped onion

Mrs. Alfred E. T. Rusch

Cornbread Stuffing for Roast Turkey

Yield: Enough for a 12 to 15 pound bird
and to fill an 8-inch pan

Body Cavity

4 cups chopped celery
2 cups minced onion
Chicken or turkey broth (fresh or
 canned)
¼ pound butter
7 cups toasted and crumbled
 bread

7 cups crumbled fresh cornbread
1 tablespoon salt
2 teaspoons freshly ground pepper
2 teaspoons sage or poultry seasoning
1 cup finely chopped fresh parsley
5 eggs, beaten

Place celery and onion in a large saucepan. Add broth to cover plus stick of butter. Simmer very slowly about 1½ hours and let cool. In the meantime, combine in a large bowl the toasted bread and cornbread. Pour vegetables and liquid into bread mixture, add seasonings, parsley and eggs and mix thoroughly with hands until texture is smooth (adding more broth for greater moisture).

Additional ingredients might include one or two of the following:

4 cups whole or chopped
   fresh oysters
4 cups whole or chopped clams
2 cups sliced and sautéed
   mushrooms

2 cups roasted and chopped chestnuts,
   pecans, almonds or filberts
2 cups chopped black olives
2 cups fresh whole cranberries, cooked
½ cup bourbon

Neck Cavity

2 pounds sausage meat
1½ teaspoons salt
1 teaspoon thyme
1 teaspoon Tabasco

1 teaspoon ground coriander
1 teaspoon freshly ground pepper
¾ cup pine nuts
½ cup finely chopped fresh parsley

Combine all ingredients, mix well, cook over medium heat till brown (stirring occasionally and breaking up with a fork). Drain off excess fat.

Mrs. Thomas J. Stanton

Swiss Turkey and Ham Bake

Preheat: 400 degrees
Serves: 6

½ cup chopped onion
5 tablespoons butter
3 tablespoons flour
½ teaspoon salt
¼ teaspoon pepper
1 3-ounce can sliced mushrooms,
   undrained
1 cup half and half

2 tablespoons sherry
2 cups cubed, cooked chicken
1 cup cubed, cooked ham
1 5-ounce can water chestnuts,
   drained and sliced
½ cup shredded Swiss cheese
1½ cups soft bread crumbs

In skillet cook onion in two tablespoons of butter. Blend in flour, salt, and pepper. Add mushrooms, half and half and sherry. Cook and stir until bubbly. Add chicken, ham and water chestnuts. Pour into 1½-quart casserole. Top with Swiss cheese. Mix bread crumbs with 3 tablespoons melted butter. Sprinkle around edges. Bake 25 minutes at 400 degrees.

Note: Double this recipe to fill a 9 x 13-inch casserole.

Mrs. J. F. Moring

Brandy-Buttered Cornish Hens

Preheat: 350 degrees
Serves: 6

6 1 to 1½-pound Cornish hens
Salt and pepper
½ cup melted butter or margarine

¼ cup apricot, peach, or plum flavored
brandy

Pecan Stuffing

1 cup unsweetened apple juice
¼ cup apricot, peach or plum
flavored brandy
¼ cup butter or margarine

1 8-ounce package cornbread stuffing
mix
¾ cup chopped pecans

Remove giblets from hens. Sprinkle cavity of each with salt and pepper. Combine apple juice, brandy, and butter in a large saucepan; cook over medium heat, stirring occasionally, until butter melts. Add stuffing mix and pecans, stirring lightly. Lightly stuff cavity of hens; close with toothpicks. Brush hens with butter and sprinkle generously with pepper. Combine remaining butter with brandy. Place hens, breast side up, in a large shallow baking dish. Bake at 350 degrees for 1 to 1½ hours, depending on size of hens. Baste every 10 minutes with brandy mixture.

Mrs. Donald P. Burchell

Tangerine and Yam Stuffing for Roast Duck

Yield: for 5 or 6-pound duck

3 tablespoons butter
⅓ cup scallions, minced
⅓ cup carrots, diced and blanched
1½ cups yams or sweet potatoes,
cooked, peeled and mashed
1 egg, beaten
1½ cups dry bread crumbs

¼ cup finely chopped fresh parsley
2 tangerines, cut in sections, plus
some finely grated rind
Sprinkling of rosemary or thyme
Dash of salt
1 tablespoon brandy

Sauté scallions and carrots in butter until tender. Beat egg into yams until fluffy, add scallions, carrots and all other ingredients. Mix thoroughly.

Mrs. Joseph E. Hinds

Over the Coals

Washboiler Clambake

Serves: 8

Seaweed, well washed
1 quart water
4 Idaho potatoes, wrapped in foil
2 chickens, cut up and parts
  wrapped in cheesecloth

2 1½-pound lobsters
4 ears of corn, husked and wrapped in
  foil
24 steamer clams

Fill the bottom of a washboiler or a large enamel pot with seaweed, add water, and place over high heat. When the water boils, add more seaweed and the potatoes. Cover and cook for 15 minutes. Add a layer of seaweed and the chicken, cover and cook 15 minutes. Add seaweed, then lobster, then more seaweed. Cover and cook 8 minutes. Add the corn and cook 10 minutes. Add clams and cook, steaming, until clams open. Serve with butter and kettle liquid.

Note: Great with cold beer or jug of white wine.

Mrs. E. Darryl Barnes

Chutney Spareribs

Serves: 3 to 4

1 cup chutney
¼ cup chili sauce
2 tablespoons vinegar
1 tablespoon Worcestershire sauce
1 teaspoon onion salt

1 teaspoon dry mustard
Dash of hot pepper sauce
3 to 4 pounds pork spareribs
Salt

Chop any large pieces of chutney. In saucepan combine the chutney, chili sauce, vinegar, Worcestershire sauce, onion salt, mustard and pepper sauce; heat through. Sprinkle ribs with salt. Lace ribs accordian-style on spit; secure with holding forks. In covered grill place slow coals on both sides of a foil drip pan. Grill for one hour or until done in covered grill. During last 15 minutes of cooking brush meat with chutney sauce. Heat remaining sauce to pass with ribs.

Mrs. Johan Morrison

The Friendship Firehouse

Organized in 1774, the Friendship Fire Company counted George Washington as an enthusiastic member. For Washington, fire-fighting was almost a passion, beginning in his youth at Mt. Vernon and continuing throughout his career. Through the years, the honor roll of this historic association has included U.S. Presidents, Senators and Congressmen, Governors of the Commonwealth, astronauts and other great Americans.

In George Washington's day, the big bell in the cupola of Friendship Firehouse signaled to the town that something was burning. White-helmeted volunteers briskly donned their red flannel shirts, slammed the firehouse doors, and ran down the cobblestone streets to their appointed tasks.

Alexandria's first fire engine is housed in Friendship Firehouse for inspection today. Purchased by George Washington in 1775 and given to the city for its use, it cost 80 pounds, 10 shillings—approximately $400, an astronomical amount at the time.

Marinated Grill-Broiled Chicken

Serves: 4

½ cup soy sauce
¼ cup lemon juice
¼ cup oil
¼ cup wine vinegar

1 teaspoon dried oregano, crushed
Dash of pepper
2 2½ to 3-pound broiler/fryer chickens,
    split lengthwise

Combine soy sauce, lemon juice, oil, wine vinegar, oregano and pepper. Place chicken in shallow baking dish; pour marinade over. Marinate in refrigerator overnight, turning occasionally. Drain, reserving marinade. Place chicken, bone side down, on grill over *SLOW* coals. Brush with marinade. Grill 30 minutes. Turn skin side down and grill till done, 20 to 30 minutes, brushing frequently with marinade. May also be broiled in conventional oven.

Mrs. E. Darryl Barnes

Stuffed Turkey Breast

Serves: 6-8

4 to 5-pound turkey breast
1 pound ham or pork sausage,
    cooked
2 small apples, chopped

3 or 4 slices of bacon
Butter
Salt and pepper

Bone the turkey breast just as you would a chicken breast and remove the skin. With cut side up, flatten on a board to an even thickness with a mallet. Smear cut side with a generous amount of butter, salt and pepper liberally. Arrange cooked sausage and apples at one end of the breast and roll tightly. Tie with a cord every 2 inches. Insert meat thermometer. Lay bacon on the top for self basting.

Roast in the kettle grill with drip pan in center and coals on the sides for 1 to 1½ hours or until thermometer reads 170. Let stand 10 to 15 minutes before carving.

Mrs. Robert G. Lineberry

Lemon Chicken

2 chickens, cut in pieces	Salt
1 16-ounce bottle lemon juice	Pepper
1 teaspoon rosemary	1 18-ounce bottle barbecue sauce

Combine lemon juice, salt, pepper and rosemary; set aside. Skin chicken and soak in enough lemon juice to cover chicken halfway. Soak overnight, turning occasionally. Place on outdoor grill and cook slowly. Just before removing from grill, brush with barbecue sauce.

Mrs. Renny H. Barnes

Chinese Chicken

Preheat: 350 degrees
Serves: 4

4 large chicken breasts	½ teaspoon salt
⅓ cup catsup	¼ cup sherry
⅓ cup soy sauce	1 teaspoon powdered ginger
⅔ cup sugar	1 clove garlic, chopped fine

Mix all ingredients. Add chicken. Marinate at least 2 hours. Remove chicken from marinade and grill outside or bake at 350 degrees for 45 minutes.

Mrs. Kleber S. Masterson, Jr.

Tournedos

Serves: 4

1 to 1½ pounds beef, good quality steak or tenderized flank steak	1 teaspoon garlic salt
½ pound bacon	½ teaspoon ground pepper
	2 tablespoons parsley

Pound steak to even thickness—about ½ inch thick. Cook bacon until almost done but not crisp. Sprinkle steak with garlic salt, pepper and parsley. Place bacon strips lengthwise on steak. Roll up jellyroll fashion, skewer with toothpicks at one inch intervals. Cut in one inch slices. Grill over medium coals for 15 minutes turning once for rare.

Note: May be served with béarnaise sauce but is equally delicious without.

Mrs. John Smithers

Eye of the Round on the Grill

Serves: 8

⅓ cup salt
⅓ cup pepper

1 tablespoon dry mustard
1 eye of the round

Mix dry ingredients together. Roll meat in mixture. Set aside to rest at least two hours. Put roast over coals which are grey. Turn three times at twelve minute intervals. Turns out crusty on the outside, pink inside.

Mrs. Thomas C. Brown, Jr.

Tom's Delicious Never-Fail Flank Steak

Serves: 4

1 flank steak
⅓ cup oil
⅓ cup soy sauce
1 tablespoon ground ginger

⅓ cup dry wine or gin, vodka or
   sherry
2 cloves garlic, minced, or garlic salt
1 teaspoon sugar

Combine all ingredients in long shallow dish just large enough to contain steak. Marinate steak 4 or 5 hours, turning occasionally. When the rest of the dinner is nearly ready, place steak in oven broiler close to heat and cook approximately 7 minutes on one side and 5 minutes on the other. Transfer steak to carving board and slice in a thin, cross-grain manner. Serve immediately.

Note: This is one steak that can be cooked well done and still taste good. The cutting produces ample juices, excellent for dunking crusty bread.

Mrs. Thomas F. Shea

Flank Steak Teriyaki

Serves: 4 to 6

¾ cup cooking oil
¼ cup soy sauce
¼ cup honey
2 tablespoons cider vinegar

1 large clove garlic, minced
2 tablespoons chopped onion
1½ teaspoons ground ginger
1 to 2 pounds flank steak

Combine all ingredients and pour over steak. Marinate at least four hours. Turn occasionally. Broil or barbecue about five minutes on each side for medium rare. Carve into thin slices across the grain.

Mrs. Wilson Livingood

Sharp's Steak

Serves: 4

1 flank steak
3 tablespoons minced scallions or
   shallots
1½ tablespoons soy sauce
2 tablespoons olive oil

½ teaspoon thyme
Big pinch of pepper or drops of
   Tabasco
Juice of ½ lemon

Mix the marinade ingredients in a bowl. Lay the flank steak flat in the bottom of your broiling pan and spread on half the marinade. Turn the steak and spread with the rest of the marinade. Cover with wax paper and leave for at least 20 minutes, or refrigerate for several hours or a day or two. When cleaning up between courses, set the steak, just as it is, as close as possible under a hot broiler and leave for 3 minutes. Then turn and broil the other side for 2 to 3 minutes. Steak should be rosy rare. Carve in very thin slices across the grain of the meat.

Note: This steak may be preceded by potage cressoniere or fettucini and served with a vegetable and broiled cherry tomatoes for an easy and delicious dinner that can be prepared ahead of time.

Mrs. Stephen A. Sharp

Quick Flank Steak

Serves: 4 to 6

2 pounds flank steak
2 cloves garlic, crushed
4 tablespoons soy sauce
2 tablespoons tomato paste

2 tablespoons peanut oil
1 teaspoon freshly ground pepper
1 teaspoon oregano

Rub the steak with a paste made of the above ingredients. Broil according to taste. Carve on the diagonal in thin slices.

Note: The steak may be marinated for several hours, but is also tasty when prepared for a quick meal.

Mrs. Hamilton Beggs

Kettle Grilled Lamb

Serves: 6

4 to 5 pound leg of lamb or roast
Parsley
Oregano
Minced garlic

Mint leaves
Thyme
Olive oil

Clean roast and dry. Let stand and come to room temperature. Lightly score entire surface of meat. Lightly oil all over and roll in generous amount of mixture of the herbs.

Insert the meat thermometer into the thickest muscle area. Cook on a small rack set in a small close-fitting drip pan on the grill with the coals arranged at the sides of the kettle. Roast with lid closed for about 1½ hours or until meat thermometer reads 140 degrees. Remove from grill and let stand 15 minutes (the meat will actually still cook itself).

Note: It is very important that you use a meat thermometer. Different brands of charcoal, sizes of kettles, and cuts of meat make clock timing risky at best.

Mrs. Robert G. Lineberry

Grilled Leg of Lamb

Serves: 6 to 10

1 leg of lamb, butterfly cut (boned
    and rolled out like a steak,
    evenly thick)
⅓ cup olive oil
1 teaspoon oregano

½ teaspoon garlic powder
1 teaspoon dehydrated lemon peel
1 teaspoon seasoned salt
2 teaspoons dried parsley
¼ teaspoon crushed bay leaf

Mix oregano, garlic powder, lemon peel, seasoned salt, parsley and bay leaf. Rub into cut side of lamb. Pour olive oil over lamb and turn in a 9 x 13-inch dish several times. Marinate 4 to 5 hours or overnight. Broil on outdoor covered grill. Broil fat side of lamb first for 30 to 40 minutes. Turn and broil 10 to 15 minutes, maybe less depending on size of lamb. Slice on bias like London broil.

Mrs. Chris W. Ragland

Greek Leg of Lamb

Preheat: 325 degrees
Serves: 4 to 6

4- to 6-pound leg of lamb
3 to 5 garlic cloves, slivered
1 cup honey

¼ cup lemon juice
1 tablespoon oregano

Make 10 to 15 pockets in meat by piercing with knife tip. Insert garlic sliver in each pocket. Mix honey, lemon juice and oregano together and use as basting sauce. Roast lamb uncovered at 325 degrees for 35 minutes per pound. Baste frequently.

Note: May also be grilled over moderately hot coals using a meat thermometer to determine doneness.

Mrs. Robert K. Wineland

Chris' Shish Kabobs

Serves: 4

7 or 8 1½-inch cubes of pork
7 or 8 1½-inch cubes of lamb
7 or 8 1½-inch cubes of beef
1 package French's Teriyaki sauce
1 package long grain and wild rice
2 or 3 firm bananas, unpeeled

½ cantaloupe, peeled, cut in 1½-inch
   cubes
1 fresh pineapple, cut in 1½-inch
   cubes
½ honeydew melon, peeled, cut in
   1½-inch cubes

Marinate meat cubes in teriyaki sauce for 30 minutes. Skewer cubes of meat. Skewer cubes of melon, cantaloupe and pineapple. Meanwhile, cook rice according to package directions. Make a bed of rice in center of large heated platter. Cook skewers of meat on grill, about 3 minutes on each side for a total of 12 minutes. At the same time cook the skewers of fruit and the unpeeled whole bananas on rack of grill. They should be throughly heated, but not cooked. Place meat and melon, cantaloupe and pineapple on rice. Peel bananas and cut in 1½-inch chunks, add to rice.

Note: Serve with a large green salad and cheese and garlic bread for a summer dinner.

Mrs. Chris W. Ragland

Prune Stuffed Pork Loin

Serves: 10

1 6½ to 7-pound pork loin roast
Dried pitted prunes, 3 per
  pocket

2½ cups orange juice (or sherry or
  both)
1 4¾-ounce jar baby food prunes

Have butcher crack loin bones to make carving easier. Make deep pockets through meaty side of loin every 1¼ inches. Soak prunes in mixture of orange juice and strained prunes for at least 2 hours or until plump. Stuff prunes into pockets; tie lengthwise to keep pockets closed. Cook in kettle grill over an even bed of hot coals (350 degrees) and hickory chips for about 2 hours or until meat reaches a temperature of 170 degrees. Baste 4 or 5 times with remaining orange prune marinade.

Mrs. Donald M. McNamara

Vegetable Kabobs

Serves: 8

8 small new potatoes
4 medium-sized zucchini
4 medium-sized yellow squash
8 large fresh mushrooms
2 large tomatoes
2 large green peppers

¼ cup butter or margarine
2 teaspoons chopped chives
1 teaspoon dillweed
1 teaspoon salt
¼ teaspoon lemon pepper

Scrub potatoes; cut off a band of skin around middle of each. Trim zucchini and squash, but do not pare; cut into 1-inch slices. Parboil potatoes in boiling salted water for 10 minutes; add zucchini and squash and cook 5 minutes. Drain. Wash mushrooms, trim ends and halve. Cut each tomato into 8 wedges. Halve green peppers, and cut into strips. Thread potatoes, zucchini and squash onto 4 long skewers. Thread mushrooms, tomato wedges and pepper strips onto 4 long skewers. Melt butter; stir in chives, dillweed, salt and lemon pepper. Grill potato-squash kabobs 6 inches from coals, turning and brushing several times with butter mixture, for 15 minutes; place tomato-mushroom kabobs alongside. Continue grilling 15 minutes or until tender.

Mrs. E. Darryl Barnes

Ratatouille

Serves: 6 to 8

1 medium eggplant, sliced
2 onions, thinly sliced
2 cloves of garlic, pressed
4 small zucchini, sliced
2 tomatoes, peeled, sliced and cut
   in wedges

2 green peppers, seeded and sliced
   in rings
½ cup olive oil
1 teaspoon dried basil
Salt and pepper

Cut 6 or 8 large squares of heavy duty foil. Divide ingredients equally among the foil squares. Seal tightly. Grill for 45 to 60 minutes. Check on packet at 25 minutes to be sure cooking is proceeding.

Mrs. Robert G. Lineberry

Roast Corn

4 ears white or yellow corn
2 tablespoons sugar

½ cup melted butter
Salt and pepper

Pull back the husks from the ears of corn, but do not remove them. Pull off silk. Dissolve sugar in melted butter; brush corn on all sides. Sprinkle with salt and pepper; wrap in husks. Bake over barbecue coals or in a hot oven (400 degrees) for 25 minutes or until the corn is tender.

Mrs. Frederick McNamara

Pork Chop Marinade

Yield: 4 cups

1½ cups oil
¾ cup soy sauce
¼ cup Worcestershire sauce
2 tablespoons dry mustard
2½ teaspoons salt

1 tablespoon pepper
½ cup wine vinegar or dry white wine
1½ teaspoons dry parsley
2 cloves garlic
½ cup lemon juice

Combine all ingredients. Mix well. Place chops in shallow dish, pour marinade over chops. Refrigerate overnight, turning once. Broil or grill.

Mrs. Forrest E. Williams

Fiorino's Smoked Salmon

Serves: 10 to 12

1 8 to 14-pound salmon, split
    open as if to filet
1/4 cup wine vinegar
1 cup lemon juice
1 whole lemon, chopped in chunks
1 1/2 cups salad oil
2 cloves garlic

1/3 medium onion, chopped
1 cup white wine
2 teaspoons chopped parsley
Salt and pepper to taste
1 tablespoon soy sauce
Few drops of Worcestershire sauce

Mix all ingredients above, except salmon, in blender, ending on high speed. Place the two sides of fish in roasting pan skin side down. Pour marinade over both halves to cover. Refrigerate at least overnight. Make a tray of heavy duty aluminum foil to fit grill. Place salmon skin side down on the tray. Continue to baste fish using the marinade. Cook covered until the fish flakes easily with a fork. A kettle grill usually takes about 25 minutes.

Mrs. Alfred E. T. Rusch

Savory Stuffed Trout

Serves: 6

6 fresh or frozen rainbow trout
    (about 3 pounds)
1 cup sliced mushrooms
1/2 cup quartered cherry tomatoes
2 tablespoons chopped green
    pepper
1 tablespoon chopped celery

1 clove garlic, minced
1 tablespoon chopped onion
1/4 teaspoon salt
1/4 teaspoon leaf thyme, crumbled
Dash of pepper
6 slices bacon
1/3 cup butter or margarine, melted

Split trout and wipe dry. Combine mushrooms, tomatoes, green pepper, celery, onion, garlic, salt, thyme and pepper. Divide filling into six portions and stuff trout. Wrap a slice of bacon around each trout, securing with wooden picks. Brush generously with melted butter. Grill 4 inches from hot coals for 8 minutes. Brush with butter, turn and grill 7 minutes longer, or until fish flakes easily. Serve with wedges of lemon and crispy fried potatoes.

Mrs. E. Darryl Barnes

Scallops on a Skewer

Serves: 4

16 bay scallops
16 thin slices of Canadian bacon
1 green pepper

1 large onion
Butter, melted

Cut green pepper and onion each into 8 pieces. Dry the scallops. Arrange each on a slice of the Canadian bacon. Alternate pepper, scallop wrapped in bacon, and onion on the skewers. Grill over white hot coals for about 10 minutes. Baste with butter 3 times. Serve with a rice pilaf and salad.

Note: A variation is to nestle each scallop in a large mushroom cap and alternate with chunks of ham steak or country ham.

Mrs. Robert G. Lineberry

Monterey Dilled Pumpernickel

Serves: 6

1 3-ounce package cream cheese,
    softened
⅓ cup Monterey Jack cheese,
    finely shredded

2 tablespoons snipped parsley
½ teaspoon dried dill weed
½ of a 16-ounce loaf pumpernickel
    bread, cut in ½-inch slices

In a bowl combine cream cheese, Jack cheese, parsley and dill; spread on one side of each bread slice. Reassemble loaf. Wrap loaf loosely in heavy duty foil. Place on edge of grill. Grill over slow coals 15 to 20 minutes, turning frequently. (May be placed in oven at 250 degrees.)

Mrs. Donald Burchell

Fiesta Bread

¼ cup soft butter or margarine
1 cup grated Cheddar cheese
½ cup catsup
⅓ cup chopped ripe olives

⅓ cup chopped green pepper
⅓ cup chopped onion
1 large or 2 small loaves French bread

Mix all ingredients thoroughly. Split bread lengthwise in half. Spread each half with butter mixture. Wrap each half in aluminum foil; heat in oven or on grill. Cut in slices to serve.

Mrs. Brian J Bowden

Marinade for Steaks and Roasts

9 tablespoons bourbon or red wine
2 tablespoons soy sauce
2 tablespoons garlic vinegar
2 tablespoons oil

½ teaspoon salt or smoked salt
½ teaspoon any leaf herb but tarragon
½ teaspoon MSG
½ teaspoon freshly ground pepper

Combine all ingredients and mix well. Pour marinade over meat; cover and place in refrigerator for at least 3 hours (even better overnight). Drain meat when ready to cook.

Note: The bourbon imparts a special flavor.

Mrs. Lawrence O. McKnelly

Barbecue Sauce

Yield: 1½ cups

½ cup catsup
¼ cup French mustard
¼ cup brown sugar
¼ cup oil and vinegar salad
   dressing
Garlic powder, to taste

1 teaspoon Worcestershire sauce
1 teaspoon A-1 sauce
½ cup orange juice
Salt to taste
Pepper to taste
Lemon juice to taste

Mix all ingredients. Baste chicken, spareribs or pork chops.

Mrs. Jack Howard

Tennessee Barbecue Sauce

Yields: 4 cups

1 cup brown sugar, firmly packed
1½ teaspoons onion salt
½ teaspoon paprika
½ teaspoon salt
½ teaspoon pepper
Dash of garlic salt

2 cups vinegar
1 cup bottled barbecue sauce
½ cup catsup
2 tablespoons Worcestershire sauce
1 tablespoon hot pepper sauce

In saucepan stir together brown sugar, onion salt, paprika, salt, pepper and garlic salt. Combine vinegar, barbecue sauce, catsup, Worcestershire sauce and hot pepper sauce in separate bowl. Combine vinegar mixture with dry ingredients in saucepan. Cook and stir over low heat until sugar dissolves. Remove from heat; cool. Store covered in refrigerator.

Mrs. Thomas T. Bellino

Vegetables

Hopping John

Serves: 6

1 pound black-eyed peas
¾ pound cubed, parboiled salt
  pork or fat bacon
½ teaspoon salt
1 large bay leaf
1 medium onion, chopped
8 peppercorns

1 cup rice
2½ quarts boiling water
Salt
White pepper
1 20-ounce can Italian plum tomatoes
1 teaspoon basil

Wash peas. Cover with 2 inches cold water. Add pork, salt, bay leaf, onion and peppercorns, freshly ground. Cook until beans are tender. Add more boiling water if necessary. Meanwhile cook rice until tender and season with salt and pepper. While rice is cooking, heat tomatoes with basil. Serve rice and black-eyed peas separately; pour peas over a mound of rice and surround with tomatoes.

Mrs. John P. Glynn

Port City Sweet Potatoes

Preheat: 350 degrees
Serves: 6

3 medium sweet potatoes or yams
⅔ cup light brown sugar
1 teaspoon salt
3 tablespoons butter or margarine

3 bananas, peeled and sliced
⅓ cup orange juice
¼ cup shredded coconut

Cook sweet potatoes in boiling water to cover about 25 minutes or until tender but firm. Cool, pare, and cut into ¼-inch slices. Arrange layer of potatoes in buttered 1-quart casserole. Sprinkle with sugar mixed with salt. Dot with butter. Top with layer of bananas. Repeat layers. Pour orange juice over layers. Sprinkle with coconut. Bake 20 minutes in 350 degree oven or until top is lightly browned.

Mrs. Hugh C. Newton

George Washington National Masonic Temple

The most prominent structure in Alexandria is the towering monument erected by the Masonic Fraternity of the United States to honor George Washington and to house the relics in possession of Lodge Number 22. Shooter's Hill, named for a hill near London, England, from which "shooters" hunted, is an ideal location, for Washington knew every foot of the ground surrounding the shrine in every direction.

The Alexandria Lodge was organized in 1783. George Washington was its first Worshipful Master, serving while President of the United States. The Alexandria Masons helped lay the cornerstone of the United States Capitol in 1793, and in 1824 they entertained General Lafayette during his visit to the United States.

The cornerstone of the memorial was laid in 1923 with the same trowel used in the U.S. Capitol cornerstone ceremony. President Herbert Hoover helped dedicate the shrine in an elaborate ritual in 1932. The Washington family Bible and a clock stopped by Washington's attending physician at the time of his death are included in the outstanding collection of memorabilia in the George Washington Museum.

187

Artichoke Spinach Casserole

Preheat: 350 degrees
Serves: 6

2 10-ounce packages frozen
  chopped spinach, thawed and
  drained
8 ounces cream cheese, softened
¼ pound margarine, softened
3 tablespoons lemon juice

Salt
Pepper
Dash of nutmeg
1 10-ounce package frozen artichoke
  hearts, cut in half
Buttered bread crumbs

Butter casserole. Mix cheese and margarine. Add seasonings and drained spinach. Place artichokes in bottom of casserole. Cover with spinach mixture. Top with buttered bread crumbs. Bake at 350 degrees for 45 minutes.

Mrs. Kleber S. Masterson, Jr.

Cheese Asparagus Pie

Preheat: 350 degrees
Serves: 6 to 8

1 8-ounce package crescent rolls
1 16-ounce can cut asparagus,
  drained

½ cup mayonnaise
1 cup packed, grated Cheddar cheese
1 teaspoon lemon juice

Unroll and separate dough into 8 triangles. Place on an 8-inch or 9-inch pie plate. Press together to form crust covering bottom and sides of plate. Combine remaining ingredients, tossing lightly. Spread mixture in unbaked crust. Bake 35 minutes at 350 degrees.

Mrs. F. Eugene Brown, Jr.

Asparagus Amandine

Preheat: 300 degrees
Serves: 8

2 1-pound cans green asparagus
1 10¾-ounce can cream of
  mushroom soup
½ teaspoon salt
¼ teaspoon pepper

1 cup grated American cheese
1 cup bread crumbs
4 tablespoons melted butter
¼ cup blanched almond halves

Drain (or cook, if fresh) the asparagus, saving the liquid. Lay asparagus in 9 x 13-inch casserole. Mix soup with ½ cup asparagus liquid, salt and pepper. Pour soup mixture over asparagus. Sprinkle with cheese. Combine crumbs and butter. Sprinkle over casserole. Top with almonds. Bake at 300 degrees for 45 minutes.

Mrs. Richard Rhame

Barley Casserole

Preheat: 350 degrees
Serves: 6

½ cup butter or margarine
½ pound fresh mushrooms, thinly
  sliced
1 cup coarsely chopped onion

1⅓ cups pearl barley
6 chicken bouillon cubes
5 cups water

In 2 tablespoons butter, sauté mushrooms. Set aside. Sauté onion in remaining butter until golden and add barley. Cook over low heat until golden. Dissolve bouillon cubes in water. Put barley mixture into greased 2-quart casserole with 2 cups of chicken bouillon broth. Cover and bake 30 minutes. Stir in 2 additional cups of broth and bake 30 more minutes. Stir in remaining cup of broth and bake 20 minutes.

Note: The stirring is very important.

Mrs. Philip A. Wells

Broccoli Soufflé

Preheat: 325 degrees
Serves: 8

¼ cup minced onion
6 tablespoons butter
2 tablespoons flour
½ cup water
3 eggs, well beaten

2 10-ounce packages frozen chopped
  broccoli
1 8-ounce jar processed cheese spread
Bread crumbs

Sauté onions in 4 tablespoons of butter until soft. Stir in flour, add water. Cook over low heat until mixture thickens. Stir in cheese. Meanwhile, boil broccoli until slightly cooked, then drain well. Stir broccoli into cheese sauce. Add eggs. Mix gently until blended. Place mixture in greased casserole. Cover with bread crumbs. Bake at 325 degrees for 40 to 50 minutes. If refrigerated before baking, add 15 minutes to baking time.

Mrs. David W. Dellefield

Party Broccoli

Serves: 6 to 8

2 tablespoons butter
2 tablespoons minced onion
1½ cups sour cream
2 teaspoons sugar
1 teaspoon white vinegar
½ teaspoon poppy seed

½ teaspoon paprika
¼ teaspoon salt
Dash of cayenne pepper
2 10-ounce packages frozen broccoli
⅓ cup chopped cashews

Cook broccoli until just tender and drain. Melt butter in small saucepan; sauté onion. Remove from heat and stir in sour cream, sugar, vinegar, poppy seed, paprika, salt and cayenne pepper. Arrange broccoli on heated platter and pour sour cream sauce over the stalks. Sprinkle on cashews.

Mrs. John B. Allen

Rødkaal Red Cabbage

Serves: 6

2 pounds red cabbage
2 tablespoons butter
1 tablespoon sugar

3 tablespoons red currant jelly
2 tablespoons vinegar

Remove outer leaves and quarter cabbage. Remove core and rinse with cold water and drain. Shred cabbage very finely. Melt butter in large saucepan. Add sugar, jelly and vinegar; then blend. Add shredded cabbage. Cover tightly; simmer until cabbage is very tender. stirring occasionally.

Mrs. Henry E. Thomas IV

Blender Hollandaise

Serves: 6

½ cup butter
3 tablespoons lemon juice
¼ teaspoon salt

4 egg yolks
Dash of pepper

Heat butter until bubbly. Meanwhile place egg yolks, lemon juice, salt and pepper in blender. Turn blender on and off quickly. Then turn to high speed and slowly add butter in a very thin but steady stream. Serve immediately.

Mrs. Timothy R. Geary

Broccoli Divine

Preheat: 350 degrees
Serves: 8

3 10-ounce packages frozen
  broccoli
1 6-ounce package cream cheese
  with chives

2 10-ounce cans frozen cream of
  shrimp soup
Juice of 1 lemon
Paprika

Cook broccoli as directed on package; drain. Mix together cream of shrimp soup, cream cheese and lemon juice. In a greased 2-quart casserole, alternate layers of broccoli and soup mixture. Sprinkle top with paprika. Bake at 350 degrees for 30 minutes.

Mrs. Stephen R. Shaffer

Alpine Bean Casserole

Preheat: 350 degrees
Serves: 8

2 10-ounce packages frozen green
   beans, cooked and drained
2 tablespoons butter
2 tablespoons flour
1 teaspoon salt
¼ teaspoon pepper

5 teaspoons sugar
2 teaspoons grated onion
2 8-ounce cartons sour cream
½ cup grated Swiss cheese
1 cup crushed corn flakes

Place green beans in buttered 1½-quart casserole. In a double boiler, melt butter; stir in flour, salt, pepper, sugar, onion and sour cream. When mixture is hot, add cheese. Pour sauce over green beans. Top with corn flakes and dot with butter. Bake 20 minutes in 350 degree oven.

Mrs. E. David Doane

Beets in Sour Cream

Serves: 4

3 cups cooked or canned sliced
   beets
½ cup cultured sour cream
1 tablespoon prepared horseradish

1 tablespoon chopped chives
1 teaspoon grated onion (optional)
Salt to taste

Combine all ingredients in the top of a double boiler and heat slowly until flavors combine.

Mrs. Donald Burchell

Lucille's Lima Beans

Preheat: 350 degrees
Serves: 4 to 6

1 pound dried lima beans
1 cup brown sugar

1 large can pear halves
2 tablespoons butter

Wash beans. Soak beans overnight. Next morning simmer in some water for 1 hour or until beans are tender, but not mushy. Salt to taste. Drain beans. Butter a large casserole (2-quart). Melt butter and brown sugar. Add 1 cup of pear juice. Place in casserole: layer of beans, then a layer of pear halves, cover with part of syrup. Repeat, ending with pears and syrup. Bake covered at 350 degrees for 3 to 4 hours, uncover for last half hour.

Note: May be made 1 or 2 days ahead and reheated. Especially good with pork or sausage dishes. Very popular at church suppers.

Mrs. Robert L. Calhoun

Carrot And Cheese Ring

Preheat: 325 degrees
Serves: 8

3 cups finely shredded fresh
* carrots*
⅓ cup finely diced celery
1 cup finely chopped onion
½ cup fine dry bread crumbs
1 cup shredded Cheddar cheese

1½ cups medium white sauce
¾ teaspoon salt
⅛ teaspoon pepper
3 eggs, separated
1 cup cooked peas 'n onions

Combine carrots, celery, onion, bread crumbs, cheese, white sauce, salt and pepper. Beat egg yolks and add to carrot mixture; mix well. Beat egg whites until they stand in soft, stiff peaks. Fold egg whites into carrot mixture. Pour into well-greased 1½-quart ring mold. Place in a pan of hot water. Bake at 325 degrees for 1 hour and 15 minutes. Remove from oven and let stand for 10 minutes. Turn onto serving plate. Fill center with buttered, cooked peas 'n onions.

Note: Preparation time is greatly reduced with the use of a food processor.

Mrs. James R. Skidmore

Cauliflower-Onion Bake

Preheat: 350 degrees
Serves: 8

1½ cups water
1 10-ounce package frozen
  cauliflower, thawed
2 10-ounce packages frozen onions
  in cream sauce
2 tablespoons margarine

¾ cup (3 ounces) shredded sharp
  cheese
¼ cup toasted slivered almonds
1 tablespoon snipped parsley
½ cup canned French fried onions,
  crumbled

Cut cauliflower into bite-sized pieces. In saucepan, place water, margarine and onions. Cover, bring to a boil, reduce heat and simmer for 4 minutes stirring occasionally. Remove from heat, stir until sauce is smooth. Add cauliflower, cheese, almonds and parsley. Turn into 1½-quart casserole. Bake uncovered in 350 degree oven for 35 minutes or until bubbly and heated through. Top with French fried onions. Bake 5 minutes more.

Note: Goes well with roast beef.

Mrs. Renny H. Barnes

 Cauliflower keeps white if you put a tablespoon of lemon juice or white vinegar in the cooking water.

Baked Swiss Cauliflower

Preheat: 350 degrees
Serves: 6

1 large head cauliflower
½ cup bread crumbs
2¾ cups shredded Swiss cheese
1½ cups half-and-half
3 egg yolks, beaten

¼ teaspoon ground nutmeg
½ teaspoon salt
¼ teaspoon pepper
¼ cup melted butter or margarine

Wash cauliflower and discard green leaves; break into flowerets. Cook, covered, 10 minutes in a small amount of boiling salted water; drain. Place cauliflower in a buttered 1½-quart shallow baking dish. Combine remaining ingredients except butter, and pour over cauliflower. Drizzle butter over top. Bake at 350 degrees for 15 to 20 minutes.

Mrs. Donald Burchell

Baked Carrots and Apples

Preheat: 375 degrees
Serves: 6

8 medium carrots, pared and cut
in one-inch pieces
1 20-ounce can pie-sliced apples,
drained

½ cup sugar (brown or white)
2 tablespoons margarine
Paprika

Cook carrots until tender. Combine carrots and apples; turn into 9-inch pie plate. Sprinkle with sugar and dot with margarine. Sprinkle with paprika. Bake at 375 degrees for one hour.

Note: To enhance flavor, cook carrots in as little water as possible.

Mrs. Renny H. Barnes

Swiss Corn Soufflé

Preheat: 350 degrees
Serves: 4 to 6

6 ears fresh corn
6 slices bacon
¼ cup all-purpose flour
¼ teaspoon salt
Dash pepper

1 cup milk
4 egg yolks
1 cup (4 ounces) shredded processed
Swiss cheese
4 egg whites

Cut kernels from cob (you should have about 2 cups cut corn). Cook corn, covered, in a small amount of boiling, salted water for 6 to 8 minutes until done; drain and set aside. In skillet, cook bacon until crisp. Drain, reserving ¼ cup drippings. Crumble bacon and set aside. In saucepan, blend flour, salt and pepper into reserved drippings. Add milk. Cook and stir until thickened and bubbly. Remove from heat. Beat egg yolks until thick and lemon-colored. Blend a moderate amount of hot mixture into egg yolks; return to saucepan. Cook, stirring rapidly until blended. Stir in cheese until melted. Stir in corn and bacon. Remove from heat. Beat egg whites until they form stiff peaks. Fold hot mixture into egg whites. Turn into ungreased 1½-quart soufflé dish. Bake in 350 degree oven for 30-40 minutes or until knife inserted *off-center* comes out clean. Garnish with bacon curl, if desired.

Note: This can be a year-round treat; substitute one 9-ounce package frozen whole kernel corn for fresh corn.

Mrs. Ronald Ziegler

Far East Celery

Preheat: 350 degrees
Serves: 8

4 cups celery cut in 1-inch pieces
1 5-ounce can water chestnuts,
   drained and sliced thin

1 10¾-ounce can cream of chicken
   soup
½ cup chopped pimento

Mix all ingredients. Place in 5-cup casserole. Sprinkle with buttered bread crumbs. Bake at 350 degrees for 35 minutes.

Mrs. Carlyle C. Ring, Jr.

Corn Casserole

Preheat: 325 degrees
Serves: 4

¼ cup butter, melted
1 green pepper, diced
2 cloves of garlic
¼ cup flour
1 cup milk
1 teaspoon basil
1 teaspoon oregano
Salt

Pepper
¼ teaspoon red pepper
½ teaspoon sugar
1½ cups grated Cheddar cheese
1 can tomatoes, drained
1 large can corn, drained
1 can small onions, drained

Cook green pepper and garlic in butter. Add flour and stir. Add milk, salt, pepper, basil, oregano, red pepper and sugar. Heat, stirring until thick. Stir in ½ cup Cheddar cheese. Place tomatoes, corn and onions in casserole. Pour cheese mixture over vegetables and mix well. Sprinkle 1 cup of Cheddar cheese over top. Bake uncovered for 50 minutes at 325 degrees.

Note: When doubling recipe, do not double onions. Good for pot luck suppers and picnic dinners.

Mrs. Raymond T. Bond

Corn Pudding

Preheat: 375 degrees
Serves: 4

3 eggs
⅔ cup sugar
2 cups milk

1 tablespoon melted butter
Salt and pepper
2 cups corn

Beat eggs thoroughly. Add sugar, butter, salt, pepper and milk. Add corn last. Turn into buttered 1½-quart baking dish. Bake at 375 degrees for 30 to 35 minutes.

Mrs. John Denson

Bacon Cheese Grits

Preheat: 350 degrees
Serves: 4 to 6

1 cup grits
1 cup butter
1 3-ounce roll bacon cheese
   (optional)

3 eggs, well beaten
⅔ cup milk
½ cup grated Cheddar cheese
Bacon curls (optional)

Cook grits according to recipe on package. While hot add butter and bacon cheese, stir until melted. Let cool slightly, add milk to eggs, stir well into grits mixture. Pour into greased 2-quart casserole. Sprinkle with grated cheese. Bake in 350 degree oven for 45 minutes—top with bacon curls.

Mrs. Carlton L. Schelhorn

Hominy Surprise

Preheat: 350 degrees
Serves: 8

2 cups hominy grits, cooked and
   cooled slightly
1 tablespoon salt
½ cup butter
1 cup milk

2 eggs, beaten lightly
1 cup grated sharp cheese
1 tablespoon Worcestershire sauce
Freshly ground pepper

Mix together well and pour into baking dish. Sprinkle some cheese on top. Bake at 350 degrees for 40 minutes to 1 hour until it is firm.

Mrs. James W. Vaughan, Jr.

Eggplant-Tomato Casserole

Preheat: 350 degrees
Serves 4 to 6

1 medium-large eggplant
3 tablespoons butter
3 tablespoons flour
1½ to 2 cups chopped tomatoes
½ cup Parmesan cheese

1 green pepper, chopped
1 medium onion, chopped
1 teaspoon salt
2 tablespoons brown sugar
1 cup buttered croutons

Peel and cut eggplants into 1-inch cubes. Cook in small amount of water for 10-15 minutes. Drain well and place in casserole. Combine butter, flour, tomatoes, pepper, onion, salt and sugar. Cook 5 minutes, stirring often. Pour over eggplant. Sprinkle ¼ cup cheese, then croutons, then cheese on top. Bake at 350 degrees for 35 minutes.

Mrs. Temple C. Moore

 To avoid discoloration cook eggplant in enamel, glass or stainless steel.

Norma's Mexa-Hominy Casserole

Preheat: 350 degrees
Serves: 8

2 14-ounce cans hominy
3 4-ounce cans whole Mexican
  peppers (hot)
8 ounces grated Monterey Jack
  cheese

1 pint sour cream
½ cup table cream
Dots of butter
Salt
Pepper

Layer ingredients in the following order: begin at the bottom with hominy, sour cream, cheese, Mexican peppers, repeat order again. Dot top with butter, sprinkle with salt and pepper according to taste. Pour table cream on top. Bake at 350 degrees until bubbling and cheese is turning light brown.

Mrs. Hugh C. Newton

Mushroom Flambé

Serves: 4

12-15 mushroom caps
2 cups ½-inch diced onions
2 cups ½-inch diced green pepper
2 ounces butter
Garlic salt

Freshly ground pepper
¼ teaspoon marjoram
Parsley
3 ounces brandy

Sauté onions and green peppers for 5 minutes over moderate heat. Add mushrooms. Cook 5 minutes more. Add seasonings. Add brandy, which will ignite immediately. Serve immediately.

Note: Serve as a vegetable, main dish over toast points or as an appetizer. Freezes well, and recipe can be tripled!

Mrs. Michael R. Ward

Mushroom Casserole

Preheat: 325 degrees
Serves: 8

1 pound fresh mushrooms
4 tablespoons butter
8 slices white bread
½ cup chopped onion
½ cup chopped celery
½ cup chopped green pepper
½ cup mayonnaise

¾ teaspoon salt
¼ teaspoon pepper
2 eggs, slightly beaten
1½ cups milk
1 10¾-ounce can cream of mushroom
    soup
Grated cheese

Sauté mushrooms in butter. Butter 3 slices of white bread; cut in 1-inch squares and put in casserole. Combine onion, celery, green pepper, mayonnaise, salt and pepper. Add to mushrooms. Put mixture on top of bread. Add 3 more slices of buttered bread. Combine eggs and milk. Pour over bread. Refrigerate at least 1 hour. One hour before serving, spoon soup over the top. Add 2 more slices of bread diced smaller. Bake at 325 degrees for 50 to 60 minutes. Ten minutes before removing from oven, sprinkle grated cheese on top.

Mrs. Kleber S. Masterson, Jr.

Tangy Mushrooms

Serves: 4

4 tablespoons butter
1 pound sliced mushrooms
2 cups sour cream
4 teaspoons flour

2 teaspoons grated onion
1 teaspoon salt
¼ teaspoon pepper

Sauté mushrooms in butter until tender. Mix other ingredients together. Add to mushrooms. Refrigerate. When ready to serve, cook until thickened over low heat. Stir.

Mrs. Jerome J. Palermino

Okra Fritters

Serves: 6

1 cup thinly sliced okra
½ cup chopped onion
½ cup chopped tomato
¼ cup all-purpose flour
¼ cup corn meal

½ teaspoon salt
½ teaspoon curry powder
¼ teaspoon pepper
1 egg, beaten

Combine ingredients, stirring well. Drop mixture by tablespoonfuls into hot oil. Cook until golden brown, turning once.

Mrs. Lewis B. Puller, Jr.

Braised Onions

Serves: 5

1 10-ounce package frozen whole
   onions
2 tablespoons water

3 tablespoons butter
2 beef bouillon cubes

Combine all ingredients in a large skillet and bring to a boil, stirring frequently. Cover and continue cooking for 5 minutes. Remove cover, continue cooking, stirring frequently until all liquid is evaporated.

Note: Excellent with steak or beef roasts.

Mrs. Kevin Gallen

Funghi all'Olio e Limone
(Mushrooms with Oil and Lemon)

Serves: 6

1 pound small white mushrooms
½ cup olive oil
1 clove garlic

½ teaspoon salt
¼ lemon
1 tablespoon chopped fresh parsley

Peel and clean the mushrooms, and cut caps from stems. Slice off the very bottom of the stems where they are slightly dried out. Put the oil in a medium-sized frying pan; add the garlic and sauté over medium heat until golden brown, then discard. Add the mushrooms and increase the heat; cook quickly. Stir as they cook. As the mushrooms start to give up their juices, add the salt. When they are tender but still firm (about 4 to 5 minutes), squirt them with lemon, stir well, add the parsley, stir again and remove from the heat. Serve cold in their own flavored oil.

Mrs. Stephen L. Echols

Onion Cheese Pie

Preheat: 400 degrees
Serves: 12 to 16

2 9-inch unbaked pie shells
1 cup (or more) sliced onions
2 tablespoons butter
3 eggs
1½ cups milk

Salt to taste
Pepper to taste
½ teaspoon basil
2 cups grated Cheddar cheese

Sauté onion in butter. Beat eggs and add milk, salt, pepper and basil. Divide cheese in half and spread evenly in bottom of each pie shell. Divide onions in half and spread over cheese. Pour milk mixture over cheese in both pies. Bake at 400 degrees for 40 to 45 minutes. Allow 5 minutes to set before serving.

Note: Goes especially well with a roast. Can be frozen and reheated.

Mrs. Raymond T. Bond

English Peas

Preheat: 350 degrees
Serves: 8

2 cans peas (save ½ can of juice)
1 onion sliced
½ green pepper, chopped
4 stalks celery, chopped
1 4-ounce can mushrooms
  (optional)

½ cup butter
1 2-ounce can pimentos
1 8½-ounce can water chestnuts
1 10-ounce can cream of mushroom
  soup
Bread crumbs or cornflake crumbs

Sauté onions, pepper, mushrooms and celery in butter. Add soup with pea juice. Add pimentos, water chestnuts, and place in 2-quart casserole. Top with bread or cornflake crumbs. Bake at 350 degrees for 30 minutes.

Mrs. James W. Vaughan, Jr.

 To preserve green color of vegetables, add a pinch of baking soda to the boiling water.

Peas and Rice Deluxe

Serves: 4 to 6

2 cups seasoned (with salt and
  pepper) cooked rice
1 to 1½ 10-ounce packages frozen
  peas, barely cooked

2 tablespoons minced onion
½ clove garlic
⅓ cup sliced stuffed olives
3 tablespoons hot salad oil

Toss rice with peas. Sauté onion, garlic and olives in salad oil. Add sautéed mixture to rice. Check seasonings.

Note: Especially good with beef dish or meatloaf.

Mrs. Raymond T. Bond

Pine Nut Pie

Preheat: 350 degrees
Serves: 4 to 6

*1 11-inch unbaked pie crust made
    with white wine and butter
3 minced shallots, sautéed in
    butter
½ cup grated Parmesan cheese
⅔ cup cottage cheese
2 tomatoes, seeded and puréed*

*2 eggs, beaten
1 10-ounce package frozen chopped
    spinach, cooked and drained
Lemon juice
Nutmeg
¼ pound pine nuts, sautéed in butter*

Sprinkle pie crust with shallots and ¼ cup Parmesan cheese. Combine cottage cheese, tomato purée and eggs and pour in crust. Bake until it sets, about ½ hour at 350 degrees. Season finely chopped spinach with nutmeg and lemon juice to taste. On top of pie make stripes (rows) with spinach, cheese and pine nuts. Heat through.

Mrs. William Heenan

Devilish Stuffed Potatoes

Preheat: 350 degrees
Serves: 12

*6 baking potatoes
1 8-ounce package cream cheese
1 4-ounce can deviled ham*

*1 teaspoon onion flakes
4 tablespoons mayonnaise
Paprika*

Bake potatoes. Combine all other ingredients except paprika. Allow potatoes to cool. Slice each in half; scoop out pulp. Combine pulp and cream cheese mixture. Spoon back into potato shells. Sprinkle with paprika. Bake for 20 minutes. Can be prepared ahead and frozen. If frozen, increase baking time to 30-40 minutes.

Mrs. Richard L. Wallace

Potato Princess

Preheat: 350 degrees
Serves: 6

4 *large baking potatoes*
¼ *pound butter*
¼ *pound Swiss cheese*
Caraway seeds

3 *onions*
Salt
White pepper
Paprika

Parboil potatoes in unsalted water and remove skin. Sauté onions in butter; add salt and pepper to taste. Grease 1½-quart baking dish. Slice potatoes and place in baking dish, alternating layers of potatoes and onions, sprinkling with caraway seeds. Dot each layer with cheese; sprinkle completed casserole with paprika. Bake at 350 degrees until cheese melts. Serve hot.

Note: This may be frozen before cooking. Provides a German accent to your meal.

Mrs. Thomas T. Bellino

Pommes de Terre Gratin

Preheat: 350 degrees
Serves: 6 to 8

2 *pounds white potatoes, peeled,*
  sliced ⅛-inch thick
½ *pound grated Swiss cheese (or*
  more)
Salt

Pepper
Dots of sweet butter
2 *whole eggs*
1½ *cups half-and-half*

Place potato slices in cold water; drain, dry slices thoroughly with towel. Layer the potatoes in 2-quart casserole with lots of Swiss cheese, salt and freshly ground pepper to taste. Top with additional cheese and dot with butter. Beat eggs with half-and-half. Pour over the potatoes and bake at 350 degrees for 1 hour and 15 minutes.

Mrs. Lawrence O. McKnelly

Cottage Potatoes

Preheat: 350 degrees
Serves: 15

10 new potatoes
1 onion
1 green pepper
1 4-ounce can pimentos
½ pound Cheddar cheese

1 or 2 slices bread
1 cup melted butter
Cornflakes
Parsley

Cook, cool, peel and cube potatoes. Cube onion, green pepper, cheese and bread. Mix potatoes, onion, green pepper, pimentos, cheese and bread. Add butter; place in shallow baking casserole and sprinkle with crumbled cornflakes and parsley. Pour over enough milk to moisten cornflakes. Bake at 350 degrees for 45 minutes.

Note: Great for buffets

Mrs. Michael Cericola

Zesty Mashed Potatoes

Preheat: 350 degrees
Serves: 8 to 10

5 cups freshly mashed potatoes
3 cups cream style cottage cheese
1 cup sour cream
2 tablespoons grated onion

2½ teaspoons salt
¼ teaspoon pepper
Melted butter
½ cup toasted almonds

Mash potatoes thoroughly using no milk or butter. Buzz cottage cheese in a blender and mix into potatoes. Add all ingredients except butter and almonds. Spoon into 2-quart casserole. Brush surface with melted butter. Bake at 350 degrees for 30 minutes. Place under broiler for a few minutes to brown lightly. Sprinkle with almonds.

Mrs. William T. Mahood

Country Potatoes

Preheat: 350 degrees
Serves: 4 to 6

2 pounds frozen hash brown
  potatoes, defrosted
1 cup chopped onions
1 10¾-ounce can cream of chicken
  soup

1 pint sour cream
½ cup margarine or butter, melted
1 cup grated Cheddar cheese
2 teaspoons salt

Mix all ingredients together and spread in a 9 x 13-inch pan. Bake at 350 degrees for 1 hour or until it turns golden brown on top.

Mrs. F. Eugene Brown, Jr.

 To bake potatoes in half the time, let stand in boiling water for 15 minutes; then bake in a very hot oven.

Gourmet Potatoes

Preheat: 350 degrees
Serves: 8

6 medium new potatoes, parboiled
2 cups shredded Cheddar cheese
¼ cup butter
1½ cups sour cream (room
  temperature)

⅓ cup chopped onion
1 teaspoon salt
¼ teaspoon pepper
2 tablespoons butter, cut in dots

Cook potatoes in jackets. Cool. Peel and coarsely shred. Combine cheese and ¼ cup butter over low heat. Blend in sour cream, onions, salt and pepper. Fold cheese mixture into potatoes. Place in 2-quart casserole. Dot with butter. Bake at 350 degrees for ½ hour.

Mrs. William E. Elwood

Cheesy Potatoes

Preheat: 350 degrees
Serves: 4 to 6

4 cups cubed cooked potatoes
1 8-ounce carton plain yogurt
1 cup cottage cheese
½ teaspoon salt

¼ teaspoon pepper
¼ teaspoon dill weed
1 cup shredded sharp Cheddar cheese

Combine all ingredients except Cheddar cheese; spoon into a 9-inch baking pan. Top with Cheddar cheese. Bake at 350 degrees for 25 to 30 minutes.

Mrs. Renny H. Barnes

Risotto Alla Milanese

Serves: 4

2 tablespoons butter
1 small onion, minced
1 cup uncooked long grain or
* arborio rice*
3 to 4 cups rich chicken stock
¼ teaspoon crumbled saffron
* threads*

¼ cup dry white wine
2 tablespoons butter
¼ pound sliced mushrooms
½ cup freshly grated Parmesan cheese
Salt
Freshly ground pepper

Heat 2 tablespoons butter in heavy 3 to 4-quart casserole over mid to high heat. Add onion and sauté until soft and transparent. Stir in rice and continue sautéing until rice begins to appear opaque. Meanwhile, bring stock to boil in separate saucepan; stir in saffron. Pour 1 cup boiling stock into rice mixture. Cook over medium heat, stirring often, until stock is absorbed, watching carefully so rice does not burn. When stock is absorbed, add wine and then stir in another cup of boiling stock. Continue to add stock, 1 cup at a time until risotto is creamy but not soupy. *Do not cover pot and do not try to steam rice.* Just before serving, melt remaining 2 tablespoons butter in small skillet over medium to high heat. Add mushrooms and sauté briefly until softened. Stir into risotto, add cheese, salt and pepper and mix well. Serve immediately.

Note: Arborio rice is a short grained rice grown in Italy's Po Valley. Risotto aficionados claim it is the only rice to use in this classic dish. It can be found in Italian markets and specialty food shops.

Mrs. John E. Davey

Rice Delight

Preheat: 350 degrees
Serves: 6

2 cups cooked rice
1½ 14½-ounce cans asparagus
1 8-ounce jar processed cheese
   spread
1 10¾-ounce can cream of chicken
   soup

1 cup water chestnuts, sliced thin
½ cup celery
¼ cup onion
3 tablespoons butter
½ cup milk

Sauté celery and onions in butter; add soup, milk and one third of cheese spread. Layer rice, asparagus, water chestnuts and soup mixture in a buttered casserole and top with dabs of remaining cheese spread. Bake, covered with foil, 25 to 30 minutes at 350 degrees.

Mrs. John T. Miller

 Regular or processed rice swells to about 4 times its original measure when cooked. Packaged precooked rice will slightly more than double its volume when cooked.

Riso Verde

Serves: 4 to 6

2¼ cups chicken stock or broth
¾ cup minced spinach
½ cup minced scallions
3 tablespoons butter
¼ cup minced parsley

1¼ cups long grain rice
Salt
White pepper
½ cup freshly grated Parmesan cheese

In saucepan bring chicken broth to a boil. In another heavy saucepan sauté spinach, scallions, parsley in butter over low heat, stirring occasionally, for 5 minutes. Stir in rice, salt and pepper to taste and continue to stir the mixture until it is well combined. Add 1 cup of the boiling chicken stock and cook the mixture over moderate heat, stirring occasionally, until the stock is absorbed. Add the remaining stock and cook the mixture, stirring occasionally, until stock is absorbed and rice is tender. Remove from heat, toss the rice lightly with Parmesan cheese.

Cantina D'Italia Restaurant

Baked Rice

Preheat: 350 degrees
Serves: 4

½ cup raw rice
⅛ cup chopped green pepper
⅛ cup chopped onion

1 4-ounce can mushrooms
½ cup melted butter
1 10¾-ounce can beef consommé

Add all ingredients in order into a 1½-quart casserole. Stir and bake uncovered at 350 degrees for 1 hour.

Mrs. Carlton L. Schelhorn

Curried Raisins and Rice

Serves: 8 to 12

2 cups long grain rice
2 teaspoons salt
4 tablespoons butter or margarine
1 3¼-ounce package onion soup mix

1 teaspoon curry powder
2 tablespoons dry parsley flakes
5 cups chicken broth and water
1 cup raisins

Bring above ingredients to a boil and cook according to directions on box of rice. Before serving add raisins.

Mrs. Timothy J. O'Shaughnessy

Summer Squash Casserole

Preheat: 350 degrees
Serves: 8

8 medium zucchini or yellow
*   squash*
½ cup butter
1 cup Cheddar cheese
1 cup sour cream
Salt and pepper to taste

1 beaten egg yolk
Paprika
¼ cup chives, chopped
Parmesan cheese
1 cup bread crumbs

Slice squash; steam or boil for several minutes. Heat butter, cheese, sour cream, salt, pepper, egg yolk, paprika and chives until these blend and make a sauce. Pour over squash. Sprinkle bread crumbs over top. Coat with Parmesan cheese and dot with butter. Bake for approximately 45 minutes.

Mrs. C. S. Taylor Burke III

Squash Fritters

Yield: 4-6 servings

2 cups fresh squash, grated
1 small onion, grated
1 well-beaten egg
½ teaspoon salt

1 tablespoon sugar
⅛ teaspoon pepper
2 heaping tablespoons flour
1 teaspoon baking powder

Mix above ingredients in order. Fry like pancakes in hot oil. Serve hot.

Mrs. James L. Howe III

Garlic Butter

Yield: ½ cup

Cream 1 stick of softened butter. Add garlic powder and grated onion to taste. Serve with beef fondue.

Mrs. Rennie H. Barnes

Squash and Peanut Pie

Preheat: 350 degrees
Serves: 8 to 10

3 pounds tender yellow squash
⅓ cup dry bread crumbs
1 cup heavy cream
1 medium onion, grated
¼ cup melted butter

1 tablespoon brown sugar
1 teaspoon MSG
½ cup salted peanuts, coarsely
  chopped
8 slices crisp bacon, crumbled

Scrub squash well, slice it unpeeled. Cool it in boiling salted water until tender. Drain and mash it. Let mashed squash drain in colander for at least ½ hour. There should be 3 cupfuls. Cover the bottom of 2 buttered pie plates with the bread crumbs. Beat grated onion, melted butter, heavy cream, brown sugar and MSG into squash and spoon mixture over crumbs. Bake at 350 degrees for 40 to 50 minutes. Sprinkle top with peanuts and bacon just before serving.

Note: A delightful accompaniment to ham and pork dishes.

Mrs. Timothy J. O'Shaughnessy

Spinach Fettuccini

Serves: 4

½ pound fresh spinach
1 clove garlic, mashed
2 tablespoons chopped onion
½ cup butter

8 ounces medium noodles
¼ to ½ cup heavy cream
1 cup grated Parmesan cheese

Tear spinach leaves. In pan, cook garlic and onion in ¼ cup butter until golden. Add spinach, cover and cook until spinach is wilted. Meanwhile, cook noodles; drain and mix with remaining butter. Toss noodles with cream, cheese and spinach.

Mrs. H. Franklin Green III

Spinach Supreme

Preheat: 350 degrees
Serves: 6 to 8

2 10-ounce packages frozen
    spinach, cooked and drained
1 cup sour cream
½ envelope dry onion soup mix

Buttered bread crumbs
Grated Parmesan, Cheddar or Swiss
    cheese

Combine spinach, sour cream and soup mix. Place in 4-cup casserole, cover with bread crumbs, then cheese. Bake at 350 degrees for 30 minutes.

Mrs. Forrest E. Williams

Spinach Squares Hollandaise

Preheat: 350 degrees
Serves: 12

3 10-ounce packages frozen
    chopped spinach
½ cup finely chopped onion
4 beaten eggs

2 tablespoons margarine
2 cups milk
3 cups soft bread crumbs
½ teaspoon seasoned salt

Cook spinach; drain well. Sauté onion. Combine remaining ingredients, then add to spinach and onions. Spread evenly in ungreased 12 x 7 x 2-inch pan. Bake at 350 degrees for 40 to 45 minutes, or until set. Cut into squares. Use blender hollandaise recipe, stir four diced hard-cooked eggs into sauce. Pour over spinach squares.
Note: Very easy and good for dinner party buffet. Can be made a day ahead and baked just before ready to serve. Doubles beautifully.

Mrs. Renny H. Barnes

Fried Green Tomatoes

Serves 6

4 large green tomatoes (very firm)
¾ cup cornmeal, bread or cracker
  crumbs
¼ teaspoon onion salt
¼ teaspoon garlic salt

½ teaspoon pepper
1 teaspoon grated Parmesan cheese
dash of paprika
1 egg, beaten
Bacon dripping or shortening

Cut tomatoes in ¼ inch slices. Mix dry ingredients. Dip tomato slices in egg and dredge in dry mixture. Place in a heavy skillet containing bacon drippings or shortening. Fry slowly until medium brown, turning once.

Mrs. Robert G. Lineberry

Scalloped Tomatoes and Artichoke Hearts

Preheat: 325 degrees
Serves: 6 to 8

1 2 pound, 3 ounce can tomatoes
1 14-ounce can artichoke hearts
½ cup finely chopped onion
Salt and pepper to taste

2 tablespoons shallots, finely chopped
¼ pound butter
½ teaspoon basil
2 tablespoons sugar

Grease shallow earthenware casserole. Drain tomatoes and artichokes. Quarter artichokes. Sauté onions and shallots in butter until tender; add tomatoes, artichokes and basil. Heat 3 to 5 minutes. Add sugar, salt and pepper. Turn into casserole and bake for 10 to 15 minutes at 325 degrees. This can be made ahead and heated for serving.

Note: The leftovers make delicious omelets.

Mrs. Lewis B. Puller, Jr.

Sausage-Stuffed Tomatoes

Preheat: 350 degrees
Serves: 4

4 large firm tomatoes
Salt and pepper
½ cup soft breadcrumbs
3 tablespoons finely chopped celery
3 tablespoons finely chopped green pepper

½ pound mild bulk pork sausage, cooked, crumbled and drained
½ cup (2 ounces) shredded Cheddar cheese
Fresh parsley sprigs

Cut tops from tomatoes, scoop out pulp, leaving shells intact. Chop pulp; combine tomato pulp, breadcrumbs, celery, green pepper and cooked sausage, mixing well. Sprinkle inside of tomato shells with salt and pepper; spoon sausage mixture into shells. Arrange tomatoes in an 8-inch square baking pan, bake at 350 degrees for 15 minutes or until tomatoes are thoroughly heated. Sprinkle tomatoes with cheese. Bake 1 additional minute or until cheese melts. Garnish with parsley, if desired.

Mrs. E. Darryl Barnes

Curried Creamed Vegetables

Serves 4

4 or 5 stalks celery
4 medium onions
1 cup milk
1 teaspoon curry powder
¼ cup flour

3 carrots
1 cup peas
2 tablespoons margarine
½ cup shredded Cheddar cheese

Cook vegetables in water until just tender. Drain and save 1 cup of liquid from cooked vegetables. Add milk and vegetable liquid to vegetables; then add curry powder, margarine and cheese. Stir well. Sprinkle flour over vegetables. Stir lightly until vegetable liquid and flour are mixed. Cook over low heat until thickened. Stir a few times while thickening.

Mrs. Frank McCabe

Zucchini "Soufflé"

Preheat: 350 degrees
Serves: 6

6 cups grated zucchini	*1½ teaspoons salt*
9 slices Provolone cheese, grated	*1½ cups seasoned bread crumbs*
6 eggs	

Blend all ingredients together with fork and turn into greased 2½ quart casserole. Refrigerate minimum of 1 hour (can also be frozen at this point —after thawing, add 1 more egg before baking). Bake 1¼ hours at 350 degrees.

May make individual servings by heating 1 teaspoon oil in each section of muffin tin, spooning mixture in each section. Bake 20 minutes at 350 degrees.

Mrs. Emanuel A. Baker, Jr.

Zucchini Leonardo

Preheat: 325 degrees
Serves: 6

½ pound bacon, cut fine	*6 tomatoes sliced, or 2 cups chopped,*
1 cup onion, minced	*canned tomatoes*
4 tablespoons bacon grease	*2 cups cracker crumbs*
2 pounds zucchini, sliced ¼ inch	*¼ teaspoon pepper*
thick	*1 teaspoon salt*
1 pound sharp Cheddar cheese,	
grated	

Fry bacon, sauté onion in bacon grease. Mix in a 2-quart casserole, alternate, repeating three times, layers of zucchini, cheese, tomatoes, onion and bacon mixture, cracker crumbs and seasonings. Bake 1 hour at 325 degrees.

Note: May be prepared several hours before baking.

Mrs. E. David Doane

Zucchini Gaetano

Serves: 6

3 to 4 zucchini squash, thinly
  sliced
1 onion, diced
1 tablespoon olive oil
1 teaspoon oregano

1 teaspoon salt
1 teaspoon pepper
1 8-ounce can tomato sauce
8 ounces Mozzarella cheese
Grated Parmesan cheese

Brown onion in olive oil. Add zucchini along with oregano, salt, pepper and tomato sauce. Cover and cook slowly until squash is tender, about 8 to 10 minutes. Add Mozzarella cheese. Heat until cheese melts. When ready to serve, sprinkle with Parmesan cheese.

Mrs. Edward F. Kapusta

Stuffed Zucchini

Preheat: 425 degrees
Serves: 6

3 large zucchini
¼ cup diced green onion
1 tablespoon butter

½ cup sour cream
½ cup shredded Cheddar cheese

Trim stems from squash and cook in a small amount of salted water, until barely tender; cool. Cut in half, lengthwise. Scoop out centers, leaving shells (don't scoop out too much). Cook onion in butter. Add squash pulp and cook until like paste. Add sour cream and cheese. Fill shells. Arrange in a baking dish. Bake at 425 degrees for 15 to 20 minutes.

Mrs. Brian J. Bowden

Risotto Con Zucchini

Serves: 4 to 6

3 small zucchini (1 pound)
5 tablespoons butter
½ cup minced onion
1 or 2 cloves garlic, crushed
1 cup short or medium grain rice

4 cups hot chicken broth
1 cup chopped fresh parsley
Salt and pepper to taste
¼ cup freshly grated Parmesan cheese

Cut stems from zucchini; wipe dry and slice thinly. Sauté in 2 tablespoons butter in large skillet until golden (2 or 3 minutes). Remove with slotted spoon; set aside. Add and heat 2 tablespoons butter in skillet. Add onion and garlic and sauté until tender. Add rice and sauté until grains become golden. Add 2 cups broth and cook over medium heat, uncovered, stirring occasionally (10 minutes). Add 1 cup broth, zucchini, parsley, salt and pepper; continue cooking until almost all liquid is absorbed. Add last cup of broth; continue cooking until rice is tender. Stir in remaining tablespoon butter and cheese and serve at once while moist and creamy.

Mrs. Temple C. Moore

Sandra's Cranberry Casserole

Preheat: 325 degrees
Serves: 6 to 8

3 cups chopped apples
2 cups fresh cranberries
6 pats butter
½ cup oats
2 cups sugar

½ cup brown sugar
½ cup chopped pecans
1 teaspoon cinnamon
½ teaspoon nutmeg

Place fruit in 3-quart buttered casserole. Combine dry ingredients and pat on top. Dot with butter. Decorate with pecan halves. Cook, covered for 45 minutes at 325 degrees.

Mrs. Tod R. Hullin

Curried Fruit Casserole

Preheat: 325 degrees
Serves: 10

Must be made a day ahead.

1 24-ounce can peach halves
1 10-ounce can apricots
1 24-ounce can pears
1 24-ounce can pineapple pieces

10 maraschino cherries
⅓ cup melted butter
¾ cup brown sugar
4 teaspoons curry powder

Drain fruit well. Mix butter, brown sugar and curry powder. Put fruit in a 9 x 13-inch shallow baking dish, hollow side up. Dot all over with the curry-sugar mixture. Bake at 325 degrees for 1 hour, basting frequently. Cool and refrigerate for at least one day. Warm over at 350 degrees for ½ hour.

Ms. Elizabeth J. Noyes

Baked Pineapple

Preheat: 375 degrees
Serves: 4 to 6

1 20-ounce can crushed pineapple
  (do not drain)
2 tablespoons flour

¼ cup sugar
2 cups croutons
1 stick butter

Mix pineapple, flour and sugar and place in casserole. Bake at 375 degrees for 10 to 15 minutes. Melt a stick of butter and brown croutons in a skillet. Top casserole with browned croutons. Bake an additional 15 to 20 minutes.

Note: Good with ham and other pork dishes.

Mrs. F. Eugene Brown, Jr.

Hot Fruit Salad

Preheat: 350 degrees
Serves: 24

1 16-ounce can apricot halves
1 16-ounce can pear halves
1 16-ounce can pineapple chunks
1 16-ounce can wild blueberries
Butter

3 large bananas, sliced
1 16-ounce can applesauce
1 16-ounce can cranberry sauce
Brown sugar

Place fruits in colander to drain, blueberries in last. Mix cranberry sauce and applesauce until well blended. Put half of this mixture in bottom of large baking dish. Arrange fruit in dish, then pour remaining sauce over the fruit. Sprinkle with brown sugar and dot with butter. Bake at 350 degrees for 45 minutes.

Mrs. Robert J. Lasker

Brown Sugar Cream

Yield: ½ cup

⅓ cup sour cream

¼ cup brown sugar

Combine and chill. Stir in chilled fruit; such as pineapple, mandarin oranges and bananas.

Mrs. Rennie H. Barnes

Mustard Pears

Serves: 6 to 8

1 30-ounce can Bartlett pear
   halves
1 teaspoon horseradish
¼ cup sugar

¼ cup prepared mustard
2 tablespoons vinegar
Pimento pieces

Drain pear halves, reserving syrup. Combine syrup with sugar, mustard, vinegar and horseradish. Heat to boiling and pour over pears. Let stand several hours or overnight. Serve pears chilled on platter surrounding baked ham. Garnish with pimento pieces.

Mrs. Patrick J. Vaughan

Breads

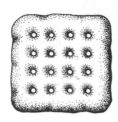

Hardtack

Add flour, with unbleached wheat, to a mixture of water and salt. Mix until a sturdy dough is produced. Roll the dough about ¼-inch thick and cut into squares measuring approximately 3 inch x 3 inch. Prick each square with holes (16 holes was the standard). Bake hardtack squares 45 to 90 minutes at 325 degrees, making sure all moisture is removed from the mixture before taking out of oven.

. . . Extract from the section, "Field and Barrack Cooking for the Army," *Soyer's Cookbook,* 1861.

Spoon Bread

Preheat: 375 degrees
Serves: 6 to 8

1 cup cornmeal	2 cups water
2 teaspoons sugar	2 cups milk
2 teaspoons salt	4 eggs
2 teaspoons butter	4 teaspoons baking powder

Mix cornmeal with water in a saucepan. Stir over medium heat until a bit thick. Add butter to melt while hot. Add salt and sugar. Set aside. Beat eggs and milk well. Add to cornmeal mixture and beat with eggbeater to mix. Last, add the baking powder. Put bacon grease or butter in 1½-quart casserole dish and melt in oven to grease dish. Then add mixture. Bake in 375 degree oven about 1 hour.

Mrs. J. F. Moring

Fort Ward

When the Civil War began in 1861, the city of Washington was practically in the front lines, vulnerable to any attack by land. On the very day of Virginia's secession from the Union, Federal troops crossed the Potomac River, seizing Alexandria and Arlington Heights. The Sixth Alexandria Battalion quickly assembled, marched to the train depot and left to join the Confederate forces.

Construction was immediately begun on a Washington defense network that would eventually include 68 forts and batteries. Fort Ward in Alexandria was the fifth largest fort in this chain, with 36 guns and 5 bastions.

The Northwest Bastion has been carefully restored to look as it did 100 years ago, and a headquarters building and officers' hut have been constructed according to Matthew Brady photographs. One of the country's largest and finest collections of Civil War items is on exhibit in the museum located in the headquarters building.

Fort Ward was named for Commander James Harmon Ward, the first Union naval officer killed in the Civil War.

Bishop's Bread

Preheat: 325 degrees
Yield: 1 loaf

1½ cups sifted flour
½ teaspoon baking powder
¼ teaspoon salt
⅔ cup chocolate chips
2 cups chopped walnuts

1 cup finely chopped dates
1 cup candied cherries
3 eggs
1 cup sugar

Line bottom of 9 x 5 x 3-inch loaf pan with waxed paper. Grease paper and sides of pan. Sift flour, baking powder and salt together. Stir in chocolate chips, walnuts, dates and cherries until well coated with flour. In a large bowl, beat eggs well, gradually add in all sugar. Fold in flour mixture and pour into loaf pan. Bake 1½ hours or until well done. Cool in pan.

Note: Made in colonial times by housewives when expecting the Bishop to visit them. Serve with tea. For a quicker method, use one of the bread mixes and add chocolate chips, walnuts, dates and cherries.

Mrs. William Hersey Bell

Grandma's Famous Cranberry Bread

Preheat: 350 degrees
Yield: 1 loaf

2 cups sifted flour
1 cup sugar
1½ teaspoons baking powder
½ teaspoon baking soda
1 teaspoon salt
¼ cup butter or margarine

1 egg
1 teaspoon grated orange peel
¾ cup orange juice
1½ cups light raisins
1½ cups chopped cranberries, fresh or
    frozen

Sift flour, sugar, baking powder, salt and soda into large bowl. Cut in margarine until mixture is crumbly. Add egg, orange peel and orange juice all at once. Stir just until mixture is evenly moist. Fold in raisins and cranberries. Spoon into greased 9 x 5 x 3-inch loaf pan. Bake in 350 degree oven for 1 hour and 10 minutes or until toothpick comes clean when inserted in center. Remove immediately from pan and cool.

Mrs. Chris W. Ragland

Banana Oatmeal Bread

Preheat: 350 degrees
Yield: 1 loaf

2 cups Bisquick
1 cup oatmeal
¼ teaspoon soda
¾ teaspoon baking powder
½ cup chopped walnuts

½ cup golden raisins
1 egg, beaten
½ cup milk
2½ ripe bananas, mashed

Combine dry ingredients in a large bowl, tossing well. Mix together egg, milk and bananas. Add to flour mixture, stirring just to blend. Turn batter into greased 9x5x3-inch loaf pan. Bake at 350 degrees for 50 to 55 minutes. Turn onto rack and cool before slicing.

Mrs. Ronald Ziegler

Lemon Pecan Bread

Preheat: 350 degrees
Yield: 1 loaf

⅓ cup melted butter
1 cup sugar
2 unbeaten eggs
½ cup sifted all-purpose flour
½ teaspoon baking powder

1 teaspoon salt
½ cup milk
Grated rind of 2 lemons
3 tablespoons lemon juice
½ cup chopped pecans or walnuts

Topping

Juice of 1 lemon and ½ cup sugar

Grease and flour loaf pan and line with waxed paper. Mix sugar, butter and lemon juice. Beat in eggs. Sift dry ingredients together and add to sugar mixture alternately with milk. Beat just enough to blend. Fold in lemon rind and nuts. Pour into 9 x 5 x 3-inch loaf pan and bake 1 hour at 350 degrees. Remove baked bread from pan while still warm. Drizzle lemon-sugar topping over the bread and into the crack that formed while baking.

Note: Best not to cut for 24 hours. Wrap in foil. May be kept 3 months in the refrigerator and up to 1 year in the freezer.

Mrs. Richard Rhame

Irish Soda Bread

Preheat: 375 degrees
Yield: 1 loaf

4 cups all-purpose flour
¼ cup sugar
1 teaspoon salt
1 teaspoon baking powder
¼ cup butter

1 cup seedless raisins
1⅓ cups buttermilk
1 egg
1 teaspoon baking soda

Mix flour, sugar, salt and baking powder. Cut in butter until it resembles coarse corn meal. Stir in raisins. Combine buttermilk, egg and soda. Add to flour mixture until just moistened. Bake in greased 1 quart pan until golden, about 45 to 50 minutes in a 375 degree oven.

Mrs. John J. Ross III

 To sour sweet milk, add 2 tablespoons of white vinegar to 1 cup of sweet milk.

Zucchini Bread

Preheat: 350 degrees
Yield: 2 loaves

2 small unpeeled zucchini, grated
3 eggs
1 cup vegetable oil
2 cups sugar
2 tablespoons vanilla

3 cups flour
1 teaspoon salt
1 teaspoon baking soda
1 tablespoon cinnamon
¼ teaspoon baking powder

In large bowl beat eggs at medium speed until light and frothy. Add oil, sugar, zucchini and vanilla; beat well. Sift remaining ingredients together. Add to zucchini mixture; blend well. Pour batter into two 9 x 5 x 3-inch greased and floured loaf pans. Bake in 350 degree oven for 50 to 60 minutes. Cool loaves in pan on wire rack for 30 mintues before removing to complete cooling.

Note: Loaves may be frozen.

Mrs. Thomas T. Bellino

Strawberry Bread

Preheat: 350 degrees
Yield: 2 loaves

3 cups flour
1 teaspoon salt
1 tablespoon cinnamon
1 teaspoon baking soda
2 cups sugar
3 eggs, beaten

1¼ cups cooking oil
2 10-ounce packages frozen sliced
   strawberries, thawed and drained
1¼ cups chopped pecans

Combine all dry ingredients in large bowl. Make a well in the center. Add eggs and oil. Stir until moistened. Stir in strawberries and pecans. Put mixture in 2 lightly greased loaf pans. Bake at 350 degrees for one hour or until done.

Mrs. Robert Silver

Pumpkin Bread

Preheat: 350 degrees
Yield: 2 loaves

3⅓ cups sifted flour
3 cups sugar
1 teaspoon nutmeg
1 cup oil
1 teaspoon cinnamon
2 teaspoons soda

1½ teaspoons salt
⅔ cup water
4 eggs
2 cups pumpkin
1 cup chopped pecans

Mix all ingredients together. Pour into 2 greased and floured 9 x 5 x 3-inch loaf pans. Bake at 350 degrees for 1 hour.

Note: Delicious with cream cheese or whipped butter.

Mrs. Carlyle C. Ring, Jr.

Apricot Bread

Preheat: 350 degrees
Yield: 2 loaves

1 6-ounce package dried apricots
1 cup boiling water
4 tablespoons butter
1½ cups sugar
2 lightly beaten eggs

3 cups flour
2 teaspoons soda
½ teaspoon salt
1 cup nuts

Cover apricots with water and let stand 15 minutes. Cream butter with sugar; add eggs, apricots and water. Mix flour, soda, salt together and blend into apricot mixture. Add nuts. Pour into 2 greased 9 x 5 x 3-inch loaf pans. Bake at 350 degrees for 45 to 60 minutes. Serve with butter or cream cheese.

Mrs. John Smithers

Mama's Corn Bread

Preheat: 425 degrees
Serves: 8 to 12

1½ cups yellow corn meal
½ cup flour
¼ cup sugar
½ teaspoon salt

3 rounded teaspoons baking powder
1 cup milk
¼ cup oil
1 egg

Place corn meal, flour, sugar, salt and baking powder in large bowl. Add milk, oil and egg and mix until blended and not lumpy. Bake in hot greased 11¼ x 7½ x 1½-inch pan at 425 degrees for 15 to 20 minutes.

Mrs. William Sanders, Jr.

Dilly Bread

Preheat: 350 degrees
Yield: 1 loaf

1 package cake yeast
¼ cup warm water
1 cup cottage cheese, heated to
 lukewarm
2 tablespoons sugar
1 tablespoon instant minced onion

1 unbeaten egg
1 tablespoon butter
2 teaspoons dill seed
1 teaspoon salt
¼ teaspoon soda
2¼ cups flour

Soften yeast in water. Combine in large mixing bowl: yeast, cottage cheese, sugar, onion, butter, dill seed, soda, salt and egg. Add flour gradually, beating well after each addition. Cover and let stand until double in size, about 50 to 60 minutes. Stir dough down, turn into well greased 9 x 5 x 3-inch pan or 1-quart round casserole. Let dough rise again for 40 to 50 minutes until it's light in consistency. Bake 45 to 50 minutes at 350 degrees; top will be very brown. Immediately upon removing from the oven, brush the top with butter and sprinkle with salt.

Mrs. Donald Burchell

Herb Bread

Preheat: 350 degrees
Yield: 1 loaf

½ pound butter or margarine
1½ tablespoons Italian Seasonings
1 tablespoon garlic salt
1 loaf French or Italian bread

Soften butter and thoroughly mix in seasonings. Slice loaf into 1-inch slices. Butter both sides of each slice with the herb butter. Wrap loaf in heavy duty aluminum foil, sealing all edges. Bake 30 minutes at 350 degrees; unwrap foil and bake an additional 5 minutes.

Note: Great with lasagna, spaghetti, stroganoff, etc.

Mrs. Carlyle C. Ring, Jr.

Beer Bread

Preheat: 350 degrees
Yield: 1 loaf

3 cups self-rising flour
2 tablespoons sugar
1 bottle or can (12-ounce) beer at room temperature

Mix (only 17 to 20 strokes) all ingredients. Place in greased 9 x 5 x 3-inch loaf pan. Bake in oven preheated to 350 degrees for 1 hour — possibly 15 minutes longer if not browned. Bake until lightly browned on top and sides of loaf pull away from the pan. Brush with butter halfway through baking time.

Note: So easy, you can have hot bread with almost no preparation time!

Mrs. Michael E. Delnegro

Veteflätor
(Swedish Coffee Bread)

Preheat: 375 degrees
Yield: 2 braids

2 packages dry yeast
¼ teaspoon ginger
1 teaspoon sugar
¼ cup warm water
1 cup milk

1 tablespoon butter
½ teaspoon salt
½ cup sugar
1 egg (¾ in dough, ¼ reserved)
3½ to 4 cups flour

Dissolve yeast in warm water with ginger and one teaspoon sugar. (Ginger chemically reacts with yeast; let it bubble about 15 minutes; it makes bread moist.) Melt butter and add milk; chill until lukewarm. Mix all ingredients with half of flour until smooth and elastic, adding more flour gradually, saving about 1 cup of flour. Sprinkle dough with small amount of flour. Cover with a towel and let rise in a warm place until double in bulk, approximately 50 to 60 minutes. Punch down dough and turn onto floured board. Knead until smooth, adding small amounts of flour gradually, if necessary. Divide dough into two parts to make two braids. Cut each portion into three equal parts. Shape parts into strands, 12 inches long. Braid. Place on greased sheet. Cover and let rise until double, about 45 minutes. Brush with beaten egg. Bake in 375 degree oven for 20 minutes.

Mrs. Renny H. Barnes

Shredded Wheat Bread

Preheat: 325 degrees
Yield: 2 loaves

4 shredded wheat biscuits,
   crushed
2 teaspoons salt
¼ cup shortening
1 pint milk

1 pint water
1 cup molasses
2 packages dry yeast
5 cups whole wheat flour
5 or more cups all-purpose flour

Scald milk, add water, molasses and shortening. Add 3 cups whole wheat flour, yeast, salt and shredded wheat. Mix 2 minutes at medium speed. Work in remaining whole wheat flour and about 5 cups of white flour. Knead well. Place in large greased bowl to rise until double in bulk (about 2 hours). Work down and place in greased bread pans to double in size again. Bake for 50 to 60 minutes at 325 degrees.

Mrs. Chris W. Ragland

Grandmother's Never-Fail Popovers

Yield: 1 dozen

1 cup flour
1 cup milk

2 eggs
½ teaspoon salt

Thoroughly grease muffin tins. Add milk to eggs and beat well. Gradually add flour and salt. Pour into muffin tins until ½ full. Place in cold oven. Turn oven to 450 degrees and bake for 35 minutes. Serve immediately piping hot.

Mrs. E. Darryl Barnes

Sally Lunn Bread

Preheat: 350 degrees
Yield: 2 loaves

2 cups milk, scalded
½ cup sugar
2 teaspoons salt
½ cup plus 2 tablespoons
  shortening

2 packages yeast
3 eggs, beaten until very light
6 cups flour

Pour scalded milk over sugar, salt and shortening. Stir until dissolved. Cool to lukewarm. Stir in yeast and eggs. Stir and beat vigorously after adding flour in 1 cup increments. Beat until smooth. Cover and let rise until double in bulk, about 1 hour. Stir down batter and place in well greased 10-inch tube pan or 2 loaf pans. Cover and let rise again until doubled, about 1 hour.

If you prefer rolls or buns, grease a muffin tin and shape into balls and place in muffin tins. Bake in a 350 degree oven for about 30 minutes. Turn out on a rack and cool slightly. Serve warm with butter.

Mrs. E. Darryl Barnes

Raisin Bran Muffins

Preheat: 400 degrees
Yield: 8 dozen

3 cups sugar
5 cups flour
5 teaspoons baking soda
1 tablespoon pumpkin pie spice
2 teaspoons salt

4 beaten eggs
1 cup melted butter or margarine
1 quart buttermilk
1 15-ounce box raisin bran cereal

Mix all ingredients together. Fill 2-inch muffin tins two-thirds full and bake at 400 degrees for 15 to 20 minutes.

Note: Dough will keep in refrigerator up to 6 weeks. Great to have on hand for house guests.

Mrs. Patrick J. Vaughan

Blueberry Muffins

Preheat: 375 degrees
Yield: 28 muffins

½ cup butter
1 cup sugar
2 eggs
1¾ cups sifted flour
1 teaspoon baking powder
¾ teaspoon soda

¼ teaspoon salt
¼ teaspoon nutmeg
Dash of ground cloves
¾ cup buttermilk
¾ cup blueberries
⅓ cup sugar and grated orange peel

Cream butter and sugar until light. Add eggs one at a time; beat well. Sift all dry ingredients; add to creamed mixture alternately with buttermilk. Beat well. Fold in blueberries. Fill paper-lined 2-inch muffin pans two-thirds full. Bake 20 to 25 minutes at 375 degrees. Dip muffin tops in melted butter and then in the sugar and orange peel mixture.

Note: Also works well in miniature muffin tins.

Mrs. James R. Skidmore

Sweet Potato Muffins

Preheat: 400 degrees
Yield: 24 muffins

1¼ cups sugar
1¼ cups cooked, mashed sweet
  potatoes (fresh or canned)
½ cup butter, room temperature
2 large eggs, room temperature
1½ cups flour
2 teaspoons baking powder
1 teaspoon cinnamon

¼ teaspoon nutmeg
¼ teaspoon salt
1 cup milk
½ cup chopped raisins
¼ cup chopped walnuts or pecans
2 tablespoons sugar mixed with ¼
  teaspoon cinnamon

Thoroughly grease 24 muffin cups. Beat sugar, sweet potatoes and butter until smooth. Add eggs and blend well. Sift together flour, baking powder, spices and salt. Add alternately with milk to sweet potato mixture, stirring just to blend. Do not overmix. Fold in raisins and nuts. Spoon into 2-inch muffin cups and sprinkle each with sugar and cinnamon mixture. Bake 25 to 30 minutes or until muffins test done. Serve warm.

Note: May be frozen

Ms. Elizabeth J. Noyes

Applesauce Puffs

Preheat: 400 degrees
Yield: 24 to 30

2 cups packaged biscuit mix
¼ cup sugar
1 teaspoon cinnamon
½ cup applesauce

¼ cup milk
1 slightly beaten egg
2 tablespoons oil

Glaze

¼ cup sugar
2 tablespoons melted butter

¼ teaspoon cinnamon

Beat all ingredients together 30 seconds. Fill greased 2-inch muffin pans two-thirds full. Bake at 400 degrees for 12 minutes. Cool slightly. Dip tops in cinnamon glaze.

Mrs. Wallace W. Edens

Spoon Rolls

Preheat: 350 degrees
Yield: 2 dozen

1 package dry yeast
2 cups very warm water
½ cup margarine

¼ cup sugar
1 egg, beaten
4 cups self-rising flour

Place yeast in warm water. Melt margarine and cream with sugar in large bowl. Add beaten egg and dissolved yeast to creamed mixture. Add flour and stir until well mixed. Place in airtight bowl and refrigerate. To bake, drop by spoonfuls into well-greased 2½-inch muffin tins and bake for 20 minutes or until browned. Dough keeps for several days.

Mrs. Alfred E. T. Rusch

Cinnamon Rolls

Preheat: 375 degrees
Yield: 3 dozen

⅔ cup milk
½ cup sugar
⅓ cup shortening
1¼ teaspoons salt
⅔ cup warm water

2 packages dry yeast
2 tablespoons sugar
3 eggs, beaten
6 cups all-purpose flour

Scald milk; add ½ cup sugar, shortening and salt, stirring until sugar dissolves and shortening melts. Cool mixture to lukewarm. Meanwhile, combine water, yeast and 2 tablespoons sugar in a large bowl; let stand 5 minutes. Stir in milk mixture, eggs, and 3 cups flour; beat until mixture is smooth. Add remaining flour, one cup at a time, stirring well until a soft dough is formed. Turn dough out on a floured surface, knead until smooth and elastic (5 to 8 minutes). Place in a well- greased bowl, turning to grease top. Cover tightly, and let rise in a warm place, free of drafts, for 1 to 1½ hours or until doubled in bulk. Punch dough down and divide in half. Roll out into a rectangle about ¼ inch thick. Spread with butter and sprinkle with cinnamon, sugar and add raisins if desired. Roll up in jelly roll fashion. Cut into rolls. Let rise until double in size. Bake at 375 degrees for 30 minutes.

Mrs. Philip A. Wells

Sticky Pull-Apart Rolls

Preheat: 350 degrees
Yield: 2 loaves

1 3¾ or 4-ounce package regular
butterscotch pudding mix
1 cup chopped walnuts or pecans
½ cup brown sugar

4 tablespoons butter, softened
1 teaspoon cinnamon
2 16-ounce loaves frozen bread dough,
thawed

In mixing bowl combine all ingredients except dough. Stir until crumbly. Cut bread in half lengthwise, then in 8 pieces crosswise (16 pieces per loaf). Sprinkle ¼ of the topping into each of 2 greased 9 x 5 x 3-inch loaf pans. Arrange 16 dough pieces in each pan. Sprinkle each with ½ of the remaining topping. Cover and let rise in a warm place until almost double, about 1 hour. Bake in 350 degree oven for 35 to 40 minutes. Turn out of pans immediately. Serve warm.

Mrs. Donald Burchell

Oatmeal Applesauce Bread

Preheat: 350 degrees
Yield: 1 loaf

1½ cups all-purpose flour
1 cup applesauce
½ cup brown sugar
⅓ cup oil
2 eggs
1½ teaspoons salt

1 teaspoon baking soda
1 teaspoon baking powder
1 teaspoon cinnamon
1½ cups quick cooking oats, uncooked
1 cup seedless raisins

Using medium speed of electric mixer, mix flour, applesauce, sugar, oil, eggs, salt, soda, baking powder and cinnamon until well blended. Stir in oats and raisins. Bake 1 hour at 350 degrees in greased 9 x 5 x 3-inch loaf pan.

Mrs. Richard Rhame

Hot Cross Buns

Preheat: 400 degrees
Yield: 36

1 cup milk
2 tablespoons butter
1 package dry yeast
¼ cup warm water
4 cups sifted unbleached
  all-purpose flour
⅓ cup sugar
¾ teaspoon salt

¾ teaspoon cinnamon
¼ teaspoon cloves
¼ teaspoon nutmeg
¾ cup currants
½ cup diced dried apricots
2 eggs, well beaten
1 egg yolk diluted with 1 teaspoon
  water

Scald milk, stir in butter and cool until lukewarm. Dissolve yeast in water. Sift flour again with sugar, salt and spices. Combine flour mixture with currants and apricots. Stir in eggs, cooled milk and yeast. Blend well. Turn dough out on lightly floured board and knead until smooth and elastic. Place in greased bowl; cover and let rise in a warm place until doubled in size, about 1½ hours. Stir down dough, pinch off pieces and form smooth rounded balls about 1¼ inches in diameter. Place the balls of dough on a lightly greased cookie sheet about 2 inches apart. Cover and let buns rise in a warm place until doubled in bulk, about 20 minutes. Brush each bun lightly with egg yolk and water topping. Bake at 400 degrees for about 10 minutes or at 350 degrees for 20 minutes or until lightly browned. Cool on racks for 5 minutes. With a spoon, drizzle lemon frosting on top of each bun to form a small cross. Serve warm.

Lemon Frosting

1 cup sifted confectioners' sugar
2 teaspoons lemon juice

1 teaspoon water

Add ingredients and beat until smooth. May add 1 tablespoon rum if desired.

Note: May be frozen, but omit frosting. Heat frozen buns in 400 degree oven for 3 to 5 minutes. Cool and drizzle frosting on top.

Mrs. Joseph E. Hinds

Orange French Toast

Serves: 1 to 2

1 egg
½ cup orange juice
3 tablespoons sugar
1½ teaspoons orange rind

¼ cup butter
Sliced bread
Powdered sugar
1 orange, peeled and sliced

Beat egg with orange juice. Add sugar and orange rind. Mix well. Dip slice of bread in egg mixture. Brown on both sides in butter over low heat. Garnish with orange slice on each piece of toast. Sprinkle with powdered sugar.

Note: Sugar substitute can successfully be used to reduce calories.

Mrs. James W. Vaughan, Jr.

Special Breakfast Popovers

Preheat: 425 degrees
Yield: 8 to 12

1 cup all-purpose flour
½ teaspoon salt
¾ cup milk

2 tablespoons honey
1 tablespoon melted butter
2 large eggs

Sift flour and salt together. Add the milk, honey and melted butter. Stir to blend. Beat in the eggs. Fill greased 2 or 2½- inch muffin tins just under half full. Bake 25 to 30 minutes at 425 degrees (watch carefully) or until sides are rigid and the top and sides of the popovers are brown. Do not open the oven until you think they are done, or the popovers will fall and not rise again. If popovers are preferred dry inside, slit each with a sharp knife and bake 5 minutes longer. Serve with honey butter.

Note: This is a great breakfast treat for children. For regular popovers omit honey and butter.

Mrs. Ronald K. Ziegler

Sour Cream Coffee Cake

Preheat: 350 degrees
Serves: 12

1 cup granulated sugar
½ cup soft shortening
2 eggs
½ pint sour cream
1 teaspoon vanilla
2 teaspoons cinnamon
2 tablespoons soft butter

2 cups flour
1 teaspoon baking soda
1 rounded teaspoon baking powder
½ teaspoon salt
⅓ cup brown sugar
½ cup chopped walnuts or pecans

Blend granulated sugar, shortening, eggs, sour cream and vanilla. Sift together flour, baking soda, baking powder and salt. Stir flour mixture into sugar mixture and beat well. In a small bowl, mix brown sugar, nuts, cinnamon and butter with a pastry blender. Put one half of batter into greased tube pan. Sprinkle one half of nut mixture over batter in pan. Add remaining batter and top with remaining nut mixture. Bake 45 to 50 minutes in pan.

Mrs. Robert K. Wineland

Soft Pretzels

Preheat: 425 degrees
Yield: 12

1 package dry yeast
1½ cups warm water
⅛ teaspoon ground ginger
1 tablespoon sugar
1 teaspoon salt

4 cups flour
1 egg, slightly beaten
Coarse salt
Sesame seed (optional)

Dissolve yeast in warm water, and stir in ginger. Add sugar and salt. Blend in flour. Turn out dough on lightly floured surface. Knead until smooth. Cut into 12 pieces. Roll into ropes and twist into pretzel shapes. Arrange on a lightly greased cookie sheet. Brush with beaten egg. Sprinkle generously with salt and sesame seeds. Bake at 425 degrees for 15 minutes or until browned.

Note: Should be eaten the same day.

Mrs. Robert L. Calhoun

Desserts

George Washington Cake, 1780

Preheat: 350 degrees

1 cup butter or margarine
1½ cups sugar
2 eggs, separated
2 cups sifted all-purpose flour
2 teaspoons baking powder
½ teaspoon ground mace
½ teaspoon ground cinnamon

½ teaspoon salt
½ cup milk
½ cup seedless raisins, cut in pieces
¼ cup currants
3 tablespoons finely chopped citron
1 tablespoon flour

Cream butter and sugar until smooth. Beat in egg yolks. Sift flour, baking powder, mace, cinnamon and salt together. Add to butter mixture alternately with milk, beginning and ending with dry ingredients; blend well. Combine fruits with one tablespoon flour. Toss until fruits are covered with flour. Stir into batter. Beat egg whites until stiff but not dry. Fold into batter. Spread in two 8-inch greased layer-cake pans lined with greased wax paper. Bake 55 minutes or until top is golden brown and cake is firm. Cool 10 minutes, then remove from pans. Cool thoroughly. Frost with Butter Cream Icing.

Butter Cream Icing

1 pound confectioners' sugar
½ cup butter, softened

1 teaspoon vanilla
3 to 4 tablespoons cream

Sift sugar. Blend butter, vanilla and half of the sugar. Beat in remaining sugar. Add cream gradually, adding just enough to make a smooth frosting of good spreading consistency. Frost cake. Garnish with pecan halves and cut pieces of citron if desired.

Mrs. Donald Burchell

Mt. Vernon

As a homesite, Mount Vernon was patented by the Washington family in 1674. George Washington took up residence in 1754, enlarged the main house, built several outbuildings, landscaped the grounds and thus created one of the finest and most thoughtfully designed estates of his era.

Washington was very proud of his home on the banks of the Potomac River and it was here that he and Martha entertained friends, family, and visiting dignitaries on the wide verandas and broad lawns that afforded a panorama of the river and the Maryland and Virginia countryside.

The house was enlarged in at least five different stages and Washington incorporated many of the architectural styles and conveniences popular in England at that time.

George Washington was also an astute businessman. He was one of the first planters to turn to wheat. The soil at Mount Vernon did not produce a good tobacco crop so he established a grist mill and made flour from the wheat which proved more profitable. The grist mill still operates today.

The restoration and maintenance of the estate was undertaken by the Mt. Vernon Ladies' Association in 1853. They continue in this effort today. Purchases, donations, loans and bequests have enabled many of the original pieces to be returned to Mount Vernon.

Banana Cake

Preheat: 375 degrees

2 cups sifted cake flour
1 teaspoon baking soda
1 teaspoon baking powder
½ teaspoon salt
¾ cup shortening
2 eggs

1 teaspoon vanilla
½ cup buttermilk
½ cup chopped pecans
1 cup flaked coconut
1½ cups sugar
1 cup mashed bananas

Sift together cake flour, baking soda, baking powder and salt. Cream together shortening and sugar until light and fluffy. Add eggs, one at a time, beating well after each addition. Beat in bananas and vanilla; blend well. Add dry ingredients alternately with buttermilk, beating well after each addition. Stir in pecans. Pour batter into 2 greased and floured 9-inch round cake pans. Sprinkle top of each with ½ cup coconut. Bake in 375 degree oven 25 to 30 minutes or until cakes test done. Cool in pans on racks 10 minutes. Remove from pans; cool on racks. Place first layer, coconut side down, and spread with Pecan Filling. Top with second layer, coconut side up. Spread with Fluffy Frosting on sides and about 1 inch around top edge, leaving center unfrosted.

Pecan Filling
½ cup sugar
2 tablespoons flour
½ cup light cream
2 tablespoons butter or margarine

½ cup chopped pecans
¼ teaspoon salt
1 teaspoon vanilla

Combine sugar, flour, cream and butter in small heavy saucepan. Cook over medium heat, stirring constantly until thickened. Add pecans, salt and vanilla. Mix well. Cool well.

Fluffy Frosting
1 egg white
¼ cup shortening
¼ cup butter or margarine

1 teaspoon vanilla
2 cups sifted confectioners' sugar

Combine egg white, shortening, butter and vanilla. Beat until smooth and creamy. Gradually add confectioners' sugar, beating until light and fluffy.

Gordon L. Cluka, Chef
Cates Restaurant and Bakery

Ada's Boston Cream Pie

Preheat: 350 degrees
Serves: 8 to 10

Cake

1 cup sifted flour
½ teaspoon salt
1 teaspoon baking powder
1 tablespoon shortening

½ cup milk
2 eggs
1 cup sugar
1 teaspoon vanilla

Sift flour, baking powder and salt. Set aside. Add shortening to milk and heat in a double boiler. Beat eggs until thick and light, beat in sugar gradually. Add vanilla, then blend in hot milk. Fold flour mixture into liquid. Pour batter into greased 9-inch cake pan. Cook at 350 degrees for 25 to 30 minutes. Split while warm.

Custard

¼ cup sugar
¼ cup flour
¼ teaspoon salt
2 cups milk

2 tablespoons butter
2 eggs, beaten
1½ teaspoons vanilla

Mix flour, sugar, and salt in double boiler. Add milk slowly to make a smooth mixture. Stir and cook over hot water until thick, cover and cook 10 minutes. Add butter and beaten eggs, mixing quickly. Cook one minute more, cool, add vanilla.

Frosting

1 square unsweetened chocolate
2 teaspoons butter
¼ cup milk

1 cup confectioners' sugar
½ teaspoon vanilla

Melt chocolate and butter slowly in milk and let stand until lukewarm. Add sugar and vanilla.

Assembly: Frost top of one half of cake with custard, top with second cake layer and frost top only with chocolate mixture. This cake is supposed to be very heavy.

Mrs. William Heenan

Carrot Cake

Preheat: 350 degrees

1 yellow cake mix
1 3-ounce package vanilla instant
  pudding
4 eggs
⅓ cup oil
3 cups grated carrots

½ cup raisins
½ cup chopped walnuts
2 teaspoons cinnamon
Pinch of salt
⅓ cup water

Mix all ingredients well. Put in a greased and floured Bundt pan. Bake at 350 degrees for 45-50 minutes.

Mrs. John Fitch, Jr.

Carrot Cake Icing

1 8-ounce package cream cheese
1 stick margarine
1 pound box confectioners' sugar

1 teaspoon vanilla
1 cup chopped pecans

Beat all ingredients well. Spread on cake.

Gordon L. Cluka, Chef
Cates Restaurant and Bakery

Blueberry Batter Cake

Preheat: 375 degrees
Serves: 6 to 8

2 cups blueberries or 2 cans
  packed in water, drained
3 tablespoons butter
Juice of ½ lemon
1¾ cups sugar
1 cup flour

1 teaspoon baking powder
1 teaspoon salt
½ cup milk
1 tablespoon cornstarch
1 cup boiling water

Wash blueberries and pour into large iron skillet or 8 x 8-inch cake pan. Sprinkle with lemon juice. Cream butter and ¾ cup sugar and then add flour, baking powder, ½ teaspoon salt and milk. Spread this batter over berries. Combine 1 cup sugar, ½ teaspoon salt and cornstarch. Sprinkle over batter. Pour boiling water over all. Bake 1 hour at 375 degrees.

Mrs. Stephen Shaffer

Cheesecake Supreme

Preheat: 400 degrees
Serves: 12

Crust

1 cup sifted all-purpose flour
1/4 cup sugar
1 teaspoon grated fresh lemon peel

1/2 cup butter
1 slightly beaten egg yolk
1/4 teaspoon vanilla

Combine first 3 ingredients. Cut in butter in mixture until crumbly. Add egg yolk and vanilla. Blend thoroughly. Pat 1/3 of dough on bottom of 9-inch springform pan (sides removed). Bake in hot 400 degree oven for about 8 minutes or until golden brown; cool. Attach sides to bottom; butter and pat remaining dough on sides to height of 1¾ inches.

Filling

5 8-ounce packages cream cheese
1/4 teaspoon vanilla
3/4 teaspoon grated lemon peel
1¾ cups sugar
3 tablespoons all-purpose flour

1/4 teaspoon salt
4 or 5 eggs (1 cup)
2 egg yolks
1/4 cup whipping cream

Let cream cheese stand at room temperature to soften (1 to 1⅓ hours); beat until creamy. Add vanilla and lemon peel. Mix sugar, flour and salt; gradually blend into cheese. Add eggs and egg yolks one at a time, beating after each just to blend. Gently stir in whipping cream. Turn into crust-lined pan. Bake at 450 degrees for 12 minutes; reduce heat to 300 degrees and continue baking 55 minutes. Remove from oven; cool. Loosen sides with spatula after 30 minutes. Remove sides at end of 1 hour. Allow to cool 2 hours longer.

Strawberry Glaze

2 or 3 cups fresh strawberries
1 cup water

1½ tablespoons cornstarch
1/2 to 3/4 cup sugar

Crush 1 cup of strawberries; add water and cook 2 minutes; sieve. Mix cornstarch with sugar (amount of sugar depends on sweetness of berries.) Stir into hot berry mix. Bring to boil, stirring constantly until thick and clear. Cool to room temperature. Place remaining berries atop cooled cheesecake, pointed end up. Circle with halved pineapple rings if desired. Pour glaze over fruit. Chill 2 hours.

Mrs. James R. Skidmore

Creamy Cocoa Cheesecake

Preheat: 375 degrees
Serves: 10 to 12

1 9-inch graham cracker crumb
  crust in springform pan
2 8-ounce packages cream cheese
¾ cup plus 2 tablespoons sugar

⅓ cup cocoa
2 teaspoons vanilla
2 eggs
1 cup sour cream

Combine cream cheese, ¾ cup sugar, cocoa and 1 teaspoon vanilla, mixing at medium speed. Blend well. Add eggs one at a time. Pour mixture over crumbs. Bake 30 minutes. Remove from oven. Cool 15 minutes. Increase oven temperature to 425 degrees. Combine sour cream, 2 tablespoons sugar and 1 teaspoon vanilla. Spread sour cream mixture carefully over baked filling. Return to oven for 10 minutes. Loosen cake from rim of pan. Cool before removing. Chill.

Mrs. Renny H. Barnes

Praline Cheesecake

Preheat: 350 degrees
Serves: 10 to 12

1 cup graham cracker crumbs
3 tablespoons sugar
3 tablespoons melted butter
3 8-ounce packages cream cheese
¼ cup dark brown sugar

2 tablespoons flour
3 eggs
½ cup chopped pecans
1½ teaspoons vanilla

Combine crumbs, sugar and butter. Press into bottom of 9-inch springform pan. Bake at 350 degrees for 10 minutes. Mixing at medium speed, combine softened cream cheese, brown sugar and flour until well blended. Add eggs one at a time mixing well after each addition. Blend in vanilla and nuts. Pour mixture over crust and bake at 350 degrees for 50 to 55 minutes.

Mrs. H. Franklin Green III

Chocolate Chip Bundt Cake

Preheat: 350 degrees

1 18½-ounce package chocolate
   cake mix
1 3-ounce package chocolate
   instant pudding

2 eggs
1½ cups milk
1 12-ounce package chocolate chips

Mix all ingredients together and put in a greased and floured bundt pan. Bake at 350 degrees for 45 to 50 minutes.

Mrs. John Fitch, Jr.

Chocolate Peppermint Ice Cream Cake

Serves: 10 to 12

2 layers devil's food cake
1 6-ounce package chocolate chips
1 teaspoon peppermint extract

Milk (enough to thin melted chips)
1 quart lime sherbet

Spread lime sherbet on top of one of the cooled layers and freeze. In a double boiler melt the chips and slowly add enough milk to thin the chocolate. Bring the chocolate to a boil and add the peppermint. Cool the chocolate mixture. Put the second layer on the cake and pour chocolate mixture over the 2 layer cake. Place entire cake in the freezer. Remove from freezer 10 minutes before serving.

Mrs. Daniel Little

Hot Fudge Sundae Cake

Preheat: 350 degrees
Serves: 9

1 cup self-rising flour
¾ cup sugar
¼ cup plus 2 tablespoons cocoa
½ cup milk

2 tablespoons oil
1 teaspoon vanilla
1 cup brown sugar
1¾ cups hot water

Mix flour, sugar and 2 tablespoons cocoa. Add milk, oil and vanilla. Spread evenly in ungreased 9-inch square pan. Sprinkle with brown sugar, ¼ cup cocoa. Pour water over cake mixture. Bake 40 minutes at 350 degrees. Serve warm with vanilla ice cream.

Mrs. John Smithers

DESSERTS

Crazy Chocolate Cake

Preheat: 350 degrees
Serves: 16

1½ cups all purpose flour
1 cup sugar
5 tablespoons cocoa
1 teaspoon baking soda
½ teaspoon salt

5 tablespoons oil
1 teaspoon white vinegar
1 teaspoon vanilla
1 cup water

Sift first 5 ingredients into 8-inch square baking pan and mix well. Make 3 holes in mixture and pour oil, vinegar and vanilla into holes. Add water and mix very well. Bake 30 minutes.

Frosting

2 cups confectioners' sugar
½ cup butter, room temperature
3 tablespoons cocoa

3 tablespoons hot water
½ teaspoon vanilla or strong coffee

Combine ingredients in small bowl and stir until smooth. Spread over cooled cake. Cut into squares.

Ms. Elizabeth J. Noyes

Coal Miner's Cake

Preheat: 350 degrees

4 squares unsweetened chocolate
2 cups sugar
1½ cups milk
1 teaspoon vanilla

½ cup butter
3 eggs
2 cups flour
2 teaspoons baking powder

Place chocolate, one cup of sugar and ¾ cup milk in saucepan. Cook until well combined. Let cool and add vanilla. Set aside. In mixing bowl cream butter and remaining sugar. Add eggs and mix. Add flour, baking powder and ¾ cup milk. Add cooled chocolate mixture. Pour into two 8 or 9-inch greased layer cake pans. Bake in 350 degree oven for 25 to 30 minutes. Frost with vanilla or cocoa frosting.

Note: This recipe comes from the Pennsylvania mining towns.

Mrs. John P. Glynn

Chocolate Mousse Cake

Preheat: 200 degrees
Serves: 6 to 8

36 ladyfingers
12 ounces dark sweet chocolate
5 tablespoons strong black coffee
 (if instant use 1 teaspoon per
 cup)

¼ cup sugar
2 tablespoons vanilla
6 eggs, separated
1 cup whipping cream, whipped

Line a 10-inch springform pan with ladyfingers. Set aside. Melt chocolate in metal bowl in 200 degree oven. Add coffee, sugar and vanilla. Stir until smooth, cool slightly. Beat egg yolks until light. Add to coffee mixture. Add melted chocolate, stirring by hand. Beat egg whites until stiff but not dry. Fold half of egg whites into chocolate mixture, then fold other half into whipped cream. Fold whipped cream into chocolate mixture. Pour half of mixture into lined springform pan. Place a layer of ladyfingers on top. Pour remaining mixture on top. Refrigerate. Top with nuts or chocolate shavings when ready to serve.

Note: Makes a nice presentation for entertaining.

Mrs. Timothy Geary

Harvey Wallbanger Cake

Preheat: 340 degrees

1 box yellow cake mix
1 3¾-ounce box vanilla instant
 pudding
1 scant cup oil

4 eggs
¼ cup vodka
¼ cup Galliano liqueur
⅔ cup orange juice

Combine above ingredients and beat well for 4 minutes. Pour into greased bundt or tube pan. Bake in 340 degree oven for 55 minutes. Cool 30 minutes in pan.

Glaze

¼ cup water
½ cup butter

1 cup sugar
¼ cup orange juice

Mix above ingredients in small saucepan. Boil 4 minutes. Pour glaze over cake while warm and still in pan. Cool for 30 minutes and turn out on cake plate.

Mrs. James W. Vaughan, Jr.

Gateau Au Citron

Preheat: 350 degrees
Serves: 8

1 fresh lemon
½ cup granulated sugar
½ cup unsalted butter

2 large eggs
1 cup less 2 tablespoons flour
1 teaspoon baking powder

Peel lemon taking only yellow. Use steel knife. Add peel and start pouring granulated sugar through feed spout of food processor. Process 20 seconds after all sugar is in. Add butter cut in 4 pieces, and eggs one at a time processing about 15 seconds or until smooth after each addition. Scrape down as needed. Fill a measuring cup half full of flour and stir in the teaspoon of baking powder. Add remaining flour. Remove the cover and add flour to mixture. Replace cover; turn machine off and on 2 or 3 times until flour just disappears. Place batter in a buttered and floured 8-inch cake pan. Bake at 350 degrees in center of oven for 25 minutes or until light golden brown and springy to touch. Let stand a few minutes and remove to a rack to cool. Prepare Lemon Glaze.

Lemon Glaze

Juice of 1 lemon   ½ cup confectioners' sugar

Mix lemon juice with confectioners' sugar. Spoon some of this mixture over the cake. Repeat while cake is cooling until all of lemon juice mixture is used up.

Note: This cake keeps well, covered in the refrigerator.

Mrs. Robert Anderson

Pecan Pound Cake

Preheat: 325 degrees
Serves: 15

1 cup butter
2 cups sugar
5 eggs
2 cups all-purpose flour

1 teaspoon vanilla
1 teaspoon butter flavoring
1 cup chopped pecans

Cream butter and sugar until light and fluffy. Add eggs, one at a time; beat well after each addition. Beat in flour. Add flavorings and pecans. Pour into greased and floured tube pan. Bake at 325 degrees for 1 hour. Remove from pan immediately.

Mrs. Alan E. Mowbray

Hummingbird Cake

Preheat: 350 degrees

3 cups flour
2 cups sugar
1 teaspoon salt
1 teaspoon soda
1 teaspoon cinnamon
3 eggs, beaten

1½ cups salad oil
1½ teaspoons vanilla
1 8-ounce can crushed pineapple
 (undrained)
2 cups chopped pecans or walnuts
2 cups chopped bananas

Combine dry ingredients in large bowl, add eggs and salad oil stirring until moistened. Do not beat. Stir in vanilla, pineapple, 1 cup chopped pecans, and bananas. Spoon batter into 3 well-greased and floured 9-inch cake pans. Bake at 350 degrees for 25 to 30 minutes or until done. Cool in pans 10 minutes. Remove from pans and cool completely. Spread cream cheese frosting between layers and on top of cake. Sprinkle with one cup of chopped pecans.

Cream Cheese Frosting

6 ounces cream cheese
6 tablespoons butter

3 cups confectioners' sugar
1 teaspoon vanilla

Cream butter and cheese. Add sugar and vanilla. Mix until smooth.

Mrs. Robert Silver

Kentucky Jam Cake

Preheat: 350 degrees

1½ cups softened butter
1 cup packed brown sugar
3 eggs
1¾ cups sifted flour
1 teaspoon baking soda
1 teaspoon ground nutmeg

1 teaspoon cinnamon
½ teaspoon ground cloves
1 12-ounce jar blackberry jam
3 tablespoons buttermilk
½ cup golden raisins
½ cup chopped walnuts

Cream butter and sugar until light and fluffy. Beat in eggs one at a time, beating well after each addition. Combine flour, baking soda, nutmeg, cinnamon and cloves. Add flour mixture alternately with jam and buttermilk to butter mixture, beating well after each addition. Stir in raisins and walnuts. Pour into greased and floured 9-inch tube pan. Bake at 350 degrees for 55 to 60 minutes. Unmold immediately onto wire rack. Cool. Frost with caramel frosting.

Mrs. H. Franklin Green III

Plum Cake

Preheat: 350 degrees

2 cups self-rising flour
1 cup oil
2 cups sugar
1 teaspoon cinnamon
1 teaspoon nutmeg

2 small jars plums with tapioca baby
   food
3 beaten eggs
1 or 2 cups chopped pecans

Mix flour, sugar and spices together. Add plums, oil and beaten eggs. Add nuts. Just mix this cake; *do not beat*. Bake at 350 degrees for 1 hour in a greased floured tube pan.

Topping

4 tablespoons margarine
1 cup confectioners' sugar

Juice of one lemon
Grated rind of one lemon

Melt butter, add sugar, juice and rind. Pour half of mixture on cake before removing from pan. Remove cake from pan when cool, and pour remaining half of mixture over top of cake.

Mrs. Alfred E. T. Rusch

Rum Cake

Preheat: 325 degrees

1 package yellow cake mix
1 package vanilla instant pudding
½ cup light rum
½ cup water

½ cup oil
4 eggs
½ cup crushed pecans

Place all ingredients except pecans into bowl. Beat until creamy about 2 minutes. Grease and flour large tube pan. Spread nuts over bottom of pan. Pour in batter. Bake 60 minutes at 325 degrees. Glaze while hot.

Glaze

¼ cup light rum
¼ cup water

½ cup butter
1 cup sugar

Cook butter, water and sugar in small pan for 3 to 4 minutes bringing to a boil. Add rum. Pour hot glaze over cake while still hot. Let stand in pan 2 hours. Invert cake on plate.

Mrs. Emanuel A. Baker, Jr.

Queen Elizabeth II Cake

Preheat: 325 degrees
Yield: 9 x 13 sheet cake

1 cup boiling water
1 cup chopped dates
1 teaspoon soda
1 cup sugar
½ cup butter
1 beaten egg

1 teaspoon vanilla
1½ cups sifted flour
1 teaspoon baking powder
⅓ cup chopped nuts
1 teaspoon salt

Icing

10 tablespoons cream
4 tablespoons butter
10 tablespoons light brown sugar

Coconut
Chopped nuts

Pour boiling water over chopped dates and soda and let stand while fixing the following. Cream sugar and butter, add beaten egg and vanilla. Sift in flour, baking powder and salt. Mix well. Add nuts and date mixture. When well blended pour in greased 9 x 13-inch pan and bake 35 minutes. Cool. Boil cream, butter and brown sugar for 3 minutes and spread on cake. Sprinkle coconut and nuts on top icing.

Note: This is the only cake the Queen makes herself. Her request is that the recipe not be passed on, but sold for 10 cents by church groups or civic projects.

Mrs. Alfred E. T. Rusch

Old-Fashioned Raisin Cake

Preheat: 350 degrees

1½ pounds raisins
1 cup butter
2 cups sugar
1 cup sour milk (2 tablespoons of vinegar in milk, let stand 30 minutes)

1 teaspoon cinnamon
½ teaspoon nutmeg
2 eggs
4 cups flour
2 teaspoons baking soda (dissolved in 2 tablespoons water)

Boil raisins in enough water to cover for 20 minutes. Drain in collander. Mix all ingredients, stirring raisins in last. Pour into greased and floured tube pan. Bake at 350 degrees for one hour.

Mrs. Emanuel A. Baker, Jr.

Sunshine Cake

Preheat: 325 degrees

1 18½-ounce yellow cake mix
½ cup salad oil
4 eggs

1 11-ounce can mandarin orange
    sections, undrained

Combine cake mix, oil, eggs and oranges; mix at medium speed of electric mixer 1 to 2 minutes or until almost smooth. Spoon into 3 greased and floured 9-inch cakepans. Bake at 325 degrees for 15-20 minutes or until done. Cool cake in pans for 10 minutes; remove from pans, and cool *completely* on wire racks. Spread frosting between layers and on top and sides of cake. Store in refrigerator.

Frosting

1 20-ounce can crushed pineapple,
    undrained
1 tablespoon sugar
1 10½-ounce package cheesecake
    filling mix

1 8-ounce carton sour cream
1 9-ounce container frozen whipped
    topping, thawed
1 cup flaked coconut (optional)

Combine pineapple, sugar, cheesecake filling mix and sour cream. Stir until mixture thickens. Fold in whipped topping, mixing thoroughly.

Mrs. Alan E. Mowbray

Banana Bars

Preheat: 350 degrees
Yield: 4 dozen

1 cup flour
1 cup whole wheat flour
2 teaspoons baking powder
½ teaspoon salt
¾ cup butter
⅔ cup sugar

⅔ cup brown sugar
1 teaspoon vanilla
1 egg
2½ mashed, ripe bananas
6 ounces chocolate chips

Sift flours, baking powder and salt. Cream butter, sugars and vanilla. Add to flour mixture. Beat in egg with bananas. Add chocolate chips. Grease 13 x 9 x 2 inch pan. Bake at 350 degrees for 30 to 40 minutes.

Note: Especially nice to serve at a coffee or tea.

Mrs. Frederick McNamara

Texas Sheet Cake

Preheat: 400 degrees

½ cup shortening
½ cup butter
1 cup water
4 tablespoons cocoa
2 cups sugar
2 cups flour

1 teaspoon soda
1 teaspoon salt
2 eggs
1 teaspoon vanilla
½ cup buttermilk (or ½ cup whole
    milk and ½ teaspoon vinegar)

Bring shortening, butter, water and cocoa to boiling point. Place flour, sugar, soda and salt in a mixer bowl. Pour hot cocoa mix over flour mix. Beat one minute on medium speed. Add eggs, vanilla and buttermilk. Beat one minute. Pour into large 12 x 18-inch greased cookie sheet and bake 20 minutes at 400 degrees.

Icing

½ cup butter
4 tablespoons cocoa
6 tablespoons milk

1 pound confectioners' sugar
1 teaspoon vanilla

Bring butter, cocoa, and milk to boiling point, remove from heat and add confectioners' sugar and vanilla. Beat well until smooth. Ice cake while it is warm.

Mrs. Marjorie S. Cook

Orange-Lemon Sauce

Serves: 8 to 10

2 eggs
¾ cup sugar
Juice of 1 orange

Juice of 1 lemon
8 ounces whipping cream

Beat eggs and sugar in top of double boiler. Add juice of each fruit. Place over heat, stirring constantly until thick. Cool mixture. Whip cream and add to mixture. Serve on slices of sponge or angel food cake.

Mrs. Albert Hudson

Fresh Apple Cake

Preheat: 300 degrees
Serves: 8

2 eggs, beaten
2 cups sugar
1½ cups oil
1 tablespoon vanilla or almond
 extract
3 cups chopped raw apple

3 cups flour
½ teaspoon salt
2 teaspoons cinnamon
1 teaspoon soda
1 teaspoon nutmeg
1 cup chopped pecans

Mix ingredients in order given. Bake in greased and floured tube pan for 1¼ hours.

Mrs. Bernard Corbett

Black Bottom Cupcakes

Preheat: 350 degrees
Yield: 3 dozen

1½ cups flour
1⅓ cups sugar
¼ cup cocoa
1 teaspoon soda
1 cup water
⅓ cup cooking oil
1 tablespoon vinegar

1 tablespoon vanilla
1 8-ounce package cream cheese
1 egg
⅛ teaspoon salt
1 cup semi-sweet chocolate chips
Confectioners' sugar
¼ to ½ cup chopped nuts

Sift flour, 1 cup sugar, cocoa and soda together. Add water, oil, vinegar and vanilla. Beat well. Fill small muffin cups ⅓ to ½ full of chocolate batter. In another bowl, beat together cream cheese, egg, ⅓ cup sugar, salt and chocolate chips. Top each partially filled muffin cup with one teaspoon of cheese mixture. Bake at 350 degrees for 10 to 15 minutes. Sprinkle with confectioners' sugar and top with chopped nuts.

Mrs. David Dellefield

Tea Party Brownies

Preheat: 325 degrees
Yield: 4 to 5 dozen

4 squares unsweetened chocolate
1 cup butter
2 cups sugar
4 eggs

1 cup flour
½ teaspoon salt
1 teaspoon vanilla
1 cup chopped nuts

Melt chocolate and butter together. Add sugar. Beat eggs lightly and add to mixture. Add flour, vanilla, nuts and salt. Bake at 325 degrees for 30 to 35 minutes in a 9 x 13-inch pan.

Frosting

3 cups confectioners' sugar
4 tablespoons butter
¼ teaspoon peppermint extract

Heavy cream
Drops of green food coloring

Combine confectioners' sugar and 4 tablespoons of butter. Add enough cream to make mixture a spreading consistency. When brownies are cool, spread with frosting. When frosting is set, ice brownies. Add peppermint extract and coloring if mint frosting is desired.
Variation: Substitute orange extract and food coloring for a special Halloween treat.

Icing

4 squares semi-sweet chocolate

2 tablespoons butter

Melt chocolate with butter.

Mrs. Carlyle C. Ring, Jr.

Mexican Wedding Cakes

Preheat: 325 degrees
Yield: 2 dozen

3 tablespoons confectioners' sugar
½ cup butter
1 cup blanched almonds

1 teaspoon almond extract
1 cup cake flour

Cream sugar and butter. Add almonds and extract. Add and mix in flour, a little at a time. Form into balls. Bake for 10 to 12 minutes. While still warm, roll in additional confectioners' sugar.

Mrs. Jerome J. Palermino

Iced Cookies

Preheat: 325 degrees
Yield: Approximately 4 dozen

1 cup shortening
1 cup brown sugar
1 egg yolk

2 cups flour
1 teaspoon vanilla

Cream shortening and brown sugar. Add remaining ingredients. Roll out on greased cookie sheet. Bake 15 to 20 minutes. Ice while still warm.

Icing

4 squares unsweetened chocolate
1 to 2 squares semi-sweet
    chocolate

Slivered almonds

Melt the two chocolates together and spread over hot cookies. Sprinkle with almonds. Cool slightly; cut into squares. Refrigerate before removing from pan.

Mrs. Frank McCabe

Lemon Squares

Preheat: 300 degrees
Yield: 4 dozen

2 cups plus 6 tablespoons flour
1 cup butter
½ cup confectioners' sugar
4 eggs

⅓ cup lemon juice
1¾ cups sugar
1 teaspoon baking powder
Grated lemon rind (optional)

Melt butter; sift 2 cups flour and confectioners' sugar together in a bowl. Add butter and mix until dough is formed. Press into 9 x 13-inch pan covering the bottom and sides evenly. Bake at 300 degrees for 20 minutes. While dough is baking, beat eggs and lemon juice in a medium bowl. Sift together granulated sugar, 6 tablespoons of flour and baking powder. Add dry mixture to lemon and egg mixture. Beat well. Add grated rind if tarter lemon flavor is preferred. Pour over crust and bake 25 minutes at 350 degrees. Chill and cut in 1-inch squares.

Mrs. Simmons B. Savage III

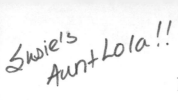
Swie's
Aunt Lola!!

Blonde Brownies

Preheat: 350 degrees
Yield: 12 to 15

1 cup sifted all-purpose flour
½ teaspoon baking powder
½ teaspoon salt
⅓ cup butter
1 cup firmly packed brown sugar
1 egg

1 egg yolk
1 teaspoon vanilla
½ cup chopped nuts
½ cup semi-sweet chocolate bits
  (optional)

Sift flour with baking powder and salt. Melt butter in large saucepan; remove from heat. Add brown sugar, stirring until dissolved. Cool. Add egg, egg yolk and vanilla; beat well. Stir in dry ingredients and nuts; mix well. Spread batter in greased 9-inch square pan. Sprinkle chocolate pieces over top if desired. Bake at 350 degrees for 25 minutes. Cool. Cut into bars. Serve plain or sprinkled with confectioners' sugar.

Mrs. Hamilton Beggs

Malayan Dream Bars

Yield: 2 to 3 dozen

¾ cup plus 1 tablespoon butter
5 tablespoons cocoa
¼ cup sugar
1 egg
1 teaspoon vanilla
2 cups graham cracker crumbs
1 cup flaked coconut

½ cup chopped nuts
2 tablespoons vanilla instant pudding
  mix
2 cups confectioners' sugar
3 tablespoons milk
3 squares semi-sweet chocolate

Stir ½ cup butter, cocoa, sugar, egg and vanilla over very low heat until butter is melted. Add graham cracker crumbs, coconut and chopped nuts. Pack mixture firmly into a lightly buttered 9 x 9 inch pan. Mix pudding mix, confectioners' sugar, ¼ cup butter and milk and spread on top of packed mixture. Let stand 15 minutes or longer. Melt chocolate and one tablespoon butter. Spread on top. Refrigerate and cut into bars.

Mrs. Donald McNamara

Seven Layer Cookies

Preheat: 350 degrees
Yield: 3 dozen

½ cup margarine
1 cup graham cracker crumbs
1 cup coconut
1 6-ounce package chocolate
  morsels

1 6-ounce package butterscotch bits
1 can sweetened condensed cream
1 cup pecans or walnuts

Melt margarine in 8 x 11-inch pan. Then layer remaining ingredients. Bake for 30 minutes at 350 degrees. Cut while warm; continue cooling.

Mrs. Donald McNamara

Peanut Blossoms

Preheat: 350 degrees
Yield: 4 dozen

1¾ cups flour
1 teaspoon soda
½ teaspoon salt
½ cup sugar
½ cup brown sugar
½ cup shortening

½ cup peanut butter
1 egg
2 tablespoons milk
1 teaspoon vanilla
48 milk chocolate kisses

Blend all ingredients except kisses. Roll dough into balls. Roll balls in sugar. Bake on ungreased cookie sheet at 350 degrees for 10 minutes. Press kiss in each cookie immediately upon taking them out of the oven, while the cookies are soft.

Mrs. John Denson

Chocolate Crinkle Cookies

Preheat: 350 degrees
Yield: 10 dozen

½ cup oil
4 squares unsweetened chocolate,
  melted
2 cups sugar
4 eggs

2 teaspoons vanilla
2 cups flour
2 teaspoons baking powder
½ teaspoon salt
Confectioners' sugar

Mix oil, chocolate and sugar. Blend in eggs, one at a time until well mixed. Add vanilla. Mix flour, salt and baking powder together and stir into chocolate mixture. Chill overnight. Form small balls about ¾ inch in diameter with chilled dough and roll in confectioners' sugar. Place 2 inches apart on greased cookie sheet. Bake 10 to 12 minutes at 350 degrees.

Mrs. Emanuel A. Baker, Jr.

Pecan/Walnut Cookies

Preheat: 325 degrees
Yield: 3 dozen

1 cup butter
1 cup brown sugar
1 cup sugar
2 eggs
1 cup chopped pecans or walnuts

1 teaspoon soda
½ teaspoon salt
2 teaspoons cinnamon
3½ cups flour

Cream butter and sugars. Add eggs and beat well. Add nuts. Sift flour, salt, soda and cinnamon 3 times. Add to butter mixture. Form a roll (2-inch diameter) and refrigerate at least 1 hour. Slice thinly and bake on ungreased cookie sheet for 10 minutes at 325 degrees.

Note: This cookie dough can be prepared and kept in the refrigerator for at least a month. Slice and bake when needed.

Mrs. Joseph E. Hinds

Rock Cookies

Preheat: 375 degrees
Yield: 4 dozen

1½ cups brown sugar
1 cup butter or margarine
3 eggs
1 teaspoon cinnamon
1 teaspoon soda

3 cups flour
1 pound seedless raisins
½ pound walnuts
½ pound candied fruit
1 cup water

Mix sugar, eggs and butter. Heat raisins in water; drain and reserve ⅓ cup juice to mix with soda. Add remaining ingredients and mix. Drop by teaspoonfuls on greased cookie sheet. Bake at 375 degrees for 12 to 15 minutes.

Mrs. James W. Keller

School Day Cookies

Preheat: 375 degrees
Yield: 4 dozen

1 cup shortening
1 cup sugar
2 beaten eggs
¼ cup orange juice
2 tablespoons grated orange rind
1 teaspoon vanilla

2 cups flour
½ teaspoon salt
1 teaspoon soda
2 cups quick oats
½ cup chopped dates
½ cup chopped nuts

Thoroughly cream shortening and sugar. Add eggs and beat well. Add juice, grated rind and vanilla. Stir in flour, sifted with salt and soda. Add oats, dates and nuts. Drop by teaspoonfuls onto greased cookie sheet. Bake at 375 degrees for 10 to 12 minutes.

Mrs. Dale G. Uhler

Monster Cookies

Preheat: 350 degrees
Yield: 12 dozen

12 eggs
2 pounds brown sugar
4 cups sugar
1 tablespoon vanilla
1 tablespoon light corn syrup
8 teaspoons soda

2 cups margarine
3 pounds peanut butter
18 cups oatmeal
1 pound chocolate chips
1 pound M & M's

Mix in dishpan in order given. Drop by large scoop on cookie sheet and flatten (can also drop by tablespoonfuls and flatten for smaller cookies). Bake 12 minutes at 350 degrees. Be careful not to overbake.

Note: Lots of work—but worth it; kids love to help make and eat these cookies!

Mrs. Michael E. Delnegro

English Toffee Cookies

Preheat: 300 degrees
Yield: 5 dozen

1 cup butter (or ½ butter and ½
   margarine)
1 cup sugar
1 teaspoon vanilla

2 cups sifted flour
1 egg white, beaten stiff
½ cup finely chopped nuts

Cream butter and sugar. Add vanilla and flour, mix until well blended. Spread mixture on lightly greased 14 x 17 inch jelly roll pan with rim. Top with beaten egg white, then nuts. Press latter with spatula. Bake 30 to 45 minutes or until golden brown. Cut while warm and remove from pan. To cut in diamond shapes, first cut inch-wide strips the length of pan and then cut in inch-wide strips diagonally.

Mrs. Alfred E. T. Rusch

Starlight Mint Surprise Cookies

Preheat: 375 degrees
Yield: 4 dozen

3 cups sifted flour
½ teaspoon salt
1 teaspoon soda
1 cup butter
1 cup sugar
½ cup brown sugar

2 eggs
1 tablespoon water
1 teaspoon vanilla
2 packages chocolate mint candy
   wafers
48 pecan halves

Sift flour, salt and soda. Cream butter and gradually add sugars, mixing well. Add eggs, water and vanilla. Beat well. Gradually add sifted dry ingredients. Mix fhoroughly. Cover and chill 2 hours. Shape 1 tablespoon of dough around each wafer. Top with pecan half. Place 2 inches apart on ungreased cookie sheet and bake 10 to 12 minutes at 375 degrees.

Mrs. John P. Glynn

Applesauce Spice Squares

Preheat: 350 degrees

2 cups sifted flour
2 teaspoons soda
¾ teaspoon cinnamon
¼ teaspoon cloves
¼ teaspoon nutmeg
½ cup soft butter
1 cup sugar

2 eggs
1 teaspoon vanilla
1½ cups applesauce
1 cup chopped nuts
1 cup raisins
Confectioner's sugar

Sift flour with soda and spices. Cream butter and sugar until light and fluffy. Add eggs and vanilla. Beat well. Beat in flour mixture. Add applesauce, nuts and raisins. Mix well. Pour into greased 10 x 16-inch pan. Bake 25 minutes at 350 degrees. Sprinkle with confectioner's sugar when cool.

Mrs. Edward F. Kapusta

Molasses Cookie Men

Preheat: 350 degrees
Yield: 30 medium cookies

4 cups sifted flour
1 teaspoon salt
1 teaspoon baking soda
2 teaspoons baking powder
2 teaspoons ginger
1 teaspoon cloves

1 teaspoon cinnamon
1 teaspoon nutmeg
1 cup shortening
1 cup sugar
1 cup molasses
2 eggs

Sift all dry ingredients. Cream shortening, add sugar gradually and beat until fluffy. Add molasses and eggs. Thoroughly mix in flour mixture. Chill until dough can be easily handled, 2 hours or more. Roll out small portion of dough ¼-inch thick on lightly floured board or pastry cloth. Cut with gingerbreadman cutter. Can use any size cutter. Place on ungreased baking sheet. Bake at 350 degrees for about 10 minutes for 8-inch cookie. Cool 2 minutes before removing from baking sheet.

Icing:
1 pound confectioners' sugar
3 to 4 tablespoons Crisco
1 teaspoon vanilla

Small amount of milk
Pinch of salt
Chocolate chips or raisins

Beat well until spreading consistency. Ice cookie using chocolate chips for eyes, nose and buttons.
Note: These cookies are particularly nice for children's Christmas parties or to give to friends at Christmas.

Mrs. John B. Denson

Lemon Chess Pie

Preheat: 375 degrees

2 cups sugar
1 tablespoon flour
1 tablespoon cornmeal
4 unbeaten eggs
¼ cup melted butter

¼ cup milk
Grated lemon rind to taste
¼ cup lemon juice
Pinch of salt
1 9-inch unbaked pie crust

Mix sugar, flour, and cornmeal together with a fork. Beat eggs, butter, milk, lemon juice, rind and a pinch of salt. Add dry ingredients and beat until smooth. Pour into pie shell. Bake at 375 degrees for 35 to 45 minutes or until golden brown.

Mrs. John B. Denson

Bourbon Pie

Preheat: 400 degrees
Serves: 8 to 10

1½ cups crushed vanilla wafers
½ cup melted butter
1 tablespoon sugar
½ cup pecans, crushed

1 cup butter (don't substitute)
1 pound confectioners' sugar
6 eggs
½ cup bourbon

Crust
Combine vanilla wafers, butter, sugar and pecans. Press into a 10-inch pie plate. Bake for 5 minutes at 400 degrees. Cool completely.

Filling
Cream butter and sugar. Add eggs, one at a time, and mix well after each addition. (If using a small, portable mixer, use only 5 eggs). Add bourbon in slow stream. The filling will look curdled at first but will become smooth and creamy. Turn into crumb crust and chill or freeze overnight. If making more than a day ahead, freeze and thaw before serving.

Mrs. Lewis B. Puller, Jr.

Buttermilk Pie

Preheat: 450 degrees
Serves: 6 to 8

1 cup raisins
1 cup sugar
1 tablespoon flour
½ teaspoon cinnamon
½ teaspoon cloves

½ teaspoon nutmeg
2 eggs, slightly beaten
4 tablespoons butter
1 cup buttermilk
1 9-inch unbaked pie crust

Boil raisins 5 minutes in enough water to cover. Drain. Combine remaining ingredients; place in pie crust. Bake at 450 degrees for 15 minutes; reduce to 350 degrees for 45 minutes longer or until a knife inserted comes out clean.

Mrs. Frank McCabe

Chocolate Almond Pie

Serves: 6 to 8

1 9-inch baked pie crust
½ cup butter
¾ cup sugar
1 square unsweetened chocolate

1 teaspoon vanilla
¼ teaspoon almond extract
2 eggs

Cream sugar and butter. Melt and cool chocolate. Add chocolate to butter mixture with vanilla and almond extract. Add eggs one at a time, beating 5 minutes after each addition. Pour into cooled crust.

Topping

½ pint whipping cream
Almond extract

2 tablespoons sugar
Sliced almonds

Whip cream with sugar; flavor to taste with almond extract. Top pie filling and garnish with almonds. Refrigerate several hours.

Note: Can be made a day ahead. It's very rich.

Mrs. Charles Everly

Chocolate Macadamia Cream Pie

Serves: 8

¾ cup sugar
⅓ cup cornstarch
3 squares unsweetened chocolate,
    chopped
½ teaspoon salt
2½ cups milk

1 9-inch baked pie shell
3 egg yolks
2 teaspoons crème de cacao liqueur or
    vanilla flavoring
¼ cup chopped macadamia nuts
Fresh whipped cream

In top of double boiler, combine sugar, cornstarch, chocolate and salt. Mix together. Gradually stir in milk. Stir constantly over boiling water until chocolate mixture is thick, about 10 to 15 minutes. Cover and cook 10 minutes longer, stirring frequently. Meanwhile, beat egg yolks in a separate bowl. Stir in half of hot chocolate mixture. Return mixture to double boiler and cook for another 5 minutes, stirring constantly. Cool slightly. Add crème de cacao. Cool. Fold in macadamia nuts. Pour into 9-inch pie shell and chill at least 4 to 5 hosrs. At serving time, decorate with slightly sweetened whipped cream. Sprinkle with grated chocolate and additional ground macadamia nuts.

Note: You may flavor with crème de cacao or rum.

Mrs. Thomas T. Bellino

Exquisite Pie

Preheat: 350 degrees
Serves: 6 to 8

1 unbaked 9-inch pie shell
½ cup margarine, melted
1 cup sugar
3 eggs, slightly beaten
½ cup coconut

½ cup raisins
½ cup chopped pecans
1 teaspoon vinegar
1 teaspoon vanilla

Mix margarine, sugar and eggs together. Add coconut, raisins, nuts, vinegar and vanilla. Mix well. Pour into pie shell, and bake approximately 35 minutes or until crust is brown and custard fairly firm.

Mrs. Alfred E. T. Rusch

Grasshopper Pie

Serves: 6 to 8

18 to 24 crushed Oreos
3 to 4 tablespoons butter, melted
24 large marshmallows
⅔ cup milk

½ pint heavy cream, whipped
1 ounce crème de menthe
½ ounce crème de cacao

Mix crushed cookies and butter, reserving a few crumbs for topping. Press into an 8 or 9-inch pie pan. Melt marshmallows in milk in double boiler, cool. (1 cup miniature marshmallows = 10 large ones). Combine whipped cream and liqueurs and add to marshmallow mixture, stirring gently. Pour into pie shell. Top with reserved cookie crumbs. Chill 6 hours or overnight.

Note: If desired, 1½ ounces crème de menthe may be used and crème de cacao omitted.

Mrs. Alan E. Mowbray

Macaroon Pie

Preheat: 350 degrees

1 cup graham cracker crumbs
½ cup shredded coconut
½ cup chopped pecans or walnuts
4 egg whites

¼ teaspoon salt
1 teaspoon vanilla
1 cup sugar
½ pint whipping cream

Mix crumbs, coconut and nuts. Beat egg whites with salt and vanilla until soft peaks form. Gradually add sugar and beat until stiff peaks form. Fold crumb mixture into egg white mixture. Spread into well greased 8-inch pie pan. Bake for 30 minutes at 350 degrees. Serve garnished with whipped cream.

Mrs. James W. Vaughan, Jr.

Peach Chiffon Pie

Serves: 6 to 8

¾ cups sugar
1½ cups mashed peaches
1 tablespoon unflavored gelatin
¼ cup cold water
½ cup hot water

1 tablespoon lemon juice
Dash of salt
1 cup heavy cream, whipped
1 9-inch baked pie crust

Add sugar to peaches and let stand 30 minutes. Soften gelatin in cold water and dissolve in hot water. Cool. Add peach mixture, lemon juice and salt. Chill until partially set. Fold in whipped cream. Pour in 9-inch baked pie crust and chill thoroughly.

Note: 1½ times the recipe makes a really deep and high pie.

Mrs. Donald Burchell

 To overcome the soggy crust problem when a juicy filling is added to a flaky baked crust, brush the bottom crust with an egg white while still hot.

Glorious Pumpkin Pie

Preheat: 450 degrees
Serves: 8

2½ cups cooked, strained pumpkin
1 cup brown sugar, firmly packed
1½ teaspoons cinnamon
½ teaspoon nutmeg
½ teaspoon ginger
¼ teaspoon salt

3 egg yolks, slightly beaten
1 cup evaporated milk or cream
½ cup melted butter
3 stiffly beaten egg whites
1 unbaked 10-inch pie shell

Combine pumpkin, sugar and spices. Add beaten egg yolks, milk and butter to pumpkin mixture. Blend well. Fold in stiffly beaten egg whites. Put in unbaked pie shell. Bake 10 minutes at 450 degrees. Reduce heat and bake at 350 degrees for an additional 35 minutes or until knife inserted in center comes out clean.

Mrs. Alfred E. T. Rusch

Frozen Pumpkin Pie

Serves: 6

1 cup canned pumpkin
½ cup brown sugar or honey
½ teaspoon salt
1 teaspoon cinnamon
⅛ teaspoon cloves

¼ teaspoon nutmeg
1 quart rich vanilla ice cream, softened
1 graham cracker crumb pie crust
½ pint whipping cream
Pecans

Mix filling and put into crumb crust. Freeze. Garnish with whipped cream and pecans.

Mrs. Herbert Stewart

Strawberry Glaze Pie

Serves: 8

2 or 3 pints strawberries, washed
    and capped
1½ cups sugar
3 tablespoons cornstarch
Dash of salt

1½ cups boiling water
4 tablespoons strawberry jello
1 tablespoon butter
1 teaspoon lemon juice
1 10-inch baked pie shell

Combine sugar, cornstarch, salt and boiling water. Bring to a boil. Cook 2 minutes stirring constantly until clear. Remove from heat. Add butter, jello and lemon juice. Cool. Place berries in pie shell, point side up. Pour glaze over berries evenly. Refrigerate.

Mrs. Frank McCabe

Rum Pie

Preheat: 350 degrees
Serves: 12

1 package thin chocolate wafers
6 egg yolks
1 cup sugar
⅓ cup melted butter
1 cup dark rum

½ cup shaved bitter chocolate
¼ teaspoon cinnamon
1 tablespoon gelatin
½ cup cold water
1 pint heavy cream (whipped)

Crush wafers (will yield 1½ to 2 cups). Add ⅓ cup melted butter and cinnamon. Press mixture on a 9-inch springform pan. Bake crust 8 minutes in 350 degree oven. Beat eggs until light. Add sugar and set aside.

Pour gelatin into water and place over low flame until mixture begins to boil. Add to yolk/sugar mixture, beating vigorously. Whip cream and fold into egg yolk/gelatin mixture. Add the rum. Sprinkle pie with chocolate and refrigerate until ready to serve.

Mrs. William T. Mahood

French Peach Tart

Serves: 6 to 8

8 baked 3-inch tart shells or 1
   9-inch baked pie crust
1 3-ounce package French vanilla
   instant pudding mix
1 cup milk
1 pint sour cream

¼ teaspoon almond extract
3 peaches, sliced or 1 can (1 pound 14
   ounce) sliced cling peaches, drained
1 jar apricot preserves
¼ cup water
Flaked coconut (optional)

Combine pudding mix with milk, sour cream and almond extract in a medium-sized bowl; prepare following label instructions. Pour into cooled tart shells or pie crust. Let stand at room temperature 5 minutes or until set. Arrange slices overlapping on top of pudding, close to pastry edge. Save some for center. Heat apricot preserves and ¼ cup water; cook stirring constantly until mixture bubbles. Cool slightly, then spoon over peaches to glaze. Chill. Just before serving, may sprinkle with flaked coconut.

Mrs. Donald Burchell

Yankee Tart Shells

Preheat: 350 degrees
Serves: 6 to 8

2 tablespoons butter
½ cup brown sugar
1 slightly beaten egg
¼ cup finely chopped pecans

⅓ cup cake flour
¼ teaspoon vanilla
Few grains of salt

Cream butter and brown sugar. Add egg and beat thoroughly. Add pecans, then remaining ingredients. Mix well. Make and bake one cookie at a time. Work fast. Put 2 level tablespoons of batter on a very well-greased cookie sheet. Spread very thin with a spoon. Bake at 350 degrees for 8 to 10 minutes. Remove from cookie sheet immediately and hold in palm of hand (wear thin gloves if you wish) a few moments until firm enough to shape over the bottom of a greased custard cup. When all the cookies are cooled, the shells may be filled with ice cream and fresh fruit.

Note: A very elegant meal ending. Strawberries are especially nice.

Mrs. Hugh Newton

Tart Shells with Lemon or Pecan Filling

Preheat: 325 degrees
Yield: 24

6 tablespoons butter, softened
3 ounces cream cheese, softened

1 cup flour

Blend butter and cream cheese. Add flour Chill one hour, covered. Shape into approximately 2 dozen 1-inch balls; place in ungreased 1¾-inch muffin pans. Press dough against bottom and sides. Add filling.

Lemon Filling
3 eggs
1 cup sugar

2 lemons, grated rind and juice

Beat eggs until light, add sugar and lemon. Pour mixture into tart shells. Bake at 325 degrees for about 25 minutes, or until brown.

Pecan Filling
1 large egg
1 tablespoon butter, softened
¾ cup brown sugar

1 teaspoon vanilla
Dash of salt
⅔ cup chopped pecans

Beat egg. Add butter, brown sugar, vanilla and salt and continue to beat until smooth. Divide half pecans among tart shells. Pour egg mixture over pecans. Place remaining pecans on top of egg mixture. Bake in 325 degree oven for about 25 minutes or until filling begins to set.

Mrs. Lawton Rogers

Boiled Custard

Serves: 6

1 quart milk
2 eggs
1 cup sugar

4 teaspoons cornstarch
¼ teaspoon salt
1 teaspoon vanilla

Scald milk in top of double boiler. In bowl, beat eggs well. Add sugar, cornstarch, salt and vanilla. Mix well. Stir this mixture into milk. Cook 15 minutes over medium heat until it coats a spoon. Cool and chill.

Mrs. Charles Beatley

Cherry Flan

Preheat: 350 degrees
Serves: 6 to 8

3 cups drained, canned pitted
  bing cherries, or frozen sweet
  cherries, thawed
¼ cup kirsch or cognac
⅔ cup sugar

1 cup milk
3 eggs
1 tablespoon vanilla
⅛ teaspoon salt
⅔ cup sifted all-purpose flour

Let cherries stand in liqueur and ⅓ cup sugar for 1 hour. Drain cherries, reserve liquid. Place in this order in blender: milk, ⅓ cup sugar, eggs, liqueur and sugar mixture drained from cherries, vanilla, salt and flour. Cover and blend at top speed for 1 minute. Pour ¼ inch layer of batter in a 7 to 8-cup buttered baking dish about 1½ inches deep. Set over moderate heat for a minute or 2 until a film of batter has set in the bottom of the dish. Remove from heat. Spread the cherries over the batter. Pour on the rest of the batter and smooth the surface with the back of a spoon. Place in middle position in 350 degree oven and bake about one hour. Flan is done when it is puffed and browned and a knife plunged in the center comes out clean. Serve warm (it will sink down slightly as it cools). Sprinkle with confectioners' sugar just before serving or serve with whipped cream.

Mrs. Donald Burchell

Pineapple Mousse

Serves: 8

1 16-ounce can crushed pineapple
2 3-ounce packages lemon gelatin

1 pint whipping cream
Juice of ½ lemon

Drain pineapple well. Place juice from pineapple in pan with gelatin and heat until dissolved. Allow to cool, but not set. Whip chilled cream to stiff peaks. Beat in lemon juice and cooled gelatin mixture. Fold in pineapple. Chill in 8 individual soufflé cups or 6-cup mold.

Mrs. William F. Clayton

Black Cherry Pudding

Preheat: 350 degrees
Serves: 8

1 cup flour
1 cup sugar
1 teaspoon baking soda
1 egg

1 tablespoon melted butter
1 cup chopped pecans or walnuts
1 16-ounce can dark sweet cherries,
    drained and chopped

Mix ingredients together in a bowl. Grease a 7½ x 12-inch baking dish. Spoon batter in. Bake 30 minutes at 350 degrees.

Sauce

½ cup butter
1 cup sugar

½ cup whipping cream
1 teaspoon vanilla

Melt butter in double boiler. Add sugar, cream and vanilla. Mix and stir over hot water until sugar is dissolved. Serve sauce warm over warm or cold pudding.

Note: Terrific winter dessert. Make the pudding a day ahead.

Mrs. David Bernabucci

Fresh Strawberry Mousse

Serves: 6

1 pint strawberries
2 3-ounce packages strawberry
    flavor gelatin

¼ cup sugar
1 pint whipping cream

Crush the strawberries. Drain and reserve the juice. Add enough water to the juice to make 1½ cups. Bring the juice to a boil and stir in gelatin. Dissolve and cool. Add strawberries and sugar. Whip cream until it stands in soft peaks and fold into strawberry mixture. Pour into 2-quart ring mold or 1½-quart soufflé dish with a 2-inch collar. Chill several hours or overnight.

Note: 2 10-ounce packages of frozen strawberries can be substituted for fresh strawberries. Omit sugar if frozen berries are used.

Mrs. Robert E. Applegate

Overnight Strawberry Dessert

Serves: 10 to 12

3 envelopes Dream Whip
1 large angel food cake
1 20-ounce can crushed pineapple
1 10-ounce package frozen
   strawberries
2 tablespoons lemon juice

2 envelopes gelatin
2 tablespoons cold water
1 cup sugar
1 cup boiling water
Coconut (optional)

Mix gelatin with cold water. Add boiling water to dissolve. Add sugar, undrained pineapple, lemon juice and strawberries. Allow mixture to begin to set in refrigerator. Whip 2 envelopes of Dream Whip according to package directions and add to fruit mixture. Line 9 x 13-inch pan with broken pieces of cake. Cover with half of gelatin mixture. Add another layer of cake. Cover with remainder of mixture. Chill overnight. Whip one envelope of Dream Whip and "ice" cake. Sprinkle with coconut. Chill.

Note: Good for bridge luncheons

Mrs. Thomas F. Johnson

Blender Chocolate Mousse

Serves: 4

6 ounces semi-sweet chocolate
2 tablespoons Kahlua
1 tablespoon orange juice
2 egg yolks

2 eggs
1 teaspoon vanilla
¼ cup sugar
1 cup heavy cream

Melt chocolate in Kahlua and orange juice over very low heat. Set aside. Put egg yolks and eggs in top of blender with vanilla and sugar. Blend 2 minutes at medium speed. Add heavy cream and blend for another 30 seconds. Add the melted chocolate mixtures; blend until smooth. Pour into individual cups. Refrigerate.

Mrs. David Bernabucci

Bananas Foster Flambé

Serves: 6 to 8

½ cup butter
¾ cup brown sugar
½ cup light rum

2 to 3 bananas, sliced lengthwise
Vanilla ice cream

Place a large scoop of ice cream in 6 to 8 sherbet dishes and keep in freezer until ready to serve. Melt butter in pan over a fondue burner; add brown sugar. Stir constantly until melted and caramelized. Add sliced bananas and gently fold in caramel mixture. Gently pour in rum around edges, to warm the rum. Ignite rum while tilting to one side. Swirl pan at this time until flame goes out. Immediately serve over the vanilla ice cream.

Mrs. Chris W. Ragland

Biscuit Tortoni

Serves: 12

¾ cup crushed macaroons (dry in
   oven, crush in blender)
1¾ cups cream
¼ cup sifted confectioners' sugar
Pinch of salt

1 teaspoon vanilla or 2 tablespoons
   dark rum
Maraschino cherries
Unsalted almonds

Combine macaroons, ¾ cup cream, sugar with salt and let stand for 1 hour. Whip 1 cup cream, fold whipped cream into the macaroon mixture after adding desired flavoring. Place in paper muffin cups in muffin tin and put in freezer. When partly frozen decorate tops with cherries and almonds.

Note: To freeze for several days, whip cream only to point where forms soft peaks. Remove from freezer 30 minutes before serving.

Mrs. Stephen Echols

Chocolate Layer Dessert

Preheat: 325 degrees

1 cup flour
1 cup nuts
½ cup margarine or butter
8-ounce package cream cheese
1 cup confectioners' sugar
1 6-ounce package chocolate
   instant pudding

4¼ cups milk
1 6-ounce package vanilla instant
   pudding
1 large container Cool Whip

Melt margarine, add flour and nuts. Put into bottom of 9 x 13 inch pan. Bake 20 minutes at 325 degrees. Cool thoroughly. Mix cream cheese, confectioners' sugar, and 1⅓ cup Cool Whip. Spread mixture over cooked cooled crust. When set, proceed with next layer.

Mix package of chocolate pudding with 2⅛ cups milk and spread on cream cheese layer. Repeat same process with vanilla pudding and spread fourth layer. Spread 2 cups Cool Whip for the last layer. Sprinkle with chocolate shavings or nut dust.

Mrs. Carlton L. Schelhorn

Savoy Trifle

Serves: 8 to 10

6 egg yolks
½ cup sugar
2½ cups milk
2 cups heavy cream

¾ cup dry sherry
1½ packages (11-ounce) jelly rolls
Candied cherries
Angelica or citron

Beat egg yolks slightly with sugar in top of double boiler. Stir in milk and 1 cup of cream. Cook mixture stirring constantly over simmering water for 25 minutes or until thickened and coats a spoon. Strain custard into bowl; cool slightly. Stir in ¼ cup sherry. Cut each jelly roll into 8 slices; place 12 slices on cookie sheet (save remaining for another use); sprinkle with remaining ½ cup sherry. Line bottom and sides of an 8-cup glass bowl using 8 slices. Pour part of custard over jelly roll slices. Place remaining 4 slices over custard; pour in remaining custard. Cover with plastic wrap; refrigerate 4 hours or overnight. Beat remaining cream in a medium-size bowl until stiff, pipe rosettes around edge of trifle. Garnish with candied cherries or angelica.

Note: A 1 pound jelly roll may be cut into 8 slices.

Mrs. Stephen Shaffer

Traditional Christmas Pudding

Serves: 8 to 10

3 cups all-purpose flour
¼ teaspoon salt
1 teaspoon soda
2 teaspoons ground cinnamon
½ teaspoon ground allspice
½ teaspoon ground cloves

2 cups raisins
1 cup peeled, chopped apples
1 cup dates, chopped
1 cup light molasses
1 cup cold water
2 cups finely chopped suet

Combine flour, soda, salt and spices in a large mixing bowl; mix well. Stir in raisins, apples and dates. Combine molasses, water and suet; add to dry ingredients, mix well. Spoon mixture into a well-buttered 10-cup mold; cover tightly. Steam pudding for 3 hours. Unmold. To serve flambé with ½ to ¾ cup boiling rum poured on pudding and light; then pass hard sauce.

Hard Sauce

½ cup butter, softened
1 cup powdered sugar

4 tablespoons rum

Combine butter and sugar, beating until smooth. Add rum; beat until fluffy. Chill.

Notes: Use food processor to finely chop suet with steel blade for 2-3 seconds. Also use processor to chop apples and dates.
Pudding may be made several days ahead, wrapped in aluminum foil and refrigerated. Preheat by steaming 30 minutes in foil.
Hard sauce should be made in the morning so it may chill.

Mrs. E. David Doane

Frozen Custard

Yield: 2 quarts

2 cups milk
3 egg yolks
1 cup sugar

¼ teaspoon salt
2 cups light or table cream
4 teaspoons vanilla

Scald milk in a double boiler. Beat egg yolks, sugar and salt. Pour scalded milk over beaten mixture. Return to double boiler and cook until it coats a spoon. Allow mixture to cool. Add cream and vanilla and place in ice cream freezer. Operate freezer according to instructions.

Mrs. Donald Burchell

Crème Brulée

Serves: 4 to 6

¼ cup sugar
1 tablespoon cornstarch
2 cups light cream
5 egg yolks

¼ teaspoon salt
¼ teaspoon almond extract
1 tablespoon brown sugar

Combine sugar and cornstarch in top of double boiler. Add cream. Heat over boiling water, stirring constantly, until slightly thick. Beat egg yolks with salt and almond extract. Add about ½ cup of the hot mixture to eggs and then add to remaining mixture in double boiler; cook over simmering water, stirring constantly, until mixture is slightly thick and coats a metal spoon. Pour into 1 quart casserole. Chill until set, about 1 hour. Sprinkle with brown sugar. Place under broiler 2 to 5 minutes, until sugar is caramelized. Serve cold, plain, or as a sauce over peaches, bananas or apricots.

Mrs. Hamilton Beggs

 Ice cream contains all of the important nutrients that are in milk, but in different proportions.

Rum Pudding

Serves: 4

1 pint heavy whipping cream
3 eggs separated
8 tablespoons sugar

4 tablespoons rum
1 teaspoon vanilla
1 teaspoon nutmeg

Beat cream until stiff and set aside. Beat egg yolks until foamy. Add 4 tablespoons sugar, rum, vanilla and nutmeg to beaten yolks. Beat egg whites until stiff and forming peaks; add 4 tablespoons sugar. Lightly blend the egg yolk mixture and whipped cream into beaten egg whites. Pour into individual large souffle cups and freeze. Serve frozen.

Mrs. Jerome J. Palermino

Country Vanilla Ice Cream

Yield: 4 quarts

4 eggs, beaten
2¼ cups sugar
5 cups milk

4 cups heavy cream
4½ teaspoons vanilla
½ teaspoon salt

Add sugar gradually to beaten eggs. Continue to beat until mixture is very stiff. Add remaining ingredients and mix thoroughly. Pour into gallon freezer and freeze as directed. For fresh fruit ice cream, substitute 4 cups pureed sweetened fruit for 4 cups of milk.

Mrs. Donald Burchell

Brandy Alexander Ice Petroleum

1 quart of good quality ice cream
¼ cup or more of brandy

Dash of nutmeg

Soften ice cream; blend in brandy to taste and rechill. Serve in brandy snifter or wine glasses. Garnish with nutmeg.

Note: This is a speciality at the Petroleum Club in Oklahoma City. Makes a great party dessert.

Mrs. Arthur M. Keleher

Cappucino Parfait

Serves: 10 to 12

½ teaspoon ground cinnamon
1 teaspoon or more grated orange
  rind

1½ cups butterscotch sauce
½ gallon coffee ice cream
Whipped cream

Stir cinnamon and 1 teaspoon of rind into sauce. In parfait glasses, alternate coffee ice cream and sauce. Freeze until time to serve. Top with whipped cream and grated orange rind.

Mrs. James W. Keller

Champagne Sorbet

Yield: One quart

2¼ cups granulated sugar
1 cup plus 1 tablespoon water

1 bottle of champagne (Fifth)
2 egg whites

In a small saucepan, dissolve 2 cups granulated sugar in 1 cup water. Cook until temperature reaches 200 degrees on candy thermometer and remove from heat. Start adding champagne, a little at a time, until mixture reaches 175 degrees. Set aside. Cook ¼ cup sugar with 1 tablespoon water until it spins a thread. Then, in a large mixing bowl, beat egg whites until stiff, pour the hot sugar syrup onto them in a thin thread, beating constantly. Continue beating until meringue is thick and peaks are well formed. Add to champagne syrup. Prepare in freezer to chill. Pour in champagne mixture. Churn according to manufacturer's directions (usually 4 parts ice to 1 part rock salt), until dasher refuses to turn. Remove the dasher, pack sherbet into can. Repack in a mixture of 4 parts ice to 1 part rock salt. Allow sherbet to "mellow" for 2 hours, then place in freezer.

Mrs. Tod R. Hullin

Minute Butterscotch Sauce

Yield: 1½ cups

½ cup butter
1½ cups light brown sugar
⅛ teaspoon salt

2 teaspoons corn syrup
½ cup heavy cream
½ cup chopped walnuts (optional)

Melt butter in saucepan; add sugar, salt and corn syrup. Bring to a boil. Cook until sugar is dissolved. Gradually add heavy cream, stirring constantly and bring to boiling point again. Cool. May add walnuts to sauce.

Mrs. James W. Keller

Fudge Sauce

½ cup butter
2¼ cups confectioners' sugar

⅔ cup evaporated milk
6 ounces unsweetened chocolate

Melt butter in top of double boiler. Stir in sugar. Pour in milk and add chocolate. Do not mix. Cover and cook over simmering water for 30 minutes. Remove from heat and beat.

Note: Can be frozen or will keep in refrigerator for 3 months.

Mrs. John Ticer

Strawberry-Banana Coupé

Serves: 4

⅓ cup light brown sugar
3 tablespoons butter or margarine
½ pint strawberries, halves
1 ripe banana, sliced

⅓ cup light rum
2 tablespoons Grand Marnier
8 dry almond macaroons
1 pint strawberry ice cream

Melt sugar and butter in small skillet, stirring often. Stir in strawberries and bananas. Heat rum and Grand Marnier slightly in small saucepan, just until warm. Ignite with match; pour over fruits (can be in chafing dish); shake pan until flames die. Crumble macaroons into 4 dessert dishes; scoop ice cream on top. Spoon hot sauce over ice cream and serve immediately.

Mrs. Windsor Demaine III

Raspberry Crème Parfait

Serves: 6

2 10-ounce packages frozen
    raspberries, thawed
2 tablespoons cornstarch
Dash of salt
5 tablespoons sugar

1 cup whipping cream
1 cup sour cream
1 teaspoon vanilla
1 tablespoon Grand Marnier liqueur

Drain raspberries, reserving the liquid. Add a small amount of the liquid to 2 tablespoons sugar and cornstarch in a saucepan to make a thin paste. Add remaining raspbery liquid, mixing well. Add a dash of salt and cook over medium heat. Cool, stirring occasionally. Carefully stir in raspberries. Chill. Whip cream until thick and add 3 tablespoons of sugar, beating until stiff. Fold in 1 cup sour cream, vanilla and Grand Marnier. Carefully spoon cream mixture into parfait glasses, alternating layers with raspberries. Begin and end with cream mixture. Garnish each parfait with a raspberry and refrigerate.

Note: This dessert can be made ahead and frozen if desired. Let it stand in refrigerator 1½ hours before serving if it has been frozen.

Mrs. Timothy O'Shaughnessy

Orange Temptation

Preheat: 325 degrees
Serves: 12 to 14

8 tablespoons grated orange peel
8 tablespoons sugar
9 egg whites
1 cup sugar
8 tablespoons Cointreau

1 11-ounce can mandarin oranges,
  drained
¼ cup toasted slivered almonds
¼ cup toasted coconut
1 cup heavy cream, whipped

Mix grated orange peel with sugar. Grease a baking mold with butter and stick mixture to mold spreading as generously as possible. Beat egg whites and when slightly stiff, add sugar gradually. Continue beating until standing in stiff peaks. Add 4 tablespoons of Cointreau, folding in carefully. Turn into mold, stand in hot water and bake at 325 degrees for 60 minutes. Let cool in oven with door closed. Marinate drained oranges in a second 4 tablespoons of Cointreau in refrigerator overnight. Several hours before serving, unmold, arrange oranges on top of, and around, the meringue. Just before serving, add toasted almonds and coconut. Serve with unsweetened whipped cream.

Note: This is beautiful on a cut glass plate. Shiny green leaves may be tucked under the oranges, if desired.

Mrs. John B. Allen

Strawberries Romanoff

Serves: 6

1 quart fresh strawberries, cleaned
  and slightly mashed
½ cup confectioners' sugar

9 tablespoons Cointreau
1 pint vanilla ice cream
1 cup whipping cream, whipped

Prepare strawberries; add sugar and 3 tablespoons Cointreau and set aside. Whip ice cream until slightly softened and fold in whipped cream and remaining Cointreau. Fold in prepared strawberries. Blend quickly and lightly and serve in chilled stemmed glasses.

Mrs. Wilson Livingood

Devonshire Cream

Yield: 1½ cups

1 cup cultured sour cream   *½ cup heavy whipping cream*

Place sour cream in jar with cover. Beat in whipping cream with fork. Cover jar. Let stand at room temperature for 8 to 12 hours, then refrigerate 24 hours. Should be almost thick enough to cut with a knife. Serve a generous dollop over a serving of berries.

Variation: May add a flavored liqueur and/or a small amount of confectioners' sugar before serving.

Mrs. C. Mason Ebhardt

Fresh Pineapple Delight

Yields: 3 cups

1 medium pineapple
1 egg, well beaten
2 to 4 tablespoons sugar
1 teaspoon flour
1 8-ounce carton whipping cream,
  whipped

1 tablespoon Falernum, Cointreau or
  other fruit based liqueur
Assorted fresh fruit

Cut a lengthwise slice from pineapple, removing one-third of the pineapple. Scoop pulp from slice; discard rind. Scoop pulp from remaining portion of pineapple, leaving shell ½-inch thick; set shell aside. Chop pineapple pulp into bite-sized pieces, discarding core. Crush 1 cup of pineapple pieces; reserve remaining pieces for dipping. Combine crushed pineapple (and juice that accumulates), egg, sugar, and flour in large saucepan. Cook over low heat until thickened; cool. Fold in whipped cream and liqueur, and spoon into pineapple shell. Serve dip with reserved pineapple pieces and other fresh fruit, cut into serving pieces.

Note: Especially nice for a tea.

Mrs. Donald M. McNamara

Gifts

Pommander Ball

1 ripe, thin skinned orange
2 ounces whole cloves

1 tablespoon orris powder
Blend of ground spices

Stud orange all over with whole cloves. Put the orange in a bowl containing a mixture of orris powder and ground spices. A traditional spice mixture includes cinnamon, allspice and cardamon. A blend of sassafras, star anise, ginger, anise, fennel and cinnamon produces a nostalgic candy scent. Leave orange in bowl for five days, rolling it in mixture daily. When orange is completely dry, wrap ribbon around it; tie with a bow and loop to hang in a closet.

Culpeper Tomato Relish

1 peck ripe tomatoes
6 medium onions, chopped
6 sweet peppers, chopped
1 ounce mustard seed
1 ounce celery seed

6 hot peppers
1 cup salt
5 cups brown or white sugar
1 quart vinegar

Peel tomatoes and cut coarsely. Add chopped onions and peppers. Add salt and mix. Let drain in cheese cloth or collander for 3 hours. Add sugar. Add vinegar, mustard seed, celery seed. Mix well; put in a crock or a jar. Stir every day for 3 days. The relish will keep one year. Stir well before using.

Culpeper Memorial Hospital Auxiliary

Old Apothecary Shop

The Stabler-Leadbeater Apothecary Shop, known in Alexandria as the Old Apothecary Shop, was founded in 1792 and remained in the Stabler family until it closed in 1933. John Leadbeater's name was added to the shop's name when he married Stabler's daughter in 1852.

George and Martha Washington, Robert E. Lee, Daniel Webster, Henry Clay and John Calhoun all patronized the 18th century drug store. But this was more than an ordinary pharmacy—it was also a meeting place where Calhoun and Webster were reported to have carried on philosophical discussions. A plaque in the shop marks the spot where Robert E. Lee was standing when he received an order to put down the John Brown insurrection at Harper's Ferry, West Virginia.

This perfectly preserved shop today houses a complete pharmaceutical collection, with hundreds of valuable hand-blown bottles, babies' nursing bottles, a cast iron sewing machine from the 1850's and other unusual items. L. Manuel Hindler of Baltimore purchased the collection at public auction in 1933 and let it remain on loan in the shop until 1948, when he donated it to the Landmarks Society.

285

Bourbon Balls

Yield: 3 dozen

1 small box vanilla wafers
1 cup chopped pecans
1 cup confectioners' sugar

2 tablespoons cocoa
1½ tablespoons white corn syrup
2 jiggers bourbon whiskey

Roll vanilla wafers into fine crumbs. Mix the crumbs with sugar, cocoa and nuts. Dissolve corn syrup in whiskey and add to dry ingredients. Mix well to blend. Mixture must be moist enough to hold together. Form into small balls and roll in additional confectioners' sugar.

Mrs. James L. Howe III

Chinese Chews

2 6-ounce packages butterscotch
   morsels

1 3-ounce can chow mein noodles
1 cup salted peanuts

Melt morsels in top of double boiler. Stir in noodles and nuts. When well blended drop by teaspoonfuls in waxpaper covered pan. Chill in refrigerator until set. Keep in tin in cool place.

Note: Chocolate and butterscotch or all chocolate may also be used.

Mrs. Alfred E. T. Rusch

Creme De Menthe Balls

Yield: 48 balls

1 cup vanilla wafer crumbs
¾ cup chopped pecans
1 cup confectioners' sugar

2 tablespoons light corn syrup
⅓ cup creme de menthe
Semi-sweet chocolate

Combine crumbs, pecans and sugar. Add corn syrup and liqueur. Roll into ½ teaspoon-sized balls. Place on wax paper and chill overnight. Dip balls in melted and partially cooled chocolate. Chill again.

Note: Good quality Swiss semi-sweet chocolate candy bars make these balls especially delicious.

Mrs. Frank McCabe

Stuffed Dates

Yield: 30-35

1 3-ounce package cream cheese,
  softened
3 tablespoons minced crystallized
  ginger

3 tablespoons toasted almonds,
  chopped
1 8 or 10-ounce package whole pitted
  dates
Confectioners' sugar (optional)

Blend cheese, ginger and almonds. Open dates with tip of paring knife and stuff with small amount of cheese mixture; press together slightly and roll in confectioners' sugar. Cover and refrigerate.

Note: To give, wrap individually in squares of plastic and pack in container.

Chocolate Truffles

Yield: 2 pounds

⅔ cup undiluted evaporated milk
1½ cups sugar
8 to 10 ounces marshmallow
  cream
¼ cup butter or margarine
½ teaspoon salt

2 6-ounce packages semi-sweet
  chocolate pieces
1 teaspoon vanilla
½ cup coarsely chopped walnuts
2 to 3 tablespoons Grand Marnier

Combine milk, sugar, marshmallow cream, butter and salt in a saucepan. Stir ingredients to blend slightly. Bring to a boil over medium heat, stirring constantly. Continue stirring and boil exactly 5 minutes. Mixture will brown slightly. Remove from heat. Immediately add semi-sweet pieces, vanilla and Grand Marnier. Stir (don't beat) until chocolate is thoroughly melted and mixture is shiny. Stir in nuts. Turn quickly into buttered 8-inch square or 9-inch round pan and swirl top. Chill. Cut into shapes when firm.

Mrs. Hugh C. Newton

Shine's Peanut Butter Squares

Yield: 45 to 60

½ cup graham cracker crumbs
1 cup chunky peanut butter
1 pound confectioners' sugar

1 cup melted margarine
2 cups milk chocolate chips

Mix crumbs, margarine, sugar and peanut butter. Spread in 3-quart casserole or 9 x 13-inch pan. Melt chocolate in top of double boiler and spread on above mixture while warm. Chill and cut in squares.

Note: If you like Reese's Peanut Butter cups, you'll love these!

Mrs. Alfred E. T. Rusch

Sugared Pecans

Preheat: 275 degrees

⅓ cup butter or margarine
¼ cup sugar
½ teaspoon cinnamon

¼ teaspoon ginger
¼ teaspoon nutmeg
1 pound pecans

In small saucepan, melt butter, stir in sugar and spices and mix well. Pour over pecans in large roasting pan and mix well to coat. Bake at 275 degree oven about 30 minutes, stirring several times during baking. Cool. Store in airtight container.

See's $1500 Christmas Fudge

Yield: 4 to 6 dozen

3 6-ounce packages chocolate chips
2 cups nuts
1 cup butter
1 8-ounce jar marshmallow whip

2 teaspoons vanilla
4½ cups sugar
Large can evaporated milk

Mix sugar and evaporated milk in saucepan, bring to a boil. Continue stirring constantly for 10 minutes. Mix chocolate chips, nuts, butter, marshmallow whip and vanilla in large bowl. Pour hot milk into cool mix, stir until melted. Pour into buttered 9 x 13-inch or jelly roll pan and cut in diamond shapes.

Note: See's is a famous California candymaker. A person is said to have requested this exclusive fudge recipe. When the recipe was received, it was accompanied by a bill for $1,500. Hence the recipe's name.

Mrs. Michael Cericola

Glazed Pecans

Preheat: 250 degrees

2 tablespoons cold water
2 egg whites
½ cup sugar
¼ teaspoon cinnamon

¼ teaspoon cloves
¼ teaspoon allspice
½ teaspoon salt
4 cups pecan halves

Beat egg whites slightly with water. Add remaining ingredients except pecans. Mix well. Add pecans and toss gently to coat on all sides. Cover a cookie sheet with foil, grease it and spread pecans evenly over the sheet. Bake at 250 degrees for 50 to 60 minutes until slightly browned. Remove from foil immediately. Place pecans on wax paper. Store in airtight containers.

Mrs. Caryle C. Ring, Jr.

Peanut Molasses Candy

Yield: 2 pounds

3 tablespoons butter
2 cups molasses

⅔ cup sugar
2 cups salted peanuts

Melt butter in saucepan. Add molasses and sugar. Boil to 256 degrees. Stir in peanuts. Pour into buttered 10 x 18-inch pan. Cool slightly and mark in squares.

Mrs. Joseph E. Hinds, Jr.

Praline Patties

Yield 3 to 4 dozen

1½ cups brown sugar
1½ cups granulated sugar
3 tablespoons dark corn syrup

1 cup milk
1 teaspoon vanilla
1½ cup pecan halves

Combine sugars, milk and syrup. Cook to soft ball stage (234 degrees). Cool 10 minutes. Add vanilla. Beat by hand for 2 minutes. Add pecans. Beat until mixture loses gloss. Drop by tablespoons on buttered foil or waxed paper.

Mrs. Charles E. Beatley
Mrs. Robert J. Lasker

Pecan Roll

2½ pounds sugar
1 cup water
1 cup milk

1 cup dark Karo syrup
1 cup margarine or butter
1 pound chopped pecans

Combine sugar, water, milk, syrup and butter in large saucepan; bring to a boil. Boil until mixture forms a soft ball in water. Stir to prevent sticking while cooking. Remove from heat and beat until mixture starts to cream. Add pecans. Blend well, then pour on a damp cloth. Roll out to form a long roll, let it set for 3 to 5 minutes. Slice in desired thickness.

Mrs. Emanuel A. Baker, Jr.

Curried Cashews

Preheat: 350 degrees

2 cups unroasted cashews
2 teaspoons seasoned salt

¾ tablespoon curry powder
¼ cup butter

Dot cashews with butter and bake in 350 degree oven, stirring occasionally for 20 minutes, or until golden brown. Remove from oven. Blend salt and curry, then sprinkle over nuts and stir. Return to oven for 5 minutes. Spread on absorbent paper to cool.

Curried Pecans

Preheat: 350 degrees

1 pound pecan halves
2 tablespoons brown sugar
¼ cup peanut oil
2 tablespoons curry powder

1 tablespoon ginger
½ cup butter
1 tablespoon chutney sauce
Salt to taste

Place pecans on cookie sheet and toast in oven for 10 minutes. Do not let pecans brown. Leave the oven on. Melt butter and oil in a large skillet. Add brown sugar, curry powder and ginger; blend well. Add pecans to skillet and stir with wooden spoon until well coated. Add chutney sauce and mix well. Turn off heat in oven. Place pecans on paper towels on cookie sheet and place in oven. Let pecans dry out in the oven for about ten minutes. Remove from oven; salt very lightly and store in airtight container when cool.

Mrs. Donald Burchell

Toasted Pecans

Preheat: 375 degrees

¼ cup butter
4 teaspoons Worcestershire sauce
1 tablespoon garlic salt

½ teaspoon hot pepper sauce
4 cups pecan halves

Melt butter in heavy skillet. Add remaining ingredients. Stir and mix well. Spread out on large flat pan and toast in 375 degree oven for 30 minutes. Stir while toasting.

Mrs. James L. Howe III

Party Snack Mix

Preheat: 250 degrees
Yield: 3 quarts

6 cups popped corn
1 6-ounce bag corn chips
2 cups bite-sized pretzels
1 cup roasted soybeans (optional)
1 3-ounce can chow mein noodles

1 stick butter or margarine
2 teaspoons Worcestershire sauce
¼ teaspoon hot pepper sauce
1 clove garlic, crushed

Put popped corn, corn chips, pretzels, soybeans and noodles in large roasting pan. In saucepan, melt butter, stir in sauces and garlic; pour over popcorn mixture and toss to mix well. Bake in 250 degree oven about 1 hour, stirring several times during baking. Cool and store in airtight containers.

Hot Pepper Jelly

¼ cup chopped hot green pepper
1½ cups chopped green peppers
6½ cups sugar

1½ cups cider vinegar
1 bottle liquid pectin
4 drops green food coloring

Blend peppers in food processor. Mix with sugar and vinegar in a large sauce pan and bring to brisk boil. Boil for 3 minutes, stirring to prevent boiling over. Add pectin and boil 1 minute longer. Remove from heat and allow to set for 5 minutes.Skim and strain, add food coloring and stir. Pour into hot sterilized jars and seal with parafin wax.

Mrs. John H. Fitch, Jr.

Homemade Kahlúa

Yield: 7 cups

1 quart water
2½ cups sugar
3 tablespoons instant coffee

1 tablespoon vanilla
2¼ cups Vodka

Bring water, sugar and coffee to a boil in saucepan. Cool. Add vanilla and vodka. Serve as after dinner liqueur or over ice cream. Bottle in decorative bottles for gifts.

Mrs. Richard L. Wallace

Corn Relish

Yield: 4 1-pint jars

1 quart whole kernel corn
2 cups finely chopped green
  cabbage
2 sweet red peppers, cut in small
  cubes
4 cups finely chopped celery,
  including heart, edible portion
  of root and tender leaves
1 large onion, finely chopped

1 small clove garlic, minced
1½ teaspoons celery seeds
1 cup sugar
1 tablespoon salt
1 teaspoon tumeric
1 tablespoon dry mustard
¼ teaspoon cayenne
2 cups cider vinegar

In a large kettle, combine the corn, cabbage, peppers, celery, onion, garlic, celery seed and a mixture of the sugar, salt, tumeric, mustard and cayenne. Blend well and stir in the vinegar. Over medium heat, bring this mixture to boiling, reduce heat and cook gently, uncovered, 15 to 20 minutes. Do not overcook. Celery should be crisp-tender and other vegetables still hold their shape. (If the consistencey of relish is too thin, combine 2 to 3 tablespoons flour with ½ cup water and blend into the relish). Bring to boiling and continue cooking and stirring until the liquid portion is thickened and smooth. Quickly ladle into hot sterilized jars and seal.

Note: Preparation time is reduced with a food processor.

Mrs. E. Darryl Barnes

Mom's Cuke Pickle

1 gallon thinly sliced baby
    cucumbers
½ cup salt
1½ teaspoon tumeric

5 cups sugar
5 cups vinegar
1 teaspoon celery seed
2 teaspoons mustard seed

Mix cucumbers with salt and bury in ice. Cover with a weight. Let stand for 3 hours. Make syrup of tumeric, sugar, vinegar, celery seed and mustard seed. Add cucumbers to syrup. Heat over low heat until scalding — do not boil.

Note: These are delicious pickles which are often eaten like a relish; well worth the effort of slicing paper thin.

Mrs. James R. Skidmore

Watermelon Preserves

Yield: 8 cups

1 medium watermelon, quartered
4 quarts water
1½ tablespoons salt
½-inch cube fresh ginger root,
    peeled
1 2-inch stick cinnamon

12 whole cloves
½ teaspoon powdered alum
9 cups sugar
2 large or 3 small lemons, thinly sliced
    and seeded

Trim dark skin and pink flesh from watermelon; cut enough of rind into 1 x ½-inch strips to make 4 pounds. Combine 2 quarts water and salt in a large, shallow glass or plastic container; add watermelon rind. Cover and chill 8 to 10 hours, stirring occasionally. Drain well. Tie ginger root and spices in a cheesecloth. Set aside. Place watermelon rind in a Dutch oven; cover with cold water, and stir in alum. Bring to a boil and boil 15 minutes. Drain, rinse with cold water. Combine 2 quarts water and sugar in a Dutch oven; bring to a boil, stirring constantly. Add the watermelon rind, lemon, and spice bag. Boil gently, stirring frequently, until watermelon rind is transparent and syrup is consistency of honey. Remove spice bag; ladle preserves into hot sterilized jars, leaving ½-inch headspace. Cover at once with metal lids, and screw bands tight. Process in boiling water bath for 10 minutes.

Mrs. Donald Burchell

293

INDEX

INDEX

INDEX

INDEX

INDEX

A Heritage of Good Tastes
P.O. Box 3614
Alexandria, Virginia 22302

Please send me _____ copies of A Heritage of Good Tastes at $9.95 per copy plus $1.50 for postage and handling. (Virginia residents add 4% sales tax.)

Enclosed is my check or money order for $_____.
☐ VISA   Account No. _____.
☐ Mastercard   Expiration Date_____.

Please print:
Name_____

Address_____

City_____State_____Zip_____
Make checks payable to: **A Heritage of Good Tastes**

- -

A Heritage of Good Tastes
P.O. Box 3614
Alexandria, Virginia 22302

Please send me _____ copies of A Heritage of Good Tastes at $9.95 per copy plus $1.50 for postage and handling. (Virginia residents add 4% sales tax.)

Enclosed is my check or money order for $_____.
☐ VISA   Account No. _____.
☐ Mastercard   Expiration Date_____.

Please print:
Name_____

Address_____

City_____State_____Zip_____
Make checks payable to: **A Heritage of Good Tastes**

- -

A Heritage of Good Tastes
P.O. Box 3614
Alexandria, Virginia 22302

Please send me _____ copies of A Heritage of Good Tastes at $9.95 per copy plus $1.50 for postage and handling. (Virginia residents add 4% sales tax.)

Enclosed is my check or money order for $_____.
☐ VISA   Account No. _____.
☐ Mastercard   Expiration Date_____.

Please print:
Name_____

Address_____

City_____State_____Zip_____
Make checks payable to: **A Heritage of Good Tastes**

Re-OrderAdditionalCopies